D0066140

Crossing Borders

Crossing Borders

Reception Theory, Poststructuralism, Deconstruction

ROBERT C. HOLUB

The University of Wisconsin Press

The University of Wisconsin Press
114 North Murray Street
Madison, Wisconsin 53715

3 Henrietta Street
London WC2E 8LU, England

5 4 3 2 1

Printed in the United States of America

Library of Congress Cataloging-in-Publication Data
Holub, Robert C.
Crossing borders: reception theory, poststructuralism, deconstruction / Robert C. Holub.
256 pp. cm.
Includes bibliographical references (p.) and index.
ISBN 0-299-13270-6 (cloth) ISBN 0-299-13274-9 (paper)
1. Criticism—History—20th century. 2. Criticism—Germany——History—20th century. 3. Criticism—United States—History—20th century. 4. Reader-response criticism—Germany. 5. Reader-response criticism—United States. 6. Literature—History and criticism.
I. Title
PN94.H66 1992
801′.95′0904—dc20 91-40251

For Renate

Contents

Preface

ANYONE who has looked at and lived through contemporary trends in theory during the eighties in Germany and in the United States cannot help but notice an odd asymmetry. The writers, critics, and philosophers who have dominated the discourse here have been all but ignored in Germany, and vice versa. While hermeneutics, communicative ethics, phenomenology, reception theory, and various forms of neomarxism have reigned supreme among German humanists, their counterparts in the United States have been more concerned with poststructuralism, deconstruction, and neopragmatism. The discrepancy between the two countries became most noticeable for me when I was preparing a monograph on reception theory in the early eighties. As a preliminary study I set out to examine how this theory, which had dominated literary criticism in Germany from the late sixties to the late seventies, had fared in the United States. I was shocked to find that not only was reception theory not very well known among literary scholars, but also that even when individual German theorists had received recognition, it was often within a framework that was quite unrelated to their activities within the Constance School. Shortly thereafter, I was able to experience at first hand the other side of the coin: German lack of interest in theories most frequently discussed in the United States. While I was a Humboldt fellow in Frankfurt from 1983 to 1985, I found that a good number of my German colleagues were more irritated than attracted by what had been imported from France and could not understand why anyone would take these "frivolities" seriously. At about the same time that I began working on reception theory I also noted a puzzling phenomenon concerning the appropriation of foreign theory. From various readings and encounters with deconstructors at universities in the United States, I was amazed at their certainty that their practice was politically radical and valuable for leftist causes. Without much investigation I was able to learn of deconstruction's origins in France during the sixties and its radical involvement institutionally in the French educational system. Again I registered a discrepancy, since during my own graduate studies and for the first years of my own teaching career I had associated deconstruction with elitist institutions and playful, apolitical exegetical practices.

These incongruities of perception and reception in different countries were obviously not due to simple misunderstandings or to a prearranged division of labor. I was observing something noteworthy in Western humanistic discourses, and it had to do with the effects of crossing borders. Although theory presents itself as abstract and applicable without regard to temporal and geographical boundaries, its appropriation and understanding were evidently bound to context. Despite the appeal to universal principles that all theoretical endeavors share, including those that abjure or call into question universals, they were apparently subject to nonuniversal criteria when it was a matter of their acceptance and evaluation in unfamiliar surroundings. This differential reception of theory helps to make sense of several conflicts, debates, and antagonisms that have developed in recent years. The lack of communication between theorists from France and Germany, for example, or among scholars who have studied different traditions in the United States seems to be due, at least in part, to an inability on the part of advocates to situate a foreign tradition in its new environment and to account for the differences that are operative in the new setting. Throughout the eighties I set out to investigate various aspects of the transformations and difficulties of border crossings in numerous essays and reviews. I have gathered, reworked, and updated the results of my rather unsystematic procedures in this volume. What I found, in the most general terms, is that what matters most in the appropriation of a theory from a foreign country is how it fits into an already established constellation in the importing country. Traditions and the possibility of assimilating something alien to a familiar frame of reference were the most important determinants of whether a given theoretical direction would be absorbed or rejected, whether it would be welcomed as an enrichment of the native heritage or rejected, ignored, or ridiculed as an unwanted intruder on foreign soil. Although I am not enough of a hermeneutic relativist to believe arguments count for nothing and that tradition is all that matters, I believe that the vicissitudes and preferences in theoretical endeavor in the United States and Germany cannot be adequately understood without reference to a notion of cross-cultural contextualization.

The sections of this volume take up the three illustrations of border crossing I described above. In the first two chapters I deal with the reception of reception theory in the United States. Perhaps the most significant postwar development in German literary theory, the Constance School of reception theory had a rather strange fate on this side of the Atlantic. As I document in the first chapter, it was largely ignored as a coherent theoretical movement until around 1980. The large fanfare that accompanied its advent in the Federal Republic was drowned out by the din of various other voices—poststructuralism, affective stylistics, deconstruction—in American criticism. In the second chapter I treat the fate of reception theory during the past decade or so and try to show how its radicality was considered not radical enough by native critics. In the second section I examine poststructuralism in the German context. After some general remarks in Chapter 3 concerning the situation in Germany and the initial appropriation of poststructuralist trends, I turn to a detailed examination of the reception of Michel Foucault. Although Foucault has been the most important French thinker for Germany, his works have encountered various barriers that have to do with his misalignment with indigenous intellectual traditions. I explore which factors have prevented a more thoroughgoing appropriation of his thought, what kind of impact his theories have had during the past fifteen years, and what the most fruitful possibilities for future Foucauldian projects may be in Germany and in the context of German studies. In Chapters 5, 6, and 7, I turn to three individuals whose writings have had an impact on German poststructuralism. In the sixties Peter Szondi was probably the first critic to appreciate the possibilities of poststructuralism for Germany; in his initial writings from the seventies and early eighties Manfred Frank was the strongest advocate for a merger of poststructuralism with the more familiar hermeneutic tradition; and Friedrich Kittler has thus far been the critic who has produced the most genial work in the poststructuralist mode.

In these initial two sections of the book I am concerned not only with the appropriation of theory across borders, but also with the political dimensions of these appropriations. In the final section of the book, in which I look at the role of deconstruction in American circles over the past fifteen years, I restrict my attention solely to political aspects of theoretical endeavor. Two particular moments in the history of deconstruction in the United States are therefore pivotal for me. The first, occurring around 1980, is marked by an attempt to politicize deconstructive theory, or perhaps more appropriately stated, to *re*politicize it for its American audience. The approaches connected with this enterprise were varied, but most included an explicit or implicit merger with the marxist tradition. In the eighth chapter I present the arguments for marxist deconstruction, analyze some representative texts in this tradition, and conclude with the unresolved, and perhaps unresolvable, problems in fashioning deconstruction as a political strategy in the United States. The ninth and final chapter looks at the second significant moment in the political history of deconstruction: its confrontation with the right-wing political pasts of Paul de Man and Martin Heidegger. The controversies surrounding both men occurred almost simultaneously in the fall of 1987, and in much of 1988 and 1989 we find writings of deconstructors, both in France and in the United States, exploring issues directly related to the politics of theory. In examining some of the more representative texts produced in response to this perceived crisis, I try to demonstrate both the difficulties of moving from philosophy to politics and the deficiencies of appropriating a Heideggerian or neo-Heideggerian schema for political evaluation. In the concluding pages of this chapter I also suggest a general framework within which the insights we have gained from deconstruction, as well as from other politically oriented criticism, could be integrated. My goal here is to eliminate the unproductive political accusations that have surrounded theoretical debates during the past decade and to establish parameters within which sincerely political, progressive critics of all persuasions can communicate with each other. Such a framework is thus designed to insure that future border crossings will not be susceptible to the types of distortions and misunderstandings that I discuss in this book.

In one form or another various parts of this book have appeared in reviews and essays in the following journals during the eighties: *German Quarterly, Textual Practice, Monatshefte, enclitic, Southern Review*. All materials, however, were reworked, some considerably, for inclusion in this volume. If I were going to thank all the people who contributed to this book, I would have to list almost every person with whom I spoke about theory since I started teaching at Berkeley. Of particular importance for me were Christian Flemmer, Gerald Graff, Renate Holub, Christopher Norris, and John Smith. In general I can say that I have learned at least as much from those with whom I disagree as from those with whom I agree. Financial support from the Alexander von Humboldt Foundation enabled me to begin investigation of several topics that eventually found their way into this book, and the University of California at Berkeley has consistently provided me with research funding. I thank both institutions for their generous assistance. I would also like to express my gratitude to the University of Wisconsin Press and, in particular, to Barbara Hanrahan for her understanding and her generosity with deadlines. Susan Tarcov was by far the best copy editor with whom I have had the pleasure to work; her careful reading improved and clarified much that was muddled and badly formulated. Special thanks go to Renate Holub for her constant encouragement and the insights into contemporary theory that she shared with me. Without her I would probably not have embarked upon this project at all.

Part One

German Theory in the United States: The American Reception of Reception Theory

1

Resistance and Rivalry

ONE of the most revealing pieces with regard to the fate of German theory in the United States was the editor's column in the *PMLA* from January of 1980. In these brief remarks Joel Conarroe gave the findings of an internal survey or "popularity poll" that he had conducted on the basis of footnotes to 35 papers discussed by the editorial board of the journal in June of 1979. The results could hardly have been surprising for students and scholars familiar with the history of literary theory in the United States during the seventies. Derrida and Barthes led the continental contingent in the Modern Language Association's version of the ratings game; the so-called Yale School, now defunct because of death and dispersion, received most numerous mention from the domestic field. Journals frequently cited included *Georgia Review*, which for a time in the mid-seventies adopted an avant-garde critical air, *Glyph*, a major organ for poststructuralist criticism that lasted for less than a decade, and *Critical Inquiry*. Among the books repeatedly footnoted were such standards as Edward Said's *Beginnings*, Jonathan Culler's *Structuralist Poetics*, the essay collection *The Structuralist Controversy*, and Lacan's *Ecrits*—to mention only those works whose authors have not already been cited.[1] No one, of course, will be astonished by this list of names and titles, but their prominence on the American critical scene is not without significance because it bespeaks a remarkable homogeneity of opinion in a country usually noted for its eclecticism and pluralism. What is most noticeable is the strong structuralist and poststructuralist profile; many, if not most, of the European and American critics referred to most often fall somewhere in this vaguely defined category. But another, undoubtedly related slant is also apparent and apt to be slightly more disturbing for those who have not been enthralled by everything that has emanated from Paris since the late sixties. For the American critical establishment of the seventies the continent seems to have stretched from the channel to the western Alps, but not beyond the Rhine; for all practical purposes it could be located almost exclusively in Paris or at least within French linguistic borders since all Swiss critics who appear on the list are from the French-speaking regions of that trilingual nation. Absent from the list were not only the older generation of Romance-language scholars, Erich Auerbach, Leo Spitzer, and Ernst Robert Curtius, all of whom had been translated into English, but also prominent leftist scholars such as Walter Benjamin, Theodor Adorno, Herbert Marcuse, and Georg Lukács. In Germany during the late sixties and seventies it would have been difficult to find an essay at a respectable journal that did not contain a citation from one of these critics. Yet from 35 submissions to the *PMLA* not one of them were referred to in more than a single essay, Conarroe's criterion for inclusion in the column.

For a student of German criticism and scholarship of the seventies, however, there is an even greater lacuna in this list. No two authors, it seems, submitted an essay in which reception theory or the so-called Constance School played a role.[2] A corresponding situation in Germany for any time during the years 1967–80 is almost unthinkable. For between the Rhine and the Elbe the hegemony of reception theory was nearly absolute among methods during that period. After Hans Robert Jauß's "provocation" to literary scholarship in his inaugural address at Constance in 1967,[3] almost every critical school of thought and practically every literary discipline responded to his challenge. A few illustrations should serve to document the proliferation of studies involved with reception theory in the German-speaking world. Just a decade after Jauß's address, Gunter Grimm was able to cite over four hundred entries in one section of a bibliography entitled "Reception Theory: Literary Communication—The History of Reception and Effect"; over fifty percent had appeared since 1967, and applications of the method were included in another section of the bibliography.[4] During the seventies a good half dozen readers or essay collections appeared in print, each treating some aspect of this methodological innovation. Several journals devoted entire issues to reception theory: *Poetica* published two tentative balance sheets *(Zwischenbilanzen).* And finally the Conference of German Teachers at Stuttgart in 1972 scheduled two entire sessions and parts of several others to examine reception and effect.[5] Applications to the literary canon were just as plentiful. In one form or another reception theory was used to discuss French troubadour lyrics, the English novel, the *nouveau roman,* surrealism, and works in the German tradition from the *Nibelungenlied* to the poetry of Paul Celan. From marxists to "formalists," from classical scholars and medievalists to modernists, virtually every methodological direction and area of literary endeavor in Germany reacted to the challenge of reception theory at some point during the seventies.

Considering the enormous impact that reception theory has had for Central European scholars,[6] the response in the United States was rather moderate. While introductions to structuralism were abundant in bookstores during the late seventies, there was no monograph-length overview of reception theory in English (although several exist in German).[7] When some of its most important theorists were anthologized in English, they were either presented vaguely as part of a "new perspective" from Germany[8] or thrown into the questionable catchall category of "audience-oriented" or "reader-response" criticism.[9] Volumes by German reception theorists, even those most influential in their own country, had difficulty getting into print in the United States during the seventies. Only the works of Wolfgang Iser were initially published, and these books, as I shall argue in a moment, were viewed less as part of a German critical movement than as an extension of more familiar American traditions. American journal articles on or by reception theorists also appeared less frequently than one might have expected in light of their continental successes. With the exception of essays in *New Literary History,* whose editorial board included both Jauß and Iser as well as Robert Weimann, an East German contributor to the debate on reception theory, the number could be counted on one's fingers; if articles by or on Iser were excluded, one hand would have sufficed. Indeed, the meager reception of reception theory in the United States during the seventies can be documented most graphically by a survey of journals I undertook in the early eighties in preparation for writing a monograph on the topic. From approximately one hundred scholarly journals published in this country dealing with English literature, French literature, comparative literature, and literary theory, I found less than twenty reviews of works by reception theorists from 1970–80. Of these more than half were devoted to books by Iser. It is little wonder then that the *PMLA* editorial board did not encounter the names of Jauß & Co. in its deliberations or that—to cite only one further illustration—in a volume from 1977 entitled *Directions for Criticism: Structuralism and Its Alternatives* there was absolutely no mention of reception theory or of any critic associated with the Constance School.[10]

The neglect of reception theory during the seventies is most evident when one considers American critics interested in similar problems and a similar change in perspective. Even in these cases the writings of the Constance School were usually ignored. A good case in point was Walter J. Ong's award-winning essay from 1975, entitled "The Writer's Audience Is Always a Fiction," which discusses several issues debated in Germany at that time without a single reference to reception theory.[11] In the first section of his essay Ong proclaims that "the time is ripe for a study of the history of the reader." This programmatic statement from the mid-seventies in the United States had been anticipated by a similar plea from Herald Weinrich in Germany during the late sixties. In fact, Weinrich's influential essay (in Germany), entitled "For a Literary History of the Reader," opens up many of the questions later covered by Ong.[12] In the second part of his essay Ong briefly treats a problem that Iser had dealt with previously in his construct of the implied reader. At issue is the role that the reader "has to play," a role that is "cast" by the author and "seldom coincides with his role in actual life." Although Iser's theoretical position allows for considerably more leeway in the reader's response, the similarity between Ong's ideal, passive reader and Iser's implied reader is evident. Later in the essay Ong sketches a tentative history of the reader in English literature. Again such concerns run parallel to outlines suggested by German reception theorists in the late sixties and early seventies. In fact Iser, in his most noted essay, "Indeterminacy and the Reader's Response in Prose Fiction," tries to construct a trajectory for the development of the novel based on an increase in indeterminacy.[13] By pointing to Ong's failure to cite German critics, I am not trying to condemn his research methods; nor am I calling into question the originality of his thought. Rather, I am calling attention to the rather significant fact that Ong, like most of his American colleagues in the seventies, completely disregarded contemporary developments in German literary theory. Indeed, it is noteworthy that no one on the editorial board of the *PMLA* insisted that Ong include some mention of reception theorists. Ong pays homage to Ricoeur, Barthes, Derrida, Foucault, Sollers, and Todorov, but completely ignores (or is ignorant of) the very theorists whose concerns most closely parallel his own.

Those who did not ignore the existence of the Constance School tended to minimize the uniquely German dimensions by assimilating these theorists under rubrics that are derived from or refer to American theory. There were no allusions to *Rezeptionstheorie, Rezeptionsgeschichte,* or *Rezeptionsästhetik* in the literature of the seventies. Steven Mailloux, who devoted several articles to an examination of what he termed "reader-response criticism,"removes Iser from any connection with

Germany of the late sixties and his colleagues at Constance by locating him comfortably between Norman Holland and the early Stanley Fish on a continuum from subjectivism to structuralism.[14] Iser is viewed here as a representative of a phenomenological branch of reader-response criticism, but his indebtedness to the philosophical roots of phenomenology in Germany is less interesting than his relation to more familiar American modes of thought. The introduction to *The Reader in the Text* (1980) by Susan R. Suleiman improves on this situation in some regards, but succumbs ultimately to a perspective that is unable to fathom the German critical scene. Suleiman is aware at least that Iser is part of a larger critical trend in West Germany—for the first time we find references to *Rezeptionsgeschichte* and *Rezeptionsästhetik,* and she even mentions Weinrich, Iser, Jauß, and Karlheinz Stierle—but she too prefers to treat individual theorists under separate descriptive headings and thus breaks up national and historically related groupings. Iser is again assigned to the phenomenologists, and Jauß, because Suleiman reserves the "hermeneutical" category for metacritical considerations, is situated somewhat awkwardly and inaccurately among those advocating the "sociological-historical variety of audience-related criticism." Although such labels could be justified, they serve to obscure the breadth and depth of reception studies as a German phenomenon of the late sixties and early seventies. Thus Suleiman can write that audience-oriented criticism was a "quiet revolution," a description that probably captures accurately the appearance of such efforts in France, England, and the United States, but which certainly misses the mark with respect to Germany. In the Federal Republic and in the German Democratic Republic, the emergence of reception theory was quite definitely accompanied by the "manifestoes," "marching," and "tumult in the streets" that Suleiman misses elsewhere. Indeed, I would contend that the promulgatory and provocative aspects of reception theory are essential for an understanding of how reception theory found its place in the intellectual life of the seventies. Since this aspect eluded most American observers for so many years, commentators in the United States were effectively barred from an appreciation of the historical and sociological dimension of reception theory. As a result they could situate it only ahistorically and abstractly alongside psychological and narratological varieties of reader-oriented criticism, which are related only by dint of shared formal characteristics.

Reception theory arose as the result of a crisis in methods during the sixties, one which was no doubt closely related to larger social and political changes in Germany and the Western world at that time. The manifestations of a crisis in the literary-academic sphere were apparent in a variety of tendencies: the reexamination of the literary canon, the demand for more relevant curricula at universities, and the attempts to reform academic programs were the most noticeable of these signs of intense reevaluation. In fact, the University of Constance, where both Iser and Jauß taught beginning in the late sixties,[15] was founded at the time as an alternative to the rigid, restrictive system of higher education at most German universities. The endeavor to break down traditional methods of studying and evaluating literature was a part of the reform plans articulated by almost all those involved at Constance from its very inception[16]—and at other German universities as well during this turbulent period. What bothered most younger literary scholars about previous methods were the arcane techniques they advocated and the obsolete assumptions they made concerning the appropriate way to study literature. The main critical directions under attack included not only the various methodological vestiges of *Geistesgeschichte,* originally developed during the first quarter of the century, but also the more text-oriented methods imported from other Western nations after the Second World War. The German version of "New Criticism," represented in most people's minds by Wolfgang Kayser and the Swiss critic Emil Staiger, had propagated what was now seen as a narrow, elitist, and politically conservative approach to literature.[17] With student protests demanding a total restructuring and rethinking of institutional standards and the emergence of a generation of young scholars willing to undertake such sweeping reforms—at least in the realm of ideas and the institutions of higher education—several alternative methods became popular. Most involved some variety of marxism, and this noticeable swing to the left is reflected in most of the methodological primers and in a great deal of the scholarship in the ensuing decade. The atmosphere in departments of literature was often explosive; literature itself was under attack and at one point declared dead, or at least moribund, in a prominent left-leaning journal;[18] and manifestoes claiming to reveal the only genuine approach to literary scholarship appeared with uncanny regularity.

This was the intellectual climate into which reception theory was born, and when the birth occurred, it was not quietly announced in the appropriate section of the local newspaper, but brashly proclaimed on the front page in bold headlines. Jauß's essay, after all, was meant to be a provocation to his colleagues, the academic equivalent of a call to arms, and the weakening of the "provocation" to a mere "challenge" in the English translations is only a further reflection of how most observers in the United States misunderstood the historical self-image of reception theory. In the spoken version of the essay the affront to established methods is even more explicit because of the unmistakable allusion to Friedrich Schiller. In 1789 on the eve of the French Revolution Schiller had delivered an inaugural lecture at Jena with the title "What is and for what purpose does one study universal history" *(Was heißt und zu welchem Ende studiert man Universalgeschichte)*. When Jauß modified this title by substituting the word "literary" for "universal," the revolutionary self-understanding was apparent. Other documents from the first years of reception theory, for example Weinrich's essay (referred to above) or Iser's inaugural address, contain passages that indicate a similar concern to agitate the academic establishment. But perhaps the best illustration of the flare with which reception theory was introduced to the West German critical scene came with Jauß's less celebrated essay "Paradigm Change in Literary Scholarship," which appeared in 1969.[19] Applying Thomas Kuhn's model of scientific revolutions to literary scholarship, Jauß hypothesizes that the old formalist-aesthetic paradigm is exhausted and that the consolidation of a new paradigm is imminent. It is interesting to note that the two main competitors to Jauß's reception theory, marxism and structuralism, are dismissed as bases for a potential new paradigm. In Jauß's scheme the former belongs to the positivist-historicist model of the late nineteenth century, while the latter has not yet developed into a force that is unified enough for it to be considered "paradigmatic." With these two rival approaches eliminated from consideration, the reader, if he or she has obediently followed Jauß's line of reasoning, is forced to conclude that only reception theory (or something resembling it) can satisfy the various challenges that a new paradigm will have to face. Important here is not so much the validity of the conceptual framework as the manner in which the argument is presented. A simple suggestion for altering critical practices to include questions of influence, effect, and reception from a hermeneutic perspective would have been much too timid a proposition for the Germany of the late sixties. As a result exaggerated claims of omnipotence, implied comparisons with the Copernican revolution, and an almost total disqualification of other approaches accompany the emergence of reception theory in West Germany during its initial phase.

It is noteworthy that the crisis in literary studies at West German universities and the rise of reception theory coincide with a period of deep questioning in the United States as well. The coincidence is even more striking in that New Criticism, "formalism," or *werkimmanente*

Kritik was sent to the whipping post in both countries. But despite the similarities, the responses in the United States to the methodological crisis assumed completely different forms. Absent from most of the renewed critical discourse on this side of the Atlantic was the element of ideological conflict so pivotal in the German discussions. Probably because the structure of the American university and that of the teaching profession are so different from their German counterparts, the question of social commitment in methodology was not a central issue in the upheavals of the sixties. At German universities the literature students are in general slightly older, more specialized at an earlier age, and more sophisticated ideologically upon entrance to higher education. Moreover, they are normally only a few years away from civil service positions as teachers of language and literature. Our two-tier system of undergraduates and graduates, in which an English major might continue professional training in any field from law to journalism or even business, tends to diffuse methodological questions in the classroom. The undergraduates often either are not intellectually mature enough to cope with issues of ideology and textuality, or have no ultimate stake in a change in approaches. The graduate students have already been admitted as apprentices in a guild-like system in which they have signed on to learn the trade, not to question the techniques. As a rule methods and metacritical reflection did not play any role in undergraduate education before the seventies, and at most institutions they continue to be an optional or marginal part of the program. At the graduate level there has been more attention paid to such matters in recent years, but this certainly was not the case throughout most of the sixties and seventies. These and other reasons contributed to the interface and lack of interface between protest and methodology in Germany and in the United States respectively. In this country the student movement centered on the draft, on the Vietnam war, on university governance, and to some degree on racial issues and institutional complicity in the military-industrial complex. But unless I completely misread the situation, there was not much focus on methodology, at least not in most literature programs. As Walter Slatoff noted in 1970, at the height of campus unrest, the "challenges to traditional patterns of education" have not extended to "the way we think and talk about literature."[20] One of the reasons for this lack of progressive input into the reform of methods was that the task was left largely to the senior members of the staff. Dialogue with students and with junior faculty occurred occasionally, but rarely was it considered a necessity. Most discussion was carried out inside the ivory tower without much input from outside. As a consequence, when theory did become a topic it remained largely unaffected by student protest and political demands; *engagement* and didactic concerns, where they did exist, were coincidental, and often for the person involved active participation in such a direct fashion was considered detrimental to career development. While in West Germany the years 1967–80 saw the production of a dozen different methodological primers, often written by and always directed at students, the seventies in the United States were marked by the emergence of a series of scholarly journals in which questions of methodology were debated by an academic avant-garde often unconcerned with the relationship between criticism and politics.[21]

Another result of the particular constellation surrounding the rethinking of approaches to literature, however, was the rather meager reception of reception theory. One of the largest barriers to the acceptance of reception theory was the lack of a strong influence of German philosophy on American criticism. This was especially true for the hermeneutic tradition, for phenomenology, and for an entire range of sociohistorical studies. Literary scholars often continued to work within the basic framework in which literary studies had been conceived by New Criticism. They valorized the text as the true object of critical endeavor, albeit with a different philosophical justification for this concentration. The result was not propitious for a German-American dialogue. Indeed, at the very height of the upheaval at American universities, Geoffrey Hartman, the influential Yale professor whose background could have assisted in the introduction of German criticism, asserted the impossibility of proceeding beyond a formal textual criticism—at the very moment when German scholars were united in proclaiming its necessity. Although the title of the collection of essays *Beyond Formalism* (1970) appears to assert the opposite, the author's conclusion is, as he writes, "a skeptical one, or else critical in the Kantian sense: to go beyond formalism is as yet too hard for us and may be, unless we are Hegelians believing in the absolute spirit, against the nature of understanding."[22] Paul de Man, another of the most prominent American representatives of literary theory, reached a similarly skeptical conclusion at the end of the decade. Contemporary criticism, he contended in 1979, should seek "to outdo closeness of reading that had been held up to them and to show, by reading the close readings more closely, that they were not nearly close enough." The program he proposes thus extends textual analysis to criticism while advocating a renewed and redoubled effort of close reading for literary works. He does make a bow toward literary history, but, like Hartman's title, it appears to be contradicted by his own interpretive practice. Merely to assert that history and ethics will reemerge "at the far end of this ongoing enterprise"[23] is not very persuasive, especially when one fails to note such a breakthrough in de Man's own work. Reflecting on this situation, Jonathan Culler in his essay "Structuralism and Grammatology" provided the most cogent explanation for the predicament of modern American criticism with respect to "formalism." He examines two accounts of why it might be impossible to go beyond formalism, identifying them with structuralism and poststructuralism respectively. The first, by extending the possibilities for investigation, postpones indefinitely the closure of a conceivable nonformalist criticism. The latter denies the possibility of nonformalism because the isolation of content as referential involves the delusion of somehow evading textuality. Culler's conclusion is particularly interesting: "Structuralism and deconstruction seem in various ways opposed to one another; each of them is opposed to the New Criticism (whose faults are usually said to involve excessive formalism); nevertheless both can be identified with the impossibility of going beyond formalism."[24] The oppositions Culler detects among the various approaches most favored in the United States in the mid-seventies entail a fundamental similarity; the unwillingness or inability to escape from the prison-house of formalism, or alleged impossibility of such escape.

If one conceives of textual criticism or "formalism" as the common denominator of most criticism in the United States during the postwar era, then it is not difficult to understand why reception theory was not well received. In contrast to these various "immanent" approaches, most types of reception theory postulate a nontextual referent in either history, the reader, or the social order. For the New Criticism, which was the dominant method at American universities for the three decades after the war,[25] using such "external" factors for interpretation meant that the critic had succumbed to one fallacy or another. All interpretative tasks could be accomplished with reference to the text itself. Structuralism, as it was absorbed into literature departments during the early seventies, continued this focus on the work of art. Although for French society this movement can be located historically and sociologically as a formalist rebellion against the obsolete scholarly dogmas of the academy, analogous perhaps to the New Critical or Russian Formalist revolts in the earlier part of the century, its appropriation in the United States can be more easily understood in terms of its continuity with previous methods than as a protest against past practice. As Maria Ruegg pointed out in her observations on the reception of structuralism and poststructuralism in the United States: "In the process of assimilation, structuralism gradually came to appear, not as a radically threatening revolutionary theory, but as a kind of formalism, not unlike Chomskian linguistics, and in many respects, not even unlike New Criticism."[26] Deconstruction also focuses our attention on features of the text, often, as we have seen from the remarks by de Man, more obdurately than its predecessors. Although the practitioners of deconstruction deny the organic nature of the work of art associated with New Criticism and dispute the centeredness of the structure (structuralism), they too, even in their purportedly political variants, would not resort to what a traditional critic might term "external" factors. At most they might make intertextual connections, but the notion of a referential text has always been anathema to their critical perspective. This obsession with the text that has characterized the American critical establishment for almost forty-five years has been challenged somewhat in the past decade by critics concerned with feminism, minority criticism, and colonialism. But such alternatives were not well formulated during the early seventies, and it is the persistence of textual criticism in the United States that has been the single largest factor in preventing a fruitful dialogue with methods developed in Germany. That the American crisis of the seventies was resolved with the importation of a new "formalism" followed by a "postformalism" (which remained in the hands of literary critics "formalist"), and that these two alternatives, particularly deconstruction, occupied the critical space into which reception theory might have penetrated, must be viewed as a testimony to the tenacity and flexibility of the textualist dogma in American literary theory. In the struggle between structuralism and New Criticism, and between deconstruction and structuralism, a "nontextual" alternative like reception theory did not even enter into the fray.

Until now I have portrayed reception theory as a totally unknown quantity in American criticism of the seventies. This is of course a slightly exaggerated and distorted picture since the work of Wolfgang Iser received some attention during that decade. However, if we turn now to Iser's theory and to the manner in which he was appropriated, then I think we shall find again a peculiarly "formalist" assimilation of even this branch of the Constance School. In the first place Iser was seldom associated with German directions in criticism. In various reviews of his books, he has been identified with reader-response criticism and narrative theory; he has been linked with critics such as Barthes, Holland, Bleich, Merleau-Ponty, and Fish; and a few generous reviewers have compared his work in importance to such standard volumes as *The Rhetoric of Fiction*, *The Teller in the Tale*, and *Anatomy of Criticism*. But even to this day one rarely finds him connected with a German school of thought, with his colleague Jauß, or with the colloquia *Poetik und Hermeneutik*, to which he has been a consistent and seminal contributor. In general, German discussions of his work have been ignored,[27] and in this sense the statements about the nonreception of reception theory are not overstated at all. To be sure, Iser may foster this non-German image by referring rather sparingly to contemporary German criticism in his English works—Jauß, for example, is mentioned only in a few inconsequential footnotes in *The Act of Reading*—but that American reviewers have by and large lost sight of his German roots is a type of blindness that excludes insight into his origins and intellectual concerns. His dissociation from Constance and incorporation into American critical theory is facilitated by a number of factors. Not only does Iser deal primarily with the Anglo-American tradition—he is an *Anglist*, that is, a professor of English and American Literature—but he also writes in English. Although several reviewers ridiculed him for his plodding, awkward "German style"—this often being the only acknowledgment of his native heritage[28]—his own considerable abilities in the English language make him more accessible to American critics. Finally, Iser also relates to the American scene more closely because of his concern for narrative theory, an area that has traditionally been of more interest to American critics, probably because of its attention to textual features. Iser's first American publication, an English version of "Die Appellstruktur der Texte," was delivered at a conference devoted to narrative theory and can be viewed from an American perspective as a contribution to the construction of texts as much as a discussion of how readers respond. Indeed, one of the most important conceptual terms for Iser, his "implied reader," is apparently adapted from Wayne Booth's notion of the "implied author," although for some reason Booth was never cited when the term was introduced.

But a more fundamental reason for Iser's modicum of success in the United States at a time when other reception theorists were ignored is that his theory lends itself to the textuality so familiar to the American tradition.[29] Iser defines his concepts in order to avoid the appearance of "formalism," and such precautions may have been necessary for a German scholar presenting a new theoretical direction in the early seventies. His implied reader, for example, contains both textual and reader-related dimensions: "This term incorporates both the prestructuring of the potential meaning by the text, and the reader's actualization of this potential through the reading process."[30] But his dependence on a phenomenological foundation of "gaps" and "vacancies" *(Leerstellen)*, qualities of the text that stimulate the reader's cognition, for his theory of the reading process tends to vitiate his allegedly double-edged constructs. The reader's response, after all, cannot be ascertained with certainty, and even if it could be, as in so-called empirical studies of reception, Iser is not interested in it. The "actualization" of meaning in his theory is performed by some sort of ideal reader, one which appears to correspond closely to a well-informed contemporary of the author, although some critics have argued that the reader whom Iser imagines is the author's own ideal reader.[31] In either case, however, one is left with, on the one hand, an analysis of the rhetoric of the text in terms of "gaps" and "indeterminacies" and, on the other, conjectures on how an ideal reader (or perhaps interpreter would be a more apposite designation) is affected by, reads, or actualizes the various authorial or textual strategies. Formulated in this fashion, both of these alternatives can easily be assimilated into a tradition of textual criticism and close reading. Finding indeterminacy in texts, elucidating how they have been constructed, whether to elicit response or not, can be conceived as analogous to activities by more traditional critics who sought paradox and irony in texts. Speculating on how the reader reacts, filling in the "gaps" as it were, may be translated into the act of interpretation itself. Iser's project, when it is applied to literary works, also remains for the most part within the bounds of textual criticism, and it appears that this focus on text and reader (interpreter) has gradually eroded the traces of historical analysis—or was it the vestiges of literary history—to which Iser still adhered in his work from the late sixties. The "Appellstruktur" essay sketches an outline of literary history which *The Implied Reader* retains in unstated form. But the reflections on a history of reading or a sociology of reading disappear in the mid-seventies, yielding to an almost ahistorical phenomenology by *The Act of Reading*.[32] For these and a number of other reasons[33] Iser's reception in American criticism of the seventies was a paradoxical one: on an overt level he rejects New Criticism, yet his theory has been used to provide important support for a textual method not unlike that of his American predecessors. At the same time he remained apparently uninfluenced until around 1980 by most of what Paris had to offer. As Wallace Martin observed, Iser deserves the attention of those "who oppose deconstruction but wish to revitalize the fundamental assumptions of the New Criticism."[34] His reception in the United States thus paralleled that of structuralism and poststructuralism in that they were all assimilated to a textual criticism that had strong links to the critical tradition they were putatively supplanting.

One should note here that until the eighties most of the other names associated with reception theory could be recruited only for the first half of the task that Martin links to Iser's theoretical efforts. The work of Hans Robert Jauß, Karlheinz Stierle, and other frequent participants in the Constance colloquia, as well as the responses from the East Germans by Robert Weimann, Manfred Naumann, or Rita Schober, could also have served as alternatives to poststructuralist directions in criticism. It would have been difficult, however, to resuscitate any version of the New Criticism with these other varieties of reception theory. For common to all these critics is a conception of literary research that questions or even discards close reading as the sole proper activity for the literary scholar. Instead of textual exegesis, these theorists most frequently place literary history or the social function of literature in the foreground. The "horizon of expectation" *(Erwartungshorizont)* made popular by Jauß,[35] for example, cannot be properly reconstructed or objectified without recourse to social and political values. In connection with the third of the three factors that Jauß considers a prerequisite for determining the horizon, the interpreter is compelled to examine the opposition between fiction and reality, between the poetic and the practical function of language, since without these distinctions the reflective reader would have no basis of comparison: "The third factor includes the possibility that the reader can perceive it [a new work] within the narrower horizon of literary expectations, as well as within the wider horizon of experience of life."[36] Once the horizon has been established Jauß speaks of using it as a criterion for defining the aesthetic value of a literary work; the distance between the horizon of expectation and the work "determines the artistic character of a literary work according to an aesthetics of reception."[37] Although one can detect the tendency in Jauß's theory to survey the distance with solely literary determinants, as the Russian Formalists did in their conceptualization of "literary evolution,"[38] the inclusion of "life experience" (*Lebenserfahrung*) in the original reconstruction of the horizon lends Jauß's theory an unmistakable societal dimension. This refusal to relinquish the socially formative aspect of literature is reflected in Jauß's treatment of literature and history as well. Indeed, the penultimate paragraph of his "provocation" essay argues for a more secure bridge between literature and history based on a conception of literature as an active agent in the social process:

> The gap between literature and history, between aesthetic and historical knowledge, can be bridged if literary history does not simply describe the process of general history in the reflection of its works one more time, but rather when it discovers in the course of "literary evolution" that properly *socially formative* function that belongs to literature as it competes with other arts and social forces in the emancipation of mankind from its natural, religious, and social bonds.[39]

The pathos of this plea, as well as the somewhat overblown emancipatory claims, was typical for the incipient years of reception theory. But what is more significant is the emphasis on viewing literature as part of a larger social sphere. Iser, of course, cannot be accused of totally ignoring the social and the historical in his writings either. But what separates him from Jauß, as well as from most of the other early work in reception theory, is the equivocal role that history and society play in the reading process. An appropriation of Jauß or Weimann could not have avoided consideration of historical or societal function; with Iser either these questions can be marginalized or they can remain unthematized. And it is this adaptability of Iser to a more familiar model, coupled with the relative unavoidableness of the sociohistorical demands in the work of other reception theorists, that contributed, I believe, to the initial lopsided American reception.

The high point of Iser's reception in critical circles in the United States came with the summer 1980 issue of *Diacritics,* in which both an interview and two review essays of his books appeared.[40] The details of the discussions are revealing for the peculiarities reception theory encountered in crossing borders. In general, none of the pieces was typical for this journal, which usually features a poststructuralist or postmodernist critique. Two of the three questioners in the interview by correspondence were Norman Holland and Wayne Booth, neither of whom is known for his avant-garde credentials.[41] Moreover, the essays on Iser were a good deal more sympathetic than what he might have received from even a benevolent adherent to deconstruction. The first, by Rudolf E. Kuenzli, is perhaps most interesting for our concerns because we once again find the familiar attempt to divorce Iser from the Constance School. By relying on Iser's distinction between a "theory of response" *(Wirkungstheorie)* and a "theory of reception" *(Rezeptionstheorie)* and on his separation of meaning and significance, Kuenzli is able to present an Iser who is more acceptable to the mainstream American scholar. The message we get from Kuenzli's discussion is that Iser's work is primarily involved with meaning and the production of meaning. Significance, which means for Iser the reader's response to meaning and therefore entails sociology and history, lies outside of Iser's theoretical terrain.[42] Iser's own view of this matter, cited by Kuenzli as evidence for his presentation, affirms the radical chasm between areas of competence: "The first instance (the intersubjective structure of meaning-production) relates to a theory of literary effect, the second (the significance ascribed to meaning) to a theory of reception, which will be rather more sociological than literary."[43] Now there are, of course, substantive differences between Iser and Jauß. Indeed, I have just argued that the lopsided American reception during the seventies is due in no small part to perceived dissimilarities in their projects. Still it seems to me that Iser's distinctions and Kuenzli's acceptance of them are too neat. The separation of meaning and significance in the reading process ultimately breaks down, as Iser's own discussions often evidence. Our search for meaning in one textual segment, for example, will depend on what kind of significance we have given a previous segment. Even if an implied reader can defer the bestowal of significance for a sentence or a paragraph, it would be impossible to suspend the endowing of significance for an entire work. Furthermore, it would be difficult to fathom what this pure reading for meaning would actually entail since language itself is saturated with social and historical values. Neither Iser's theory of response nor his interpretive illustrations avoid the "extraliterary" in the form of a recourse to society or historical reality, and the pretense that they do—and that this is even possible—must be critically evaluated as an ideological moment inhering in Iser's theoretical presuppositions.

John Paul Riquelme's more skeptical reading of Iser's works challenges Iser's seemingly neat distinctions from a slightly different perspective. The dichotomies of meaning-significance, response-reception, or literary-sociological break down, he contends, once one considers the conceptual apparatus which Iser introduces to examine meaning production. In Iser's depiction of the reading process, historical context and social norms play something more than an ancillary or supplemental role. By introducing the "repertoire," which consists of social norms and literary conventions, as an instrument for producing meaning, Iser frequently makes more concessions to society and history than he cares to admit. Indeed, his readings of Fielding would be impossible without this sociological factor.[44] Riquelme succinctly summarizes the dilemma as follows:

> Despite his announced intention to deal with response, not with reception, every time Iser identifies social and philosophical norms or even suggests that they can be identified, he has recourse to an aesthetics of reception. In practice, the distinction between response and reception breaks down as soon as Iser defines the text in relation to a historical status that is not wholly distinguishable from the history of judgments about the text.[45]

The procedure of sneaking history in through the back door—Iser's swerve from textuality, which, once postulated, is retracted and attributed to his colleague Jauß—disturbed several reviewers oriented toward pure textuality.[46] But the swerve is only a temporary avoidance maneuver, a promise never fulfilled. History thus plays an ambivalent role in Iser's theory: it intrudes just enough to upset strict textual exegetes, but it is not integrated enough at the most fundamental levels of conceptuality to satisfy historically based critics. In most of his interpretive endeavors, however, this tension is resolved by a return to close reading, narrative theory, and conventional analysis in the guise of "reader-response criticism." Riquelme recognizes Iser's furtive adherence to the tradition he boasts of superseding and comments as follows: "While ostensibly about reading, Iser's comments concerning specific narratives always focus implicitly on the ambivalence in the act of writing. They do so because they invariably direct attention to the place of the narrator. And the place of the narrator must be understood with respect to the place of the problematic implied author."[47] Iser fails, in short, to escape the long shadow of Wayne Booth.

As telling as Riquelme's analysis of Iser's works is for the American reception of reception theory, his remarks concerning what direction "reader-response" criticism could take are even more so, demonstrating again the hegemony of the text on the domestic front. After lauding Iser's treatment of modern literature, especially his elucidation of Joyce's stylistic techniques for presenting consciousness, he adds: "A critical method that paid close attention to *style*, especially to its conceptual implications, could describe the *affective* impact of form in a way that Iser's theory does not accommodate." The words I have italicized indicate the drift of the thought, toward the project of affective stylistics, toward the early work of Stanley Fish, and toward a more "formal" consideration of literary texts. For Fish's works, when categorized as another "reader-response criticism," occupied the critical space in the United States of the seventies for which Iser's (and Jauß's) theory had to vie. If we find that Fish was able to ward off Iser's competitive brand of "reader-response" criticism, then this is very likely attributable to more than his mere presence in the United States. We can suspect that it is somehow connected with what seems to be the red thread running through postwar American criticism, namely the obsession with textual analysis and the disregard of "external" factors. In light of Fish's statements about the status, or rather nonstatus, of the text, it may seem exorbitant to accuse him of a rigorous adherence to textuality. It may seem that the only constant feature in the vicissitudes of his theoretical quest during the seventies was the premise that it is only the reader, and not the text, that determines meaning.[48] But his actual critical practice depends, as he shows time and again, on following closely the words printed on the page before him.[49] His readings, in other words, do not appear to rely upon the theoretical notions that have made him so controversial; his interpretations would probably be just as "interesting" without the radical flare in his theory, although undoubtedly the phenomenon Stanley Fish would not have been.

What separates Fish's model from Iser's can be used as a balance sheet for the difference between criticism in the United States and West Germany during the initial phase of the importation of reception theory. In his theory Fish is more consistent in the sense that his arguments are more easily defended, although, as Fish himself would probably concede, they are also less convincing from a commonsense perspective. While Iser is forced into the uncomfortable position of attributing meaning to a prelinguistic realm located somewhere (spatially? temporally?) between the text and its reader, Fish, by radically undermining the objectivity of the text in his theory, effectively seals himself off from critical and metacritical objections. When disagreements arise, he simply ascribes them to differences in "assumptions" or "convention."[50] But this act of making the text disappear in theory is accompanied by a meticulous attention to it in actual interpretation. Iser looses, therefore, on both counts: his reading praxis involves less stylistic and textual analysis and sometimes even encompasses historical or sociological dimensions: and his theory is less interesting because it is perceived to be less attuned to the overblown rhetoric surrounding American poststructuralism. Reception theory in the United States until 1980, largely tied to the work of Wolfgang Iser, thus found itself outflanked and misunderstood. In the critical landscape of the seventies the advent of poststructuralism, particularly deconstruction, contributed to a continued hegemony of textual criticism under an altered philosophical guise. With regard to reader-response criticism, which likewise benefited from the general turn to theoretical concerns during the seventies, reception theory was generally viewed as a weak version of more daring domestic enterprises. In short, the American reception of reception theory highlights the dominant tendencies in literary theory in the United States until 1980: a fundamental adherence to the heritage of text-centered criticism and a continued neglect of nontextual factors, particularly history. That this could occur under the auspices of an alleged rupture with critical tradition indicates perhaps only how difficult it is, even in a land of eclectic and changing fashions, to break with past practices.

2

Confrontations with Radicalness

SINCE Conarroe's popularity pole in the *PMLA* the reception of reception theory in the United States has changed to some extent. If the Constance School was effectively barred from extensive critical consideration during the seventies, then we could say that it fully arrived in the United States in the early eighties. This tardy crossing of borders was manifested in the publication of three books authored by Hans Robert Jauß[1] and in the continued efforts of several journals of criticism, among them *New Literary History* and—to a lesser degree—*Diacritics,* to mediate this branch of German criticism to an English-speaking public. The regular visiting appointment Iser enjoys at the University of California at Irvine, as well as frequent visits by Jauß and other members of the Constance community, has also assisted in introducing the American critical establishment to the full scope of reception theory. Perhaps the renewed interest in theories other than poststructuralism, a tendency that continued and became more pronounced in the course of the past decade, reflects a discontent with the monopoly that French theory held during a good part of the seventies. For what it's worth, statistical evidence could also be produced to substantiate this broadening of concern. While Jauß and Iser were not even mentioned in Conarroe's survey of submissions to *PMLA* in 1979, my own more recent and equally unscientific procedures showed that they were among the more frequently cited critics in the pages of this prestigious journal during the decade of the eighties. At the start of the nineties, therefore, it would be unusual if a fairly well informed literary theorist in the United States had not heard of or read texts by members of the Constance School.

Still I think it would be a mistake to believe that the critical establishment in the United States has accepted the precepts of reception theory or that reception theory has gained a significant following outside of German departments and German studies. Reception theory is still an optional and marginal theoretical tendency in the United States. A recent anthology of major statements in twentieth-century literary theory documents this quite clearly.[2] Significant in the first place is the underrepresentation of German theory, a feature we noted in the Conarroe poll as well; in foreign theory French and Russian authors predominate. Among contemporary German critics only Iser is included, and the absence of Lukács, Benjamin, and Adorno is remarkable. Perhaps most relevant for our concerns here is that even under the category of "reception" we encounter only a single essay, by Iser, who, we should recall, considers himself to be dealing with response and effect (*Wirkung*). In a volume reviewing major contemporary theories we find a similar neglect. The section on audience-oriented criticism by Peter J. Rabinowitz repeats all the American biases we noted in the seventies.[3] Ignoring the remarkable unity in the Constance School and the regular colloquia held there, Rabinowitz relies exclusively on the American view of a dispersed, nonunified collection of isolated critics. Only one book by Jauß is mentioned in the bibliography; and the discussion as a whole evidences no knowledge of reception theory's former importance on the continent. In the same volume Jauß and Iser make a brief appearance under phenomenological directions, but are totally ignored under hermeneutics, where at least Jauß is most obviously at home.[4] Vincent Leitch has the matter in correct perspective. In his four-hundred-page history *American Literary Criticism from the Thirties to the Eighties* the contribution of "German Reception Theory" can be described in three pages.[5] The progress that reception theory has made during the eighties is therefore perhaps not as great as we might assume from counting footnotes in *PMLA*. Although most major theorists and many coming into the field are now familiar with the general precepts of reception theory, to my knowledge there are no endeavors to extend or refine a position based on these precepts; nor are there any major studies in English—again outside of American Germanistik—which put this theory into practice. In the volume *Literary Theory Today,* the essay by Jauß is—perhaps appropriately—a retrospective on the unacknowledged prehistory of the movement he initiated, not a programmatic statement of future directions.[6] Although critics like Peter Uwe Hohendahl have done a great deal of work in English that relates to reception,[7] by and large colleagues in departments of English and American literature have continued to go their own ways.

Once again we can only speculate about the reasons for the continued disinterest displayed toward a branch of criticism which has been so popular in both Germanies. Certainly two factors I touched upon above have contributed to this neglect. The first is the lack of philosophical grounding for a reception of reception theory. Hermeneutics, especially in its Heideggerian-Gadamerian variant, and the phenomenology of Husserl and Ingarden were never topical in literature departments; indeed, with the hegemony of the analytical tradition throughout most of the United States, they have not even received much attention in most philosophy departments. Samuel Weber, in an essay devoted to a consideration of Iser's *The Act of Reading,* to which I shall return in a moment, states quite correctly that Iser's "critical position derives in large part from a tradition (Husserl, Ingarden, the group 'Poetics and Hermeneutics') that has remained outside the mainstream of North American critical theory."[8] But reception theory is a specifically Middle European phenomenon not only from the perspective of its intellectual heritage. As I have argued previously, the astounding success of reception theory first in the Federal Republic and later, in reaction to this, in the German Democratic Republic depended on a particular constellation of events in German academic life, and this may assist in explaining its diminished appeal in the United States. With regard to the West I have already mentioned in particular the student movement and its interaction with issues of methodology.[9] In the East I would point to an endeavor on the part of less orthodox theorists to break away from sclerotic notions inherited from the earlier dogmatism of socialist realism. In both Germanies reception theory appears to have offered an answer to questions not posed on this side of the Atlantic.

But it seems to me that the relative neglect of reception theory is not solely attributable to its philosophical underpinnings or its special German context. Deconstruction, after all, has had remarkable success by appealing to the same intellectual traditions (in a very different manner), and the situation at West German universities during the sixties and seventies was not so totally different from the situation in the United States. Perhaps a more fruitful way for us to understand the parameters of crossing borders is by a consideration of image and "packaging." On the academic marketplace reception theory simply appeared to be a less desirable commodity. When compared with theories that were more popular and adaptable for US scholars, it seemed drab and somewhat worn. What became increasingly apparent in the eighties was that reception theory was never perceived as a radical departure from more familiar approaches; it appeared more traditional, more conservative, and more commonplace than even the most popular forms of reader-response criticism and certainly more colorless than almost all varieties of poststructuralism, especially deconstruction. This contention is of course strange for those who remember the turbulence of the late sixties in West Germany and the various manifesto-like proclamations calling for a turn to the study of the reader and response. Indeed, in order to be heard at all among the din of voices calling for a reexamination of method, reception theory, as I have shown above, had to announce itself as a revolution in literary scholarship. But this is not the way it was perceived—or is perceived today—in the United States. In the final chapter of *Reception Theory* I staged a confrontation between this German branch of criticism and the so-called avant-garde in the United States with respect to four concepts: the text, the reader, interpretation, and history.[10] This staging was necessary in the early eighties because of the absence of native response to reception theory. Today, however, we have sufficient comments to alleviate the need for a constructed dialogue or debate. Although relatively few native critics have bothered to comment at length on reception theory, a consideration of those who have commented demonstrates why it seems to break the revolutionary promises which accompanied its rise and acceptance in German critical circles.

Let me begin with the most severe assault against a member of the Constance School and the only one which has occasioned a debate in print. It occurred in the spring 1981 issue of *Diacritics* where Stanley Fish reviewed Iser's *The Act of Reading*.[11] We will recall that Fish was originally part of the three-person mail interview *Diacritics* arranged in the summer of 1980, and from his review we can see why he preferred comment to questions. In the most general terms we could observe that Fish objects to the timidity of theorizing by his German colleague and to his protean appeal. Iser, according to him, is somehow everything to everyone; he appears to stand on both sides of all important issues, and thus never makes anyone feel uncomfortable. He is thus a kind of theoretical chameleon, and after a brief and fair summary of the chief arguments in the book, Fish sets out to examine how exactly he manages to be so inoffensive to so many potentially antagonistic camps. He thinks that he has found the answer to this enigma in Iser's use of the opposition determinacy/indeterminacy. Fish starts by questioning the validity of the first half of this pair. According to Iser the reader's activity consists largely of filling in blanks in the text. What Fish questions initially is the nature of these blanks. Whereas Iser suggests that blanks are somehow there in the text and therefore independent of the reader, Fish contends that they do not exist before a prior act of interpretation. The issue separating them here is thus really one of epistemology as much as of literary theory. Perception of any sort is for Fish a mediated activity; it is never "innocent of assumptions," while for Iser, it would appear, there are some things that simply exist and must be perceived by all viewers. Because Fish disputes this point, he also attacks Iser's repeated endeavors to distinguish between our interaction with the world and with the text. There are differences, he concedes, but they do not involve a distinction between perception and ideation, as Iser claims, nor do they entail a difference in the degree of determinacy. Both activities—interacting with a text and interacting with the world—are equally conventional and mediated. What we see or understand is always already informed by a prior perspective or framework that enables the very seeing and understanding.

If there are no determinate objects for interpretation but only interpreted objects that are erroneously called determinate, one might suppose that Fish would then validate a totally arbitrary, subjective indeterminacy, as some American reader-response critics have done. But this is most emphatically not the case. In fact, Fish disputes the notion of indeterminacy on the same grounds that he rejected determinacy. Because we are always operating inside of an interpretive framework, because we have no access to a free subjectivity unconstrained by conventions, indeterminacy, if it is conceived as the reader's individual contribution to the meaning of a text, is impossible. While Fish argued previously, therefore, that there is nothing in the text that is given—he uses the terms "given" and "determinate" synonymously—and everything is supplied, he here maintains that nothing is supplied and everything is given. Although he seems to have backed himself into a corner, he is really quite consistent. The paradox dissolves once we recognize that he, like many poststructuralist critics, has simply viewed the problem of reading texts—and interacting with the world—from the perspective of a code (or convention) that informs and determines individual response. He has raised the entire problem, as Iser had posed it, to a metacritical level. Thus he does not claim that the analysis of a text is impossible using Iser's model. An interpretation of any work could be performed using the distinction between textual givens and the reader's contributions. Indeed, Iser himself has demonstrated this time and again. But Fish claims that every component in such an account is itself the consequence of a particular interpretive strategy which possesses validity only inside of a particular system of intelligibility. Iser's perspective is, in short, limited, and Fish criticizes him by assuming a position that implicitly maintains it can overlook his and all other theoretical pronouncements.

The tone of Iser's reply to this assault shows that he was displeased with both the content and the tenor of the arguments used against him.[12] But instead of taking Fish to task at the metacritical level on which he is operating, he commits the error of clarifying his own terms in order to correct his adversary's misunderstandings. I feel this is a strategic blunder on his part because Fish has stacked his argument so that he cannot lose. It is difficult to imagine an explanation Iser could have given that would have nullified Fish's objections, since these objections apply to any theory purporting to distinguish between things that are determinate and other things that are indeterminate. Nonetheless, Iser proceeds to untangle what he feels is a central confusion by setting up a tripartite distinction: "The words of a text are given, the interpretation of the words is determinate, and the gaps between the given elements and/or interpretations are the indeterminacies."[13] With these terms he evidently thinks he can separate our interaction with the real world from our interaction with texts:

> The real world is given, our interpretation of the world is determinate, the gaps between given elements and/or our interpretations are the indeterminacies. The difference is that with the literary text, it is the interpretation of the words that produces the literary world—i.e. its real-ness, unlike that of the outside world, is not given.[14]

With these distinctions firmly in hand—or so Iser thinks—he then goes on to argue that there has to be something which restricts interpretation, some "given" that limits or constraints arbitrary, subjective response. But the very fact that he believes he must defend himself on this point just indicates that he has misunderstood what Fish has argued and the level on which he has argued it. Fish is not taking the Berkeleyan stance Iser ascribes to him; he is not claiming that only what is perceived actually exists. He too would presumably admit the existence of words or marks on a page or at least something that is there prior to interpretation. His contention is, however, that these "givens" are meaningless—they are not even "pointable to" as givens—before we endow them with meaning as "givens." We might observe, then, that Iser's confusion comes from his employing the word "givens" in two distinct ways. On the one hand, he uses the term to denote mere existence, and Fish could probably be convinced to use "givens" in this way as well. But it also designates for him the intersubjective recognizability of existing things, such as we have seen in the statements above. When he writes that "the words of a text are given," Fish might counter that marks on a page are recognizable as words only within a certain context that includes (for example), at a minimal level, literacy. Fish's point is that elements are given in the second sense of the word only if they are situated in a system in which elements can be perceived. Interpretation or interpretive conventions precede their determination as elements. Similarly Fish does not maintain that on a practical level nothing in the text restrains interpretation. He maintains rather that the very perception of constraints or the ability to constrain is possible only because the interpreter is already operating within a convention or under a set of assumptions.

Let us leave the Fish-Iser debate for a moment and turn to Paul de Man's confrontation with the reception theory of Hans Robert Jauß.[15] While Fish's attack occurred within the secure confines of a journal which exalts the "sirens of literary theory,"[16] de Man presents his objections as part of an introduction to the English edition of Jauß's works. Perhaps this is one of the reasons that the critique is so much less abrasive than Fish's. In any case he does not undertake a frontal assault, but instead, as is his habit, seeks to uncover in a gentle and careful fashion the blindness that enables the insight. Accordingly his remarks ostensibly praise his colleague's perspicuity and rigor. He is particularly laudatory with regard to Jauß's synthetic abilities. After briefly discussing the reception and shortcomings of Prague structuralism, he writes: "It is Jauß's considerable merit to have perceived and demonstrated the linkage between reception and semiotics."[17] What bothers de Man about the aesthetics of reception, however, is that, in a certain sense, it takes too much for granted. In its most general terms de Man's objection can be conceived of as directed against an inattentiveness to language, or more precisely, against an illicit equating of the phenomenal with the linguistic realm. "The hermeneutics of experience," de Man admonishes, "and the hermeneutics of reading are not necessarily compatible."[18] De Man is particularly concerned here that the notion of a "horizon of expectation," a term he identifies with the phenomenological tradition, not be made "applicable, without further elaboration, to the arts of language."[19] In more particular terms Jauß's deficiency may be attributed to his neglect of all those theorists who problematize the stability of signification and the determinacy of the signifier. At one point in the introduction de Man refers to

> Jauß's lack of interest, bordering on outright dismissal, in any considerations derived from what has, somewhat misleadingly, come to be known as the

"play" of the signifier, semantic effects produced on the level of the letter rather than of the word or the sentence and which therefore escape from the network of hermeneutic questions and answers.[20]

Those familiar with the idiom of poststructuralism will know immediately what de Man is referring to here. Jauß is being chastised for failing to integrate the insights of the most recent French theorists, in particular for ignoring the linguistically unavoidable ambiguities which accompany any text. A third way to understand Jauß's shortcoming, however, involves reexamining the grand synthetic project for which he is so heartily commended. From this perspective de Man suggests that Jauß is guilty of suppressing the potentially destructive force of rhetoric—a key term in de Man's critical vocabulary—in order to complete his unification of poetics and hermeneutics unaffected by the disruption of the letter.

The radical nature of de Man's critique, however, can be most clearly discerned in connection with his discussion of Walter Benjamin. De Man remarks that Benjamin's opposition to reception theory in the essay "The Task of the Translator" was noted by Rainer Warning.[21] But he points out that this rejection of response on the part of Benjamin should not be viewed as a conservative concession to some essentialist mode of interpretation, but rather as a recognition of the negativity inherent in the very process of understanding. De Man feels that this essay is particularly important because Benjamin deals with translation, which, as an interlinguistic process, obviates the opposition between subject and object.

Throughout the essay, Benjamin's point is that translation, as well as the insuperable difficulty that inhabits its project, exposes certain tensions that pertain specifically to language: a possible incompatibility between proposition (*Satz*) and denomination (*Wort*) or between the literal and what he calls the symbolic meaning of a text or, within the symbolic dimension itself, between what is being symbolized and the symbolizing function.[22]

This theory of a necessary interlinguistic discrepancy returns later when de Man discusses Jauß's model of reading. De Man argues that the inclusion of a horizon of expectation as the focal point for *Rezeptionsästhetik* makes it a conservative enterprise. With respect to the oppositions classical/modern and mimetic/allegorical, Jauß must be identified with the former terms: "If literary understanding involves a horizon of expectation it resembles a sense of perception, and it will be correct to the precise extent that it 'imitates' such a perception."[23] Again we should note that de Man is identifying the horizon of expectation exclusively with its roots in Husserlian phenomenology. Thus even

Jauß's category of allegoresis, which Jauß opposes to mimesis, is informed for de Man by a traditional "aesthetics of representation." By contrast, de Man hails Benjamin's "anorganic" notion of allegory, which depends on the letter. Like translation and rhetoric, the allegorical associated with Benjamin defies and questions the synthetic activity at the heart of Jauß's enterprise. Indeed, for de Man allegory is the rhetorical process which removes a text from the phenomenological realm of the world and places it in a grammatical, language-oriented realm of the letter. Thus Jauß is guilty of an illicit identification of word and world, which Benjamin carefully avoids in his early piece on translation as well as in his monograph on baroque tragedy. De Man summarizes as follows: "The debate between Jauß and Benjamin on allegory is a debate between the classical position, here represented by Jauß, and a tradition that undoes it."[24] In this confrontation, so carefully staged by de Man, *Rezeptionsästhetik* again appears as something less radical, as a method which, for all its advantages, fails to break with familiar and conservative presuppositions.

A more recent confrontation with reception theory, this time again with the work of Wolfgang Iser, occurred in 1986 in the first volume of the revitalized journal *Glyph*.[25] The editor, Samuel Weber, in a clever and well-argued essay entitled "Caught in the Act of Reading," examines in some detail how the author of the *The Act of Reading* himself reads. Weber points out that in order to construct his theory Iser has frequent recourse to both literary illustrations and other theoretical texts, and the question that he then poses concerns the status of this material. In his book Iser endeavors to dismiss the issue by claiming that his particular readings of texts are not interpretations, but merely clarifications. If his examples clarify, Weber argues, then they must clarify something, and this something must be the intentions that inform the work, i.e., what the author means to say. But what Iser qua author in fact says is something quite different, for his theory maintains that reading is tantamount to the concretization of a skeletal structure. We are thus faced with the rather unusual situation of Iser's asserting that reading necessarily entails the actualization of texts, while simultaneously insisting that his own readings escape this very general precept. By closely examining Iser's readings, Weber then demonstrates very persuasively how Iser in fact distorts the meaning of several theorists on whom he calls for support. The texts of these theorists do not control the reading, as Iser's model postulates, since he is able to derive from their theoretical pronouncements a meaning which runs counter to their express intention. His performance, therefore, comes into conflict with his own theoretical utterances on what reading necessarily entails.

Weber's point, however, is not just that Iser contradicts himself. Rather, he is interested in showing what Iser hopes to accomplish with a model of reading in which a text steers and delimits response. Without repeating his arguments in all their intricacy, let me summarize his results. First he demonstrates that Iser depends upon a notion of the text as a totality. In its complex interrelationship with the external world, a work of art encompasses all particular relationships. Literature is systematic for Iser "insofar as it constitutes a process of totalization, and it does this by incorporating what the extraliterary system, to which it responds and refers, leaves out."[26] Second, and related to the notion of totality, is Iser's affirmation of a transcendental perspective from which readers interact with texts. Implicit in Iser's theory is a terminal point for the reading process. The object is always to regain a transcendental position; the text supposedly leads us to this position, although it is only our activity which allows us to reach it. Weber's point here is that for Iser such a position is assumed to be available, at least *in potentia*. Finally, Weber argues that despite all the talk about the reader, the—perhaps unwitting—consequence of Iser's theory is to reassert the primacy of the author. This follows from the first two points. For the totality in which the reader is supposed to participate and the transcendental viewpoint she or he is called upon to regain assume some larger unifying principle. Obviously this principle cannot be the text, since it is itself open to a multitude of different concretizations. What ultimately controls the reader and the reading process is therefore the familiar notion of a self-identical authorial intention.

Weber closes his essay with an interpretation of Henry James's short story "The Figure in the Carpet." Iser used his own reading of this piece in the introductory chapter of *The Act of Reading* to validate the shift in literary criticism that he would later advocate.[27] The gist of Iser's argument in this introduction is that there are two ways to go about interpretation. The first is traditional: it treats a text as the repository of some more or less secret meaning that it is the critic's duty to ferret out. The other, which Iser's work will propose, views meaning as something emerging from an interaction with the text; it is not already there waiting to be discovered, but rather produced as part of the response to the work. Weber counters this interpretation with a psychoanalytically informed reading of the story, especially of the role of the anonymous narrator, suggesting that we have to recast our notion of criticism in terms of desire. "It is the game of the critic's desire to discover an object that is ultimately nothing other than *the desire of the critic,* in both senses of the genitive."[28] Iser, Weber claims, has fallen into the mode of critical endeavor he tells us to avoid. He has read the story and found a kernel of meaning that was presumably already there, placed in the text by the author. While it is difficult to see how Weber himself could avoid the same conclusion about his own reading—after all he too finds something in the text that substantiates his claim to describe what criticism really is or should be—he nonetheless presents us with a radically different model. Although the precepts and contours of this alternative remain elusive, we can be certain that it entails a rejection of Iser's phenomenological presuppositions. In the traditional sense embraced by Iser, "to criticize," Weber writes, "is to distinguish the truth of the work (or 'text') from its others, and this can justify itself ultimately only by construing literature to be an intentional object, the product of a sovereign and transparent self-consciousness, the idealized projection of the consciousness to which literary criticism has always aspired."[29] Although it is not clear how or why, Weber would obviously have it otherwise.

The responses of Fish, de Man, and Weber to Iser and Jauß are certainly very different. Fish, from a position of neopragmatic skepticism, attacks the notions of determinacy and indeterminacy, the very cornerstones of Iser's theory; de Man, in a more deconstructive fashion, criticizes *Rezeptionsästhetik* for its inattentiveness to language; and Weber, from a similar although slightly more Lacanian perspective, assails an obsolete manner of critical endeavor couched in the terminology of reader response. Yet I would maintain that all three share a common ground, one that can perhaps be described best by the word "radicalness." The dominant objection to reception theory in the eighties is captured by these three critics insofar as they represent alternatives that appear to undo, in a fundamental way, the projects proposed by Iser and Jauß. The question that presents itself, then, is what constitutes this radicalness. In order to investigate this we may leave aside for the moment an evaluation of the validity of each critique, since the force of the respective criticisms derives as much from the style as from the content. Let us then return briefly to the objections and formulations of Fish, de Man, and Iser in order to look more closely at the kind of radical gestures employed to confront reception theory; for in examining this radical gesturing we will also encounter major paradigms from the dominant discourse of literary theory as it has been practiced in the United States for the past two decades.

The first feature we can discern in all three confrontations might be called the metacritical maneuver. This consists in portraying the theory to be criticized as a local and confined response. The metacritic implicitly claims the ability to oversee literary theory, and from this higher, broader, and quasi-transcendental perspective the theorist under consideration appears naive and limited. We have already seen that Fish prominently employs this strategy to discredit Iser's work. A theory of response that depends on a distinction between indeterminate and determinate elements will be an efficient machine for generating readings, Fish maintains, but these readings are in no way more valid, more accurate, or more faithful than any others since they are perforce the products of an arbitrary interpretive convention. But de Man and Weber assume a similar superior position with regard to their subjects. For the former this is most obvious in his discussion of the classical trappings of Jauß's horizon of expectations. We have already seen above that de Man likens Jauß's project of interpretation to correct perception. For this reason Jauß can never fathom the radical otherness of the truly allegorical. "The negativity inherent in the Husserlian model is a negativity within the sensory itself and not its negation, let alone its 'other.'"[30] The message here, as in Fish's review, is that the aesthetics of reception operates within the strictures of a narrow framework, and that de Man is able to stand outside this framework and observe options unseen or unseeable by Jauß. The same is true of Weber's remarks. He correctly notes Iser's dependence on the construction of visual images for his theory of response, but from his privileged perspective he can envision this process of visualization as well as the nonimagistic alternatives. The point here is that American radicalness entails a certain way of disqualifying the validity of an adversarial theory. A "nonradical" approach is not so much wrong or incorrect or invalid as it is naive, limited, and limiting. Reception theory is not criticized on its own terms, for what it does, or how it performs, but placed in a perspective in which this sort of criticism is superfluous.

A second strategy employed by this brand of radicalness is to attribute to the criticized theory an unwitting retention of superannuated philosophical or theoretical tenets. Since anything old is immediately suspect, reception theorists who openly rely on tradition will appear unacceptable. This disqualification of the heritage is found most clearly in the observations of de Man and Weber. Both criticize reception theory for adhering to phenomenological models and for not paying more attention to recent developments in the theory of language, particularly in France. De Man, as we have witnessed, is especially candid about this topic. After noting the absence of "play" in Jauß's work, he writes:

> Such a concern with "the instances of the letter" is particularly in evidence, as is well known, among certain French writers not generally included within Jauß's own critical canon of relevant *Fachliteratur.* He has always treated such Parisian extravagances with a measure of suspicion and even when, under the pressure of their persistence as well as of genuine affinities between their enterprise and his own, he acknowledged some of their findings, it has always been a guarded and partial recognition.[31]

Weber makes a similar point when he contends that Iser never manages to break through to a new notion of criticism, and actually falls back into an all too familiar pattern. "It is remarkable, then," he writes, "that *The Act of Reading,* which begins precisely by questioning the traditional conception of literature as a repository of univocal meaning, nevertheless gravitates toward the very position it sets out to criticize."[32] The rhetoric of the radical avant-garde clearly valorizes novelty, rupture, and discontinuity, while it scorns progress, tradition, and dialectical process. The surest means of gaining the upper hand on an adversary, in fact, is to reveal his or her dependence on a heritage that predates the insights of Lacan or Derrida.

A final element of the American radicalness I have been describing is its negativity. If we consider that reception theory offers a positive model of how to deal with literary texts, then the result of these various confrontations has been to undercut this positivity without offering much in the way of an alternative. Fish's objections to the problem of the given and the supplied call into question not only Iser's theory of response, but any endeavor to come to terms with the reading process, including, one might add, his own. By setting the stakes at the level of the linguistic code, he undermines the coherence of any more limited approach to literary reception and effect. De Man's procedure in dealing with Jauß is similar in that he suggests the impossibility of every hermeneutic project—insofar, of course, as this project makes claims to truth. In opening up texts to an unavoidable linguistic instability, he necessarily forfeits any certainty in interpretation. All critical endeavor, including de Man's, are always already undone before they have been conceived. Finally Weber's alternative to Iser's critical model remains hazy because his assumptions allow only negation. Indeed, his final sentence speaks of a reading that "is forever caught in an act it can never quite get together."[33] But once again this avowal of futility ultimately boomerangs; with equal justification we could turn around and attack his own interpretation of "The Figure in the Carpet," or, for that matter, of *The Act of Reading* itself. In denying a transcendental position and the authority of the author, Weber would appear to cancel his own authority as well. Iser, it turns out, is not the only one "caught in the act of reading"; for according to the premises outlined by Weber this is a universal fate. It would be absurd to deny that these three critics of reception theory negate critical activity. In a paradoxical fashion the criticisms that they offer open up texts to an abundance of interpretive possibilities. But these possibilities are ultimately and fundamentally repetitions of a task whose outcome is already known. The lesson we learn is that criticism is doomed to perform an action that has been always already undone and negated before it begins.

The radicalness of American theory thus remains entangled in a self-canceling mechanism of ironic one-upmanship and a spiral of infinitely negative speculation. What is perhaps more disturbing than this Sisyphean state of affairs, however, is the rather dubious political valence of this radicalness. All three critiques make gestures in the direction of progressive politics, but it is difficult to determine whether this gesture is the sign of a greeting or a hasty departure. Fish upbraids Iser for his popularity with American academics. His theory, we are told, is "particularly well suited to the pluralism of most American literary criticism."[34] Iser embraces a safe and comfortable liberalism; no one warns against reading him (except perhaps Fish); he is not on anyone's hit list. This may very well be true, but why Fish is more dangerous and why the writers on his list pose more of a threat—and to whom?—is not clear at all. De Man's faint gesture to the political comes with his citation of Benjamin, who is called upon to play the foil to the traditional, classical Jauß. Benjamin is placed in a succession of radical subversion from Hamann to Nietzsche, but de Man conveniently ignores what precisely he was trying to subvert. No mention is made of his marxist affiliations, his ties with Brecht, or his anticapitalist views. Weber, who is most aware of the problem, nevertheless fares no better than his would-be radical colleagues. His claim to revolutionary politics exhausts itself in remarks directed against Iser's audience. He maintains, for example, that the addressees of Iser's work consist of similarly minded, transcendence-oriented professionals. Later he takes a swipe at Iser's reception "in the land that has traditionally fancied itself the home of rugged individualism." And he chastises his work for its "semblance of secular pluralism" and its "atmosphere of liberalism."[35] But his putatively more radical critique, as we have seen, offers no alternative in terms of either a positive theory or a possible politics.

American confrontations with reception theory thus disclose a deeply seated malaise in critical circles, one that I shall discuss in more detail with regard to deconstruction in the third section of this book. Forever employing a self-defeating metacriticism that attacks the very transcendental position from which it apparently makes its own categorical pronouncements, the currently fashionable radicalness heralds a permanent and self-consuming revolution of novelty and negativity. While it pretends to have political implications, when questioned about its politics, it has nothing comprehensible to say. For its element is exclusively that of the logos that it so often debunks, but is condemned to employ. Its most important objective is not to further knowledge, a proposition in which it no longer believes, but to render its own arguments impervious to attack. Perhaps this is the reason that the sophistry of the radically skeptical antitheoretical position could gain such widespread attention during the eighties as well.[36] All this does not mean that the preceding criticisms of reception theory are unjustified; nor does it let reception theorists off the hook for their abysmal ignorance of what has been going on in these avant-garde circles in the United States and France. But it does suggest that a deeper understanding of the traditions and the ramifications of the work of the best reception theorists might still play a fruitful role in American criticism. Although the border crossing of reception theory may never benefit from such an understanding, it could have the function of promoting a genuine debate concerning the possibilities and limits of radicalness.

Part Two

Poststructuralism in Germany

3

French Theory and German Scholarship

POSTSTRUCTURALISM, perhaps the dominant critical discourse in France since the late sixties and the critical rage in the United States and Britain since the middle of the following decade, never really gained much of a following in Germany during these years. While on this side of the Atlantic practically every major literary critic and every aspiring theorist have been compelled at one point to discuss some aspect of this wave of French theory, most Germans at the university have been spared any such confrontation. At first glance this absence may appear difficult to explain. After all, the French scene since at least the end of the war has been dominated by German philosophical thought. According to Vincent Descombes this hegemony can be summed up conveniently in two successive trinities. Until about 1960 the central concern was the three H's: Hegel, Husserl, and Heidegger; thereafter, the "masters of suspicion"—Marx, Nietzsche, and Freud—gradually gained ascendancy.[1] The poststructuralists, in allegedly drawing inspiration and sustenance from the latter while struggling against the former, should have been discussing issues that were at the heart of German concerns as well. While some might want to debate whether Heidegger does not belong on both sides of the two trinities, few would doubt that German thought has dominated French theory for the past two and a half decades. Nor can one cite a lack of exposure or opportunity as the reason for the scarcity of German interest in poststructuralism either. By the early eighties most of the major writers usually associated with poststructuralism had seen their works translated into German at major publishing houses. Barthes and Foucault, for example, had over a dozen volumes appear in the Suhrkamp Verlag, probably the most respected publisher of intellectual books in West Germany since the sixties. Selections from Lacan's *Ecrits* appeared in both a one-volume and a three-volume edition, making this work more accessible to the reading public in Germany than in the United States. The trio of major works that thrust Derrida into prominence in 1967—*Speech and Phenomena, Writing and Difference,* and *Of Grammatology*—were all in print in Germany by the early eighties, and a steady trickle of translations of Derrida's works has appeared as they were written. Even somewhat less renowned French writers like Gilles Deleuze and Félix Guattari, Luce Irigaray, or Julia Kristeva have been published by Suhrkamp. Indeed, if we considered just the number of translations and the promptness of their publication, we would have to conclude that German intellectuals have had a *greater* opportunity to acquaint themselves with poststructuralism than theorists in the United States. If the smaller, more specialized publishing houses like Merve in Berlin or Walter in Freiburg were included in our purview of poststructuralist dissemination in Germany, then we could extend the list of names to include writers like Jean Baudrillard, Hélène Cixous, Jean-François Lyotard, and Philippe Lacoue-Labarthe as well. And if we also catalogued the scores of essays and excerpts that have appeared in journals or anthologies, the list could undoubtedly be extended even further.

A heavy reliance on Germany philosophy and an ample exposure were not (and still are not) evidently enough to make poststructuralism anything near the vital source of theory it has become in the United States. It was obviously much easier for the French to cross the Atlantic than the Rhine. Reasons for this missing reception in prominent intellectual circles belong ultimately to the realm of speculation, but I would like to offer three possibilities that might serve as part of an explanation. They can be presented most effectively, I believe, by comparing the German state of affairs with the situation in the United States, where the impact of poststructuralism, particularly during the decade from 1975 to 1985, has been more obvious and more pervasive. In the first place, poststructuralism has found no influential advocate or advocates in intellectual and theoretical circles in Germany. While in the United States some of the most respected critics at the most august universities embraced, advanced, and disseminated French thought throughout the seventies, no German counterparts ever emerged. As I will argue on the following pages, the death of Peter Szondi was unfortunate in this regard since he had both the stature and the inclination to make poststructuralism a legitimate force in at least literary circles. The result of this dearth of advocates is that nothing corresponding to the "Yale School" emerged in the Federal Republic. There were never any literature departments or universities that were associated primarily with poststructuralist thought; the occasional groupings that did emerge at places like Freiburg and Berlin appear to be marginal and the result of initiatives on the part of younger, less established scholars.

A second and related factor has to do with the scarcity of positions at German universities following the student movement of the sixties and early seventies. One result of the protests against an antiquated and elitist educational system was the creation of new staff positions. Although most of the new professorships were less prestigious and influential than the former chairs for full professors, which traditionally carried with them considerable power and an entourage of younger assistants, they were nonetheless secure positions with tenure. The vast influx of younger scholars into the university system had the immediate effect of democratizing and enlivening the university, but it also effectively plugged up hiring for an entire generation of academicians. For the past fifteen years most of the best traditional scholars, with full support of the professorial establishment, have had difficulties securing teaching positions. Young poststructuralists, without strong backing and scholarly legitimacy, found it almost impossible to compete successfully for the few positions that became vacant. In the United States, by contrast, poststructuralist credentials have not really proven to be a barrier to employment or publication—although many poststructuralists would have us believe otherwise in order to nurture the requisite martyr complex and to promote the image of "outsider" to the establishment. In the United States poststructuralists very often graduated from the "best" schools, had the institutional authorization of renowned and established professors, and were assisted in publication in the most frequently quoted journals and most prestigious university presses. Although jobs have been scarce in the United States as well, quite often an older, more traditional department has sought someone familiar with the new "critical theory," if only to quell graduate student unrest at its antiquated theoretical practices. One could almost say that the competition for positions in Germany forced—consciously or unconsciously—young scholars to safer, more acceptable alternatives, while the literary establishment in the United States, in which poststructuralists thrived and often set standards, pushed graduate students toward a more thorough, albeit too often uncritical, adoption of French thought.

A final reason for the absence of poststructuralist influence in Germany has to do with the tradition into which it had to be absorbed. The

German philosophers that were so important for the French poststructuralists were often viewed quite differently on the other side of the Rhine. Nietzsche and Heidegger, for example, although they have had a considerable following in the postwar years, were also and always associated with a highly suspect political tradition. Their antidemocratic attitudes and association with fascism did not make them very popular among young leftist intellectuals in the student movement, precisely the group that might have been expected to show interest in poststructuralism.[2] Marx, whose work was cited frequently by the sixty-eight generation in Germany, was more traditionally conceived than the structuralist, Althusserian variant popular in France, and the poststructuralist Marx often bore no resemblance to his German counterpart. Freud, the last of the three great German thinkers to inspire the French, has never had the popularity in the German-speaking world that he has enjoyed in North America and in France, particularly since Lacan. Effectively excluded from legitimacy by National Socialism, he was never able to secure much of a following in the postwar years. The German thinkers that were so readily received by the French and exported to the United States under the Francophilic seal of approval were simply viewed through the lenses of a different cultural heritage in Germany. Moreover, poststructuralism filled distinct gaps in France and, later, in the United States that were occupied somewhat differently in Germany. While poststructuralism on its native soil was conceived as part of a rebellion connected with May 1968, it was appropriated in the United States, as I have stated above, more as a continuation of close reading and the New Criticism. It changed the trajectory of textual analysis, supplying it with a more sophisticated theoretical and philosophical profile, but it did not challenge the hallowed textualist assumptions of literary interpretation. In West Germany, this type of reception was unavailable. The politicized German citicism of the late sixties was more closely allied with the marxist tradition and with the Critical Theory of the Frankfurt School, neither of which had any obvious link to the French scene. While poststructuralism could therefore thrive in the radical atmosphere in Paris and environs and—in a less politicized form a decade later—in the American academy, lacking roots in German intellectual life and utilizing a language that is still notorious for its obscurity, it received as scant attention from oppositional critics in the Federal Republic as it did from their conservative adversaries. When the critical controversies had finally subsided toward the middle of the seventies, the situation described above—lack of noteworthy advocates and a depressed academic market—made German poststructuralism the marginal current that it remained throughout the seventies and eighties.

What nonetheless managed to take root as German poststructuralism in the late seventies was thus less a critical movement than a coterie of scholars who at some point became intrigued with French theory. As far as I can discern, they had neither a single spiritual father figure nor an intellectual center from which they originated, although Freiburg and Berlin crop up in their intellectual biographies too often to be coincidental. Nor do they appear to share a common educational experience, if we discount the obligatory pilgrimages to Paris to study with their mentors at first hand. What unites them, besides similar proclivities in theory, are age—they were all at the beginning of their careers around 1980—and initial difficulties in securing a position in the established world of German university life. Perhaps their most outstanding feature is their productivity. Since the late seventies scores of works have appeared in a variety of publishing houses, from the more established firms like Suhrkamp and Fink to more specialized smaller publishers specializing in postmodern trends. It is of course impossible for me to deal here with the diversity and breadth of German poststructuralism, which, despite its small numbers, has gained a following in fields from philosophy and German to ethnology and sociology.[3] In what follows I would therefore like to restrict my remarks to what appears to be the pioneering group that gained some prominence in the early eighties. The major writers in this group include Norbert Bolz, Manfred Frank, Werner Hamacher, Jochen Hörisch, and Friedrich Kittler,[4] all of whom received their education in German and/or philosophy during the seventies, but who, during the eighties, went in quite different directions. It is unlikely that these names will be completely unfamiliar to even the American public since Hamacher now teaches at Johns Hopkins, and both Kittler and Frank have had books translated into English.[5] By the early eighties, however, these authors had already produced a considerable body of work, including a dozen book-length studies, a half dozen collections of essays, and numerous contributions to journals and anthologies. Although they were virtually without influence at universities and foundations, the German poststructuralists, like their French mentors, were extremely visible in the intellectual book market.

Since I will look more closely at the seminal contributions of Frank and Kittler in the final two chapters of this section, I will restrict my remarks here to a general profile of this group in the early eighties, at a time when it appeared that their concerns were more unified. The studies from that period followed closely established poststructuralist patterns in both theme and form. Favorite topics were writers from the Age of Goethe, in particular romantic authors and idealist philosophers, as well as select modernists like Walter Benjamin. Footnotes reflected the active reliance on a series of names familiar to American criticism: Nietzsche and Freud from the German heritage, Foucault, Lacan, and Derrida from recent French theory. And as in many poststructuralist "literary" analyses, the texts themselves often served as starting points for metatheoretical speculation. Perhaps the most common technique in these readings was to select one passage from a longer work and to show how it potentially undermines or contradicts the dominant level of discourse. Kittler, for example, offers a persuasive analysis in this mode when he examines the figure of Lys from Gottfried Keller's *Bildungsroman, Green Henry (Der grüne Heinrich).*[6] By means of careful attention to textual detail in the description of Lys's paintings and sketches, supported throughout by frequent citations from Lacan, Kittler discovers Heinrich's repressed alter ego in the mysterious Dutch painter. For Heinrich Lee, whose name Kittler believes is the phonetic singular of Lys in Dutch, relates to women only *quoad matrem,* as mother figures. Lys's erotic and extravagant graphic work, indeed, his very appearance in the novel, is thus an indication of another type of desire, while his sudden departure represents one more obstacle overcome on the path to a repressive bourgeois education. Norbert Bolz, who has inclined more toward purely philosophical texts, provides an illustration of a slightly different technique in his treatment of Hegel's alleged suppression of the other.[7] Drawing on quotations from Hegel's entire philosophy, Bolz endeavors to show that Hegel systematically excludes forces that endanger his own totalized project. He lists the threats as "the social necessity of work, the network of power and desire, the queen of the night."[8] Hegel ignores, represses, and emarginates these factors in order to found his logic on a dialectic conceived as the appropriation of the other, rather than a becoming other *(Anderswerden).* The "tamed" other of Hegelian provenance cannot undermine the logical becoming if it always already belongs to it. Hegel's strategy is thus based on exclusion coupled with apodictic assertion to cover its own arbitrary tracks. His logic—and indeed, all logic in Western philosophy—is predicated on a denial and a forgetting or repression of origins: "Unquestionably logic does not originate on its own field, for its laws and functions must be established and commanded; but it must forget its illogical origin and perpetrate the lie that the command of the father is self-legislated."[9] As is most often the case in writings of French and American poststructuralists, an author's oeuvre becomes the site of a necessary metaphysical cover-up, which the astute detective work of the critic is designed to expose.

The preceding brief summaries of exemplary essays by Kittler and Bolz may leave the reader wondering why poststructuralists remained so emarginated in the Federal Republic. The writers they treated are certainly canonical by anyone's estimation, and the argumentative strategies seem almost straightforward. Kittler's reading is nothing more than a sophisticated psychoanalytic interpretation of an author whose works and biography lend themselves to such an approach. Bolz's discussion of an originary repression in Hegel's logic repeats with different terminology a theme familiar to readers of Nietzsche or Heidegger. It is difficult to imagine scholars repudiating either of these essays on the basis of their content. What objections to poststructuralism did critics in Germany have, then? I believe that the criticisms came less from the choice of topic and the type of argument than from the manner in which this material was presented. In many essays we encounter an excessive playfulness and disjunctive, dispersive form of argumentation that tend to befuddle even more sympathetic readers, leaving them to question whether there is really a serious point hidden among the apparent nonsense. Kittler's reliance on the wordplay "Lee-Lys" and the chiasmatic title Bolz gives to his Hegelian reflections—"Das e/Entscheidene V/vergessen" ("The Crucial Forgetting" or "To Forget the Most Crucial Thing")—are only minor illustrations of what the fertile minds of the German poststructuralists have concocted. Kittler, whose *normal* prose style is often dense and obscure, although hardly typical academic German prose, at one point dabbled in the writing of Platonic dialogues. In a "Geistergespräch" (Conversation of Spirits) entitled "Kratylos: Ein Simulacrum" (Cratylus: A simulacrum) he has Hermogenes and Socrates engaged in a debate pieced together from information drawn from selected dialogues and from Aristotle's *Metaphysics*.[10] In these early years of German poststructuralism, however, the most flamboyant of the group was probably Werner Hamacher. In his 333-page introduction to Hegel's *Geist des Christentums* (Spirit of Christianity), he delights in playing with references to food and excrement, as well as with the phonetic similarities between Hegel,

Egel (leech), and *Ekel* (disgust or nausea).[11] The following sample should provide some idea of why more conventional scholars were often exasperated, rather than impressed, by poststructuralist antics:

Der Egel fehlt auch bei Hegel nicht
Hegel—vertiert—ein Egel.
"Hegel" so lesen, das das H, mit dem er zuweilen signierte, abgezogen, in den Egel eingezogen ist.
Einen Egel schreiben, der sich an Hegel festbeißt, und noch die peristaltischen Kontraktionen seines Sphinktertrakts imitieren.
Oder einen Hegel schreiben, einen Bluthegel, der selbst noch den Ekel, den er abwehrt und den er erweckt, in sich aufsaugt.

(*The Leech [Egel] isn't missing with Hegel either*
Hegel—made into an animal—leech *[Egel].*
To read "Hegel" in such a way that the *H,* with which he sometimes signed, is withdrawn, pulled into the leech *[Egel].*
To write a leech *[Egel]* that bites firmly onto Hegel and to imitate even the peristaltic contractions of his sphincter tract.
Or to write a Hegel, a Hegel-leech *[Bluthegel],* which sucks into itself even the disgust that it fends off and that it arouses.)[12]

A subsequent Hamacher essay fragment, entitled "—in letzter Sekunde" (—in the last second) consists of over thirty pages of interrogative sentences interspersed with quotations from Schopenhauer and Nietzsche.[13] All of these pieces have serious and important points to make, and most American readers familiar with Derrida's *Glas* or Hartman's *Saving the Text* will hardly bat an eye at the strategies German poststructuralists have employed. Indeed, one can often admire the ingenuity and creativity of these interpretive texts, and reading them when they originally appeared, many younger critics agreed that they were a breath of fresh air in a tradition of dry and uninspired German scholarship. But the playfulness of these early German poststructuralist texts served only to reinforce the prejudices harbored against the "frivolity" of French theory in the critical establishment. By adopting such outrageous tactics, Hamacher and his poststructuralist cohorts appeared nonserious and impertinent. Their banner of antihumanism and their opposition to the "enlightenment," although obviously serious theoretical positions, remained misunderstood or were deemed in a simplistic fashion to be reactionary, and the sorts of textual practices they employed did nothing to dissuade those who were already leery of such provocative French slogans. For this reason we have to judge the emargination of poststructuralism in the German academy as a result of both the opponents and the advocates of French theory. In the early eighties its exile from the university was at least partially self-imposed.

And from the fringes of mainstream academia, from the outside looking in, it was easy for this group to take on the radical gesturing that we have witnessed in connection with their American counterparts. The very titles of their publications—*Austreibung des Geistes aus den Geisteswissenschaften* (The Expulsion of Spirit [Geist] from the Human [Geistes-] Sciences)[14] or *Wer hat Angst vor der Philosophie* (Who's Afraid of Philosophy)—signaled intellectual acts of defiance. Perhaps an even clearer gesture toward radical politics is included in the name selected for the journal *Fugen*, an early effort that apparently, but not surprisingly, never got off the ground. The subtitle, "Deutsch-französisches Jahrbuch" (German-French Yearbook), is obviously meant to evoke the memory of another celebrated bicultural venture from the middle of the last century. For a while, in fact, it was quite common—and at times convincing—for German poststructuralists to portray their theoretical inclinations as a radical alternative to the sterile intellectual offerings of the post-student-movement generation. Like Karl Marx and Arnold Ruge in 1844, who were the originators of the initial German-French Yearbook, they hoped to replace the dominant and obsolete mode of discourse in their own country through an appropriation of "revolutionary" French thought. Their project, not unlike that of the marxist deconstructors I shall discuss later, was to radicalize the domestic scene with French imports. As Manfred Frank argued in 1980, now that the Critical Theory of the Frankfurt School, transcendental hermeneutics, and analytical philosophy have drastically lost their credibility in intellectual circles, the hour for a productive appropriation of poststructuralism has finally struck.[15]

How the advent of French theory would actually alter the critical scene, however, and what changes would ensue from this revolutionary impulse, are perhaps best indicated by the portion of *Fugen's* subtitle that I temporarily suppressed; the complete wording is "Deutsch-französisches Jahrbuch für Text-Analytik" (German-French Yearbook for Textual Analyses). This subtitle would have us believe that radicals from the sixties were preoccupied for too long with changing the world to see that the authentic revolutionary course is to interpret it. What we could expect from this new theory, then, was "thinking in skirmishes, theory in tumult," as Bolz described it.[16] This thought should be conceived not necessarily as a turning away from the sixties, but as its continuation: "The state is not afraid of a philosophy of praxis, but of new practices of philosophy, which, as they did for the first time in the student movement, do not shy away from wild, audacious thought and which become radical diagnoses of the present."[17] By valorizing the novel and the outlandish, Bolz wants to legitimate his textual praxis as oppositional: "The state is afraid of a philosophy that no longer makes sense and for which that which exists is not everything."[18] Indeed, for him linguistic utterance as such, not calls for action, constitutes the ultimate assault on the conversative status quo: "It is not the revolutionary manifesto, but the event of speech *[Ereignis der Rede]* that seems dangerous to institutions."[19] Within the framework of a German poststructuralist politics, praxis cedes to play, and partisanship bows to gamesmanship. "What counts" for Kittler "is the relevance or pertinence in a puzzle, not the significance in a world."[20] The radicalness of the early German poststructuralists thus makes a virtue out of necessity: in the absence of a real opposition after the decline of the left, at the time of Helmut Schmidt's ascendancy in the Social Democrats and, a few years later, the switch of the Free Democrats to a conservative coalition partner, they made the retreat into textual interpretation the oppositional deed. In this they share much with their American poststructuralist colleagues, whose popularity similarly peaked when the tumultuous years were passed, during the Carter and Reagan presidencies. In both cases revolutionary gestures often were guises for powerless anarchic charades. In a literal and a figurative sense rebelliousness became more talk than action.

The following discussions of aspects of German poststructuralism emphasize what I consider some of the most interesting features of its appropriation or nonappropriation. As the chapter on Michel Foucault should make clear, his work and the potential political implications of his theory of power were not appreciated in the Federal Republic. Instead, as I outline with regard to Peter Szondi and Manfred Frank, part of the project in Germany has been to reconcile poststructuralism with the hermeneutic tradition. Szondi's attempt to do this was aborted by his death before poststructuralism could gain a foothold. Over a decade later and from a more philosophical, less literary perspective Manfred Frank began to examine the possible sites poststructuralism could occupy inside a German tradition, although he has apparently abandoned or significantly modified this project in more recent work. Finally, I look briefly at the work of Friedrich Kittler, who has taken poststructuralism, especially the work of Foucault, in a somewhat new direction for Germany by emphasizing the connections between technology and discursive systems. These discussions should by no means be mistaken for a comprehensive history of the appropriation and directions of poststructuralist thought in the Federal Republic. Rather, they are meant to demonstrate by example some of the successes, failures, and difficulties poststructuralism encountered in crossing borders.

4

Michel Foucault among the Germans

WHEN Michel Foucault died in Paris on 25 June 1984, he had achieved a popularity in the English-speaking world matched by no other contemporary theorist. Derrida may be more appealing to certain literary critics because of his stricter textual practices, Lacan may hold sway in psychoanalytic circles, and Cixous, Kristeva, and Irigaray may have more allure for feminism, but Foucault had, by contrast, acquired a much broader and more general readership. We find his work attracting attention in such diverse fields as philosophy, sociology, literature, art history, political science, and anthropology—no doubt because his own interests cut across traditional academic barriers. An indication of this interdisciplinary popularity is supplied by the number of secondary works on him in English. Since 1980 at least a dozen monographs have dealt with his work, most of them appearing since 1983.[1] Introductory readers were published in 1984 and 1986.[2] And several journals have devoted entire issues or parts of issues to his work as well. *Humanities in Society*, known for its interdisciplinary approach, has already done this twice, in 1980 and in 1982. Indeed, an annotated bibliography of primary and secondary literature from 1983 documents excellently the tremendous interest in his work, turning up a surprisingly large number of essays and reviews in English.[3] Of course all this attention does not mean that he has received universal approval. Even many of those who were influential in his introduction to a wider audience have subsequently shown signs of disenchantment.[4] Perhaps more significant is that there seem to be more books and essays about Foucault than studies which could be called Foucauldian.[5] Perhaps because such studies involve a vast amount of archival work, to date his writings have attracted more commentators than followers. Nonetheless, the sheer magnitude of the response makes it evident that Foucault has been—and in all likelihood will continue to be—a theoretical force to be reckoned with in the English-speaking world well into the next century.

Foucault's reception in Germany contrasts sharply to this enthusiastic response from the Anglo-American world. In the Federal Republic he was largely ignored;[6] when he was discussed, more often than not his work was trivialized, rejected, or ridiculed. This attitude on the part of German intellectuals may initially seem odd, especially when one considers the wide exposure the German public has had to his writings. Indeed, as early as 1965 we can find one of Foucault's essays published in *Kursbuch*,[7] a journal which at that time was the most influential publication of the left intelligentsia. A German monograph from 1986 lists twelve German translations of books by Foucault, seven collections of essays or interviews, and over a dozen miscellaneous essays.[8] All of his major works are thus available in German, and most of these have appeared in Suhrkamp Verlag in the prestigious "suhrkamp taschenbuch wissenschaft" series. Indeed, Suhrkamp, as I have stated above, has been a consistent promoter of a great variety of structuralist and poststructuralist thought during the seventies and eighties. Besides Foucault's major writings, it has been responsible for the dissemination of numerous works by Lévi-Strauss, Barthes, Lacan, and Derrida. For a time Suhrkamp was also one of the promoters of the small group of West Germans who appeared to derive their inspiration from Foucault. The collection *Urszenen: Literaturwissenschaft als Diskursanalyse und Diskurskritik* (Primal Scenes: Literary Scholarship as Discourse Analysis and Discourse Critique), perhaps the first major German work inspired by French theory, came out there in 1977, and from the subtitle it is evident that Foucault was one of the major theoretical influences. And in the mid-eighties Suhrkamp published several volumes of postmodernist reflections on various topics, the most provocative of which was *Das Schwinden der Sinne* (The Waning of the Senses).[9] Although Foucault was perhaps not the sole source for francophilic thought, his impact on the key authors of German poststructuralism, particularly in its earliest phase, cannot be denied. Directly or indirectly, therefore, the German reader has had as much opportunity to become acquainted with Foucault as his/her American or English counterpart, and it is probably safe to state that during much of the eighties he was the best known French theorist in the Federal Republic.

That Foucault's writings have nonetheless seldom found a receptive readership in Germany, particularly among university intellectuals, is manifested most evidently in the dearth of secondary literature about him and his work. Outside of a handful of dissertations, there are only a few book-length monographs that deal with his work, and most of these have appeared in either small publishing houses with limited distribution or in vanity presses that are known for publishing doctoral theses. As far as I can tell, there exists only a small number of essays on him in German-language journals, and many of these are no more than lengthy book reviews.[10] There is no popular monograph introducing his work as a whole (although one was scheduled to appear in 1988); no major German intellectual has exhibited more than a cursory interest in his writings; his influence in the seventies and eighties in Germany remained almost entirely restricted to small circles of nonorthodox leftists or anti-establishment, countercultural groups.[11] Indeed, the absence of Foucault in German intellectual life can perhaps be best demonstrated by a brief examination of research tools most often consulted by literary scholars. While in the United States he has been discussed and applauded by many major literary and cultural theorists, it is difficult to find the mere mention of his name in corresponding German circles. Anyone familiar with German literary journals can confirm that his works are seldom cited in footnotes. Up until 1984 there was not a single reference to him in the Eppelsheimer bibliography, which includes over ten thousand entries of books and journal articles from all major sources. Despite the frequent contributions of Romance-language scholars such as Jauß, Weinrich, Stierle, and Gumbrecht, he has been virtually ignored at the biannual colloquia at Constance, whose proceedings appear under the series title "Poetics and Hermeneutics." Even in the volume *Geschichte—Ereignis und Erzählung* (History—Event and Narrative), which to an outsider might seem to be an invitation to discuss Foucault's writings, his name is noted only once in passing.[12] Thus although one of the essay collections which appeared in German bore the title *Schriften zur Literatur* (1974; Writings on Literature), literary critics seem to have exhibited as little interest in him as social scientists and philosophers.

It may not have been entirely owing to the printers' strike in West Germany, therefore, that Foucault's death received so little attention in the German press. *Der Spiegel*, which had gotten a good deal of mileage out of Foucault's oppositional and iconoclastic politics in the past, printed only a one-column obituary, in which Foucault was depicted as paranoid and conceited.[13] Lothar Baier, a sympathetic and extremely knowledgeable observer of the French scene for many years, was more eloquent in his praise in an article in the weekly newspaper *Die Zeit*, but his eulogy is the exception that confirms the rule.[14] More representative was the short piece in the conservative *Frankfurter Allgemeine Zeitung,* which managed to print a more extensive essay on Foucault only some five months after his death.[15] In the obituary, written by Konrad Adam, one finds the typical German reaction. His impact, we are assured, was limited by both region and time. "Foucault has not shaped and has scarcely influenced the ongoing debates about the theory of scholarship and the history of scholarship."[16] To an American or French reader, such an evaluation of Foucault's importance must seem incomprehensible. Only in Germany, where Foucault's impact on the academic establishment has been so limited, could an intellectual have ventured such a remark in a leading national newspaper in the summer of 1984. Considering this dismissive view of Foucault's significance for current thinking on scientific and scholarly activity, it is perhaps not surprising that the subtitle of the FAZ piece speaks of the death of "Michel Foucauld."[17]

These obituaries from 1984, of course, were only the consequence of earlier intellectual notices penned throughout the seventies and early eighties. Perhaps the chief author of the damaging reports about Foucault was Jean Améry, whose reviews and commentaries on Foucault appeared frequently in the left-liberal weekly *Die Zeit* and in the important liberal journal *Merkur.* Under the guise of mediating French thought to the German public, Améry presents a mixture of distortion, misreading, and journalistic hyperbole. What bothers him, first of all, about the French philosopher is his nonconformity with respect to scholarly conventions. Although he recognizes occasionally that Foucault's style is brilliant and exercises a "not inconsiderable fascination"[18] over the reader, the overwhelming tenor of his remarks is extremely negative. He reproaches him for his "highly arbitrary terminology," his "private language,"[19] and his inaccessible concepts. While critics in France and in the United States have generally understood the necessity for Foucault's neologisms, Améry detects only philosophical fraud. What we encounter is not really philosophy at all, he contends, but rather "poesy" *(Poesie)* or "conceptual poetry" *(Begriffs-Dichtung).*[20] At times he seems to feel that these innovations are somehow connected with the "abstruseness of his argumentation," an argumentation he evidently believes one should ridicule rather than attempt to comprehend. "The convoluted thought processes of this writer are as inscrutable as the ways of God":[21] this is Améry's typical response to Foucault's dense prose. Occasionally Améry would try to persuade us that Foucault's philosophy amounts to pure charlatanry. He maintains that a combination of blind faith and divination is a prerequisite for reading his works: "Michel Foucault hypnotizes; he does not argue. Anyone not possessing the gift of a psychic medium and who is not so readily put under a spell will stand helplessly at the gates of his philosophy."[22] But more often Améry simply suggests that Foucault's ill-defined and innovative conceptual framework is just a smokescreen for a perverse and unsubstantiated theory. The most objectionable features of his thought itself are the denial of historical progress and his renowned (and misunderstood) "antihumanism," both of which are encountered throughout his oeuvre. In bringing up these sorts of objections, Améry commits an error that one frequently sees in German criticism of Foucault: he takes slogans at face value and distorts statements that were already exaggerated for effect, thereby ignoring for the most part their substantive, argumentative basis. When Foucault writes of the end of the subject or the end of man, for example, he is not referring to the annihilation of the human race, nor is he advocating the callous disregard for human life. Rather, he is maintaining that the conception of the human being that has informed what he calls the "human sciences" for the past two centuries may be only one moment in a larger history, and that this moment, like others before it, is destined to pass.[23] When he points to repressive disciplinary mechanisms in our society that were rationalized by an ideology of humanistic reform, he is not championing a return to an antihumanistic regime of torture and cruelty, but rather explaining that today power over human beings is exerted in different but perhaps more efficient and less obvious ways.[24]

The result of these willful distortions, however—and they were unfortunately shared by many other German intellectuals throughout Foucault's lifetime[25]—was a rather dubious political image of Foucault. Améry admits that in French public life Foucault is somewhere on the left; he calls him an "element of the gauchist atmosphere" *(Element der gauchistischen Atmosphäre)*.[26] And he recognizes that more often than not he has been on the "correct" side of political issues, which I presume means that he has supported causes and movements close to Améry's own left-liberal proclivities. But this partisanship is attributed to an instinctive humanism that contrasts baldly with his theoretical position. Anyone who is so ahistorical, antiprogressive, and antihumanist, we are told, must be a theoretical ally of regressive forces: "To deny progress completely and barely to shrug one's shoulders about all reforms is an inappropriate and—I am weighing my words carefully—ultimately a reactionary behavior."[27] For this reason his thought was discredited not only as eccentric, abstruse, and conceptually inadequate, but also as dangerous politically. At one point Améry states that Foucault is "the most dangerous counter-Enlightenment figure since the days of the 'lumières,' the Enlightenment, to darken the stage of the French spirit and to cast it into abysmal confusion."[28] Perhaps the most threatening dimension of Foucault's thought is manifested in his purported followers. For Améry depicts him as the sole intellectual mentor of the "New Philosophers," the "skilled to virtuoso vulgarizers" of the new structuralist Master Thinker. He is the ultimate source of this politically regressive tendency; these younger disciples simply borrowed from his intellectual "artillery." Thus, even though Améry credits him with being an "original thinker" and an "admirable character," he still finds that as a philosopher he has a reactionary effect.[29] And Améry is not alone in this sort of political denunciation. To cite only one further and significant illustration from many: In 1981 Jürgen Habermas remarked that Foucault, along with Bataille and Derrida, belonged to a group he would designate as the "young conservatives."[30] Although Habermas has modified this opinion in the intervening years and come to a more differentiated view of Foucault's writings,[31] the fact that one of the most eminent German intellectuals could categorize Foucault in this fashion as late as 1981 gives some indication of the catastrophic course of his reception in the German-speaking world.

How can we account for this kind of response? Why has there been such an enormous discrepancy between Foucault's reception in the United States and in the Federal Republic? I think it would be unfair, first of all, not to admit that Foucault's writings sometimes lend themselves to the criticism most frequently articulated in Germany. There is some truth in the objections that I have cited above, and in fact one can find similar, albeit more sympathetic, readings of Foucault in France and in the United States as well.[32] Neologisms and the creative use of concepts do create difficulties in understanding, and one must concede that often passages in his books and essays seem obscure, unnecessarily embellished with fancy verbiage, and intentionally evasive. Hayden White, who can hardly be called an adversary of French theory, has even maintained that the "*authority* of Foucault's discourse derives primarily from his style (rather than from its factual evidence or rigour of argument),"[33] a statement that comes very close to what Améry has also written about him. Since White starts from different theoretical premises, he does not necessarily find this such a serious defect or offense. Nevertheless, the "hypnotic" power of Foucault's style has received due recognition outside of Germany as well. Nor have the questionable political implications of Foucault's position been ignored by commentators in the United States. Leftist critics from a variety of perspectives have taken exception to an entire array of deficiencies, from the neglect of class analysis and the overemphasis on discourse and text, to the "metaphysical" basis of his views on social formation. Although I am not aware that he has been labeled "reactionary" or "conservative" in the United States, his political stance has been subjected to meticulous and often justifiable criticism.[34] The difference again involves the approach to his works. It seems to me that German critics have reacted to Foucault with a hostility unwarranted by anything he has written, although their arguments are ultimately based on certain statements in his texts. At a very minimum we could characterize their collective attitude as extremely uncharitable. Could we not admit, as Foucault himself has done, that there are unresolved problems in his writings, but that these problems should not negate their positive contribution toward something new and as yet undefined or cause them to be regarded as a retreat to a reactionary position? This appears to be the way most American critics have responded to him, and part of the discrepancy we have witnessed in the various receptions can be accounted for in terms of attitudinal differences.

There are other, more substantial issues at stake in the German reception of Foucault, however, and they have to do with both hasty reading habits and the biases of native intellectual traditions. A somewhat trivial but nonetheless important difficulty in many early German evaluations was the failure to recognize the tentative nature of Foucault's projects. By this I mean that despite a certain continuity in his concerns, Foucault has repeatedly altered, modified, and even totally rejected ideas from one book to the next. Indeed, we should not speak of Foucault's work as a unified whole, but rather as a series of discursive incursions undertaken from various angles with diverse conceptual instruments. If we mistakenly attribute to him an unchanging system of terminology from the early *Madness and Civilization* (1964; English trans. 1965) to his last project, the incomplete *The History of Sexuality* (1976–84; English trans. 1978–86), if we try to construct general pronouncements from a conceptual apparatus that was conceived for local and temporary application, then we will undoubtedly be able to find contradictions in his thought, but we will hardly do justice to his multifaceted oeuvre. Foucault's use of the term "episteme" is a case in point. German commentators have frequently associated it with something like a *Zeitgeist* or some other unified notion from *Geistesgeschichte*, often failing to consider Foucault's own discussions of the term.[35] As most attentive readers of Foucault already know, "episteme" enjoyed a rather brief period of favor in Foucault's arsenal of concepts. Absent in his earliest works, it emerged as a central term for describing certain discursive regularities in *The Order of Things* (1966; English trans. 1969). Three years later, in the *Archaeology of Knowledge,* it already plays a minimal role. Here it is defined as "the total set of relations that unite, at a given period, the discursive practices that give rise to epistemological figures, and possibly formalized systems."[36] After 1970 the term vanishes completely from his work; as far as I can tell, it does not even occur in *Discipline and Punish* (1975; English trans. 1977) or in the volumes of *The History of Sexuality.* Up until his death most German detractors ignored the fact that the concept "episteme" appears at a certain point in Foucault's writings, only to disappear when it is no longer useful or appropriate. But they also failed to see the limited scope of the term even where it was most important, in *The Order of Things.* Foucault makes it clear that his analyses in this book are not meant to encompass a social totality. The spirit or science of a period, he writes, is

> the very thing to which my whole enterprise is opposed. The relations that I have discussed are valid in order to define a particular configuration: they are not signs to describe the face of a culture in its totality. It is the friends of Weltanschauung who will be disappointed; I insist that the description that I have undertaken is quite different from theirs.[37]

Foucault, in short, adamantly insisted that he should not be associated with typical notions drawn from the history of ideas. He takes pains to avoid precisely the sort of illicit totalities characteristic of German *Geistesgeschichte.* For he does not examine or give credence to a "spirit" that underlies or defines a given era, but rather to a more subtle series of unifying guidelines based on discursive entities. While it may be true that his use of "episteme" cannot entirely escape some recourse to totalization,[38] Foucault has repeatedly denied this, and his elimination of the term from his active conceptual vocabulary since 1970 is very likely connected with his recognition that it could be taken to encompass precisely the type of project he seeks to critique.

Throughout the seventies and early eighties the refusal to differentiate with respect to terminology and to recognize development and change in Foucault's thought hindered a reasonable dialogue with his work in most German circles. Despite some inroads made during the latter part of the past decade, *The Order of Things* still remains his most important work there, and the tendency among most intellectuals is to derive all of Foucault from this significant but by no means terminal achievement. That Foucault himself recognized theoretical weaknesses in this book, that he sought to overcome these in the *Archaeology of Knowledge,* a work that has the express purpose of laying the groundwork for his earlier work ex post facto, and that he then abandoned even these corrections for a new direction in the seventies were and are too often ignored in the mainstream German reception of his thought. By contrast many American critics have stressed how Foucault rethought the relationship between discursive practices and social formations in his more recent writings. For this latter and penultimate stage of his development—some commentators feel that *The History of Sexuality* can be viewed as a somewhat novel point of departure—there exists no one theoretical text to which we can turn, and here again we sense the unfinished nature of his project, the "ongoing conceptualization" and "constant checking" he himself advocated.[39] Foucault's was not a finished system; indeed, his texts endeavor in a paradoxical theoretical venture to oppose all systematization. I call this venture "paradoxical" because, while opposing systemic thought, Foucault wants to describe in a coherent fashion discourses, social practices, their histories (or genealogies), as well as the role and relationship of power and knowledge. To do this he, like any theorist, is compelled to adopt a conceptual apparatus and thus something that itself resembles or mimics a system. Anyone who wishes to make statements that have some claim to accuracy must employ concepts that go beyond the particular and partake of a general or universal realm. As soon as a writer operates in this realm, however, he or she has created either a system or at least the fragment of a system. Thus the antisystemic desires, which must be understood also as a political rejection of totalizations and totalitarianisms, and the necessity for systematization in methodology inevitably come into conflict. But if only the "systemic" side of his undertaking is explored, as Habermas does in his writings on Foucault, one risks losing not only a sense for Foucault's paradoxical project, but also an appreciation for the value of his work. What I am suggesting is that a chief error in the reception of Foucault—and to an extent this error cuts across national boundaries even though it may be more endemic to German critics—is the hasty assimilation of his writings into a totalized theoretical framework. If we could possibly refrain temporarily from the leap from the particular to the general—something Foucault himself did not consistently resist—we would be in a better position to evaluate his local and considerable insights into the working of human language and society.

Up until now I have considered three factors involved in Foucault's reception in Germany: features of Foucault's texts themselves, the failure to differentiate in comments on his terminology, and the tendency to totalize local and tentative concepts. All of these have had an effect on his American reception as well, but sometimes the very factors that figure to his detriment in Germany have added to his popularity in the United States. Since the terminological field on which he operates has greater familiarity and credibility in the United States, and since he has functioned in this country as a welcome foil to systemic thought, the readings of his work are on the whole more sympathetic and favorable in American journals. What has further conditioned the unfavorable "horizon of expectation" for Foucault's writings in Germany cannot be determined with any empirical precision, but it obviously has something to do with the poor reception of poststructuralist thought in general. As I suggested above, the lack of prominent spokespersons throughout the seventies and early eighties, the parallel but distinct forms of politicization in France and Germany in the late sixties and early seventies, and the generally conservative structure of the German university and intellectual community have played a decisive role. But with respect to Foucault, who should have had a wider appeal since he works on a wider, more sociohistorical terrain than the purely "textual" poststructuralists, I would also contend that he has had difficulty gaining a following because the manner in which he approaches problems and the areas of research he prefers differ so greatly from what has been commonly recognized as legitimate in most German intellectual circles. One could rephrase this thought from a slightly different perspective by stating that other theoretical traditions have acted as barriers or interference to the reception of Foucault in West Germany, just as the acceptance of reception theory in the United States was blocked by native biases and popular imports. By calling on patterns of thought at once more familiar and more acceptable, theoretical discussions in the Federal Republic reinforce certain intellectual traditions and simultaneously obstruct the path for theories which, like Foucault's, depart from the institutional norm. Putting this in more Foucauldian terms one could say that German academic discourse has itself constituted what is apposite as scholarship and what is to be emarginated as aberrant and frivolous. Here I am thinking of two traditions in particular: phenomenological theory, represented perhaps best by the works of Alfred Schütz,[40] and Critical Theory, whose most eminent voice is undoubtedly Jürgen Habermas. Both were well received during precisely those years during which Foucault was popular in France and gaining popularity in the United States. To clarify, therefore, why

Foucault's work has encountered such formidable resistance in crossing borders into Germany, I would like to take a brief—and necessarily schematic—look at how these two traditions misalign with Foucault's thought.

We might want to note first that Foucault the archeologist and Schütz the phenomenologist have much in common. Methodologically they agree that description is the primary task for the scientific study of social reality. As Hubert Dreyfus and Paul Rabinow have pointed out, Foucault's archeological starting point can be conceived as a radicalization of the phenomenological position. Bracketing both truth claims and meaning, he analyzes statements and discourses as a kind of "metaphenomenologist."[41] In this point he converges with Schütz, who, from a Husserlian perspective, rejects explanation for pure description as well. It is also fairly evident that Schütz and Foucault share a common object of study: the composition, ordering, and constitution of what we call social reality. But the manner in which they go about their respective projects demonstrates their vast theoretical differences. Schütz proceeds by eliminating anomalous situations in order to describe an unmediated, normal social world of daily life. In the first volume of *Structures of the Life World* this enabling methodological principle is stated very succinctly from the outset: "For getting to the heart of the matter, it is important to describe the structure of the quasi-ontological areas of reality, as they are experienced by the normal adult, whereby we have to ignore the special problems of the world of children and pathological realities."[42] Foucault's procedure is not so much opposed as it is radically different. For him the concepts of normalcy, truth, and reality are products of exclusionary mechanisms, not presuppositions on which one can build a theoretical project. His entire oeuvre can be read as a questioning of our assumptions about what a "normal adult" is, for he endeavors to disclose the subterranean processes that constituted the modern subject as a normal, heterosexual, adult, white, Western male.[43] In *Madness and Civilization,* for example, he analyzes how insanity and sanity are the results of a rupture in our way of thinking; the categories "normal" and "abnormal," "sane" and "mad," and "sense" and "nonsense" are not givens, but rather historically produced and hence changeable designations. To examine the "normal" while excluding the "pathological," as Schütz proposes, is thus methodologically unsound, since both categories themselves originate in the same exclusionary gesture. For Foucault the "order of things" is always a product of history, the mediated result of a prior order of discourse and social practices; for Schütz's project the normal world is immediately accessible and describable, ahistorically, without distortion, in a language that acts as an accurate mirror of external reality.

Turning to Habermas, undoubtedly the most important theorist in postwar Germany, we could also note first a number of perspectives he shares with Foucault. Chief among these is the general concern for rationality in modern society. Both the French and the German social theorist register the oppressive effects of the form of reason that has constituted itself in the course of the nineteenth and twentieth centuries. Possibly this convergence in their thought has to do with their common historical situation. Being from the same generation (Foucault was born in 1926, Habermas in 1929), they are reacting in their writings to a similar set of circumstances: the destruction of European Jewry, the horrors of the Second World War, the failures of Eastern bloc socialism, the more general technologizing and bureaucratizing of the industrial world, and, after 1968, the collapse of the student movement and the appearance of new, more diverse forms of political opposition. We could also acknowledge that Habermas, in his debate with Hans-Georg Gadamer at least, exhibited a great sensitivity to the relationship between power and language, a theme that comes very close to Foucault's concerns after 1970. In *Truth and Method* Gadamer appears to consider language to be a pure system of exchange not subject to distortion by power or social processes. Habermas objects to Gadamer's idealized meta-institution of language, reminding us that "language is *also* a medium of domination and social power; it serves to legitimate relations of organized force."[44] Although he is primarily interested in establishing a theoretical framework based on a purified and ideal speech situation, Habermas demonstrates here that his views are not totally incompatible with French theories.

The background and trajectory of Habermas' thought, however, are at odds with significant tenets in Foucault's writings. The German theorist develops his theories against the background of the Critical Theory of the Frankfurt School and traditional sociology, while Foucault comes from a French phenomenologist and linguistic heritage. Of greatest importance for Habermas are the Weberian thesis of increasing rationalization in modern societies and Adorno and Horkheimer's views on instrumental reason, especially the pessimistic prognosis derived from them in *Dialectic of the Enlightenment* (1947). Habermas opposes to both of these views of rationality a theory that departs from the "model of consciousness" and instead depends on interactive and communicative assumptions. He divides rationality into a cognitive-instrumental variety, whose dominance has determined the direction of the modern world, and a communicative rationality, which holds the promise of emancipation. "What is paradigmatic for the latter [communicative reason] is not the relation of a solitary subject to something in the objective world that can be represented and manipulated, but the intersubjective relation that speaking subjects take up when they come to an understanding with one another about something."[45] What Habermas is appealing to is, if not a "higher rationality," at least a better one. For Foucault, who prefers to speak of local rationalities, such a move must seem illusory and illegitimate. It is ultimately a recourse to the very sort of humanism that in his view is responsible for and complicit with oppression. He could never agree with the following optimistic appraisal by Habermas: "The utopian perspective of reconciliation and freedom is ingrained in the conditions for the communicative sociation of individuals; it is built into the linguistic mechanism of the reproduction of the species."[46] For Foucault the "sciences of man" with their notion of the subject are part of the problem; for Habermas, who stands firmly on humanistic terrain here, the speaking subject in communicative action is the solution.

One could also approach the differences between the two from a slightly different standpoint, namely from their respective definitions of "discourse." Although Habermas recognizes the corruption of language by power, in postulating communicative reason he envisions a realm in which power is severed from linguistic utterance. His ideal speech situation is ultimately based on the consensus of free subjects and on a view of language as the ideal vehicle for reaching agreement: "Reaching understanding is the inherent telos of human speech."[47] Discourse is the name Habermas gives to the kind of metalinguistic interaction whose theme is the validity and truth value of other utterances.

> Only in theoretical, practical, and explicative discourse do the participants have to start from the (often counterfactual) presupposition that the conditions for an ideal speech situation are satisfied to a sufficient degree. I shall speak of "discourse" only when the meaning of the problematic validity claim conceptually forces participants to suppose that a rationally motivated agreement could in principle be achieved.[48]

The prerequisites for entering into such discursive activity are an equality among the participants and a disavowal of personal interests. In Habermas' system "discourse" thus becomes an ideal(ized) communicative action, opposed to "systematically distorted communication" and other "communicative pathologies," which are deviations from this ideal.[49] In fact, the continuity in Habermas' work from *The Structural Transformations of the Public Sphere* (1962) to his magnum opus *Theory of Communication Action* (1981), as I have argued elsewhere,[50] lies precisely in the unremitting concern for a realm in which ideas are freely exchanged by unconstrained, sovereign subjects.

It is not necessary to explore in detail Foucault's category of discourse, which he himself admits is not always clear and unequivocally employed, in order to see the disparity. The following quotation from *The Archaeology of Knowledge* should suffice to demonstrate the divergent theoretical perspectives: "Discourse is not the majestically unfolding manifestation of a thinking, knowing, speaking subject, but, on the contrary, a totality, in which the dispersion of the subject and his discontinuity with himself may be determined."[51] It is not simply that Foucault has defined his term differently; his entire perspective on linguistic utterance appears to be diametrically opposed to Habermas'. Indeed, in his later works the distance from Habermasian notions becomes even more pronounced.[52] In his writings of the seventies Foucault strengthens the ties between power and language: his contention that power is implicated in all knowledge—and vice versa—undercuts, it seems to me, the very possibility of the discursive situation Habermas needs as a ground for his theory of communicative action. One should not overlook, of course, the advantages of Habermas' position: for one thing, with his theory he is able to ground the point from which he is speaking, while Foucault, by contrast, has never been able to explain satisfactorily why his own statements should be taken more seriously than others' or how his thought escapes or defies the very mechanisms he is exposing.[53] But Habermas can situate himself beyond power and interest only by discovering in language itself an inherent and necessary rationality, which in an ideal and benevolent fashion, like Plato's philosopher kings, has the potential to control distortions, domination, and differences. In this regard Habermas has proposed, as Dreyfus and Rabinow note, "perhaps the most sophisticated counter-project available today,"[54] but with respect to Foucault's thought it remains precisely that: a "counter-project."[55]

That Habermas and those influenced by his work would have objections to Foucault's various projects was obvious even before Habermas' infelicitous reference to his "young conservative" affiliations. But perhaps more significant for the nature of Foucault's German reception is the absence of any sustained discussion of the French theorist during his lifetime. We have to wait until 1985 before we encounter the first works composed by the second and third generation of the Frankfurt School to enter into a debate with Foucault, a debate, of course, to which he was then unable to respond. Both Habermas in his *Philosophical Discourse of Modernity* and his student Axel Honneth in *Kritik der Macht* (Critique of Power) are highly critical of Foucault, but the thoroughness of their discussions reveals nonetheless the respect they have for his thought.[56] Honneth places him next to Habermas as the most important theorist of the postwar era, while Habermas devotes two of his twelve lectures to his works, while no other writer is treated in more than one. It is Habermas who provides the general framework for a critique of Foucault's work. After dealing extensively with the overriding themes of his oeuvre—the "unmasking of the human sciences" and the ubiquity of power—Habermas summarizes three areas of discontent under the headings of "presentism," "relativism," and "partisanship." Foucault is accused of "presentism" because of his rejection of hermeneutics and his affirmation of objectivity. Habermas notes the impossibility of this effort, claiming further that Foucault's method paradoxically "leads to agreement with a historiography that is narcissistically oriented toward the standpoint of the historian and instrumentalizes the contemplation of the past for the needs of the present."[57] The reproach for relativism stems from Foucault's historicist pretensions. If all truth claims are confined to the discourse in which they are located, then "they exhaust their entire significance in the functional contribution they make to the self-maintenance of a given totality of discourse."[58] Relativism also raises the question of the status of Foucault's own efforts; if genealogy is not accorded some metadiscursive privilege, then its ability to describe and dissect historical instantiations of power is effectively canceled. Finally, with regard to "partisanship," Habermas points out that Foucault's denial of normative claims undercuts any basis for his political preferences. In the all-pervasive world of power that he postulates, there is no compelling reason for resistance or even for undertaking genealogical analysis. Like many German commentators, therefore, Habermas objects to the grand scheme of Foucault's writings, to the lack of systematic consistency and coherence. While he does not deny "the importance of his fascinating unmasking of the capillary effects of power,"[59] he obviously finds his work unsatisfactory as an encompassing social theory.

Honneth's book evidences a similar reaction to Foucault. He views his early work as the attempt to develop an ethnology of one's own culture, which is then supplemented in the *Archaeology of Knowledge* by a "semiological ontology." What disturbs Honneth most is the free-floating nature of elementary utterances and the vagueness of the notion of discourse in Foucault's early work. On the one hand, Foucault wants to sever the connection between utterances and subjective intentions; but, on the other hand, he also claims their independence from objectivities. The connection that Foucault wants to establish between utterances and discourses as institutionalized practices is thus obscured. For this reason Honneth claims that Foucault's early work brought him only to the "threshold of authentic social analysis."[60] Foucault's turn to a monistic notion of power is more promising for Honneth because it proceeds, as Habermas' theory does, from an intersubjective assumption. Rejecting both the bourgeois notion of power as a contractual agreement and the marxist conception of state power, Foucault locates power in the microcosm of everyday life, where individuals interact with each other. Ultimately, however, Honneth claims that he is unable to develop an adequate social theory, in part because his conceptuality shows insufficient sophistication: his notion of action is "crude"; his critique of science is "inadequately articulated and superficial," "vague" and "ill-conceived." In general Honneth follows Habermas in criticizing Foucault's reduction of social action to its strategic variant and not considering the communicative alternative.[61] Foucault's work is eventually considered to be an insufficiently grounded French cousin of systems theory, a sociological framework developed by Talcott Parsons and refined in Germany by Niklas Luhmann. It is too "mechanistic" and "behavioristic" to account for social phenomena in the contemporary world.[62] Thus, although Honneth gives ample consideration to Foucault's writings and distinguishes between his early and late works, he finds his approach(es) unfruitful. *Kritik der Macht* begins with a discussion of Adorno's social theory and seeks to establish his successor among contemporary writers. Honneth leaves no doubt that Habermas, and not Foucault, must be accorded this honor.

As far as I can determine, Foucault's works have not been taken up again by any member of the Frankfurt School. Although he has influenced selected sociologists and some studies of literature since his death, his impact in Germany today must still be considered limited.[63] This neglect has been unfortunate, not only for German intellectuals, but in particular for scholars of German studies in the United States. Since American students of German culture and politics most often look to what is happening in Germany for guidance and inspiration, the neglect of Foucault—and, indeed, of poststructuralism in general—has contributed to a partial isolation of German theory on the American critical scene. This isolation is concretely reflected, as I have shown above, in the American reception of reception theory, but it has had other detrimental effects as well, for example, the wholesale and almost perverse misunderstanding surrounding Habermas in the humanities. Although some younger scholars have begun to bridge the gap between German and French thought, the division in contemporary theoretical discussions is as evident as it is unproductive. On the one side, poststructuralists often display an insufficient knowledge of the German sources and traditions they cite;[64] on the other side, those dealing with contemporary German thought are frequently ignorant of the seminal contributions of the French in areas that are of mutual interest. What has been needed for some time now is more cooperation and exchange between these two groups, and my plea for American Germanists to occupy themselves more with theorists like Foucault should be understood as one step toward such a fruitful and necessary theoretical partnership. Since one of the chief questions that is likely to arise concerns the reasons for dealing with Foucault at all—providing that understanding colleagues in other areas of the humanities and social sciences is not in itself sufficient reason—I would like to turn briefly to what I believe are the two most suggestive aspects of Foucault's work. To discuss this issue I am going to proceed from one of the few German manifestoes of Foucauldian thought—the introduction to *Urszenen* written by Horst Turk and Friedrich Kittler[65]—and thus examine what has been proposed for German studies in the past.

Turk and Kittler conceive of Foucault's usefulness to cultural studies primarily in terms of discursive analysis *(Diskursanalyse)*. They correctly note that this should be thought of not as a philosophical theory but rather as a subversion of theory, in particular as a critique of those disciplines subsumed under the "human sciences." The analysis of discourses subverts by exposing certain regularities and rules that texts obey, as well as showing possibilities they exclude. As we have seen, for Foucault the level of discourse is not at all similar to the spirit of an age or to a unity of themes; rather it can be thought of in a more Kantian vein as the realm of the conditions of possibility for the appearance of empirical statements. Turk and Kittler view texts accordingly not as the products of sovereign individual minds, as "small islands of coherence"[66] inside a larger circumscribed sea of spirit, but instead as knots in a vast network. Discursive analysis treats the text "as a variable dependent on the practices of utterances, which always already runs under the level of pronouncement, work, and book."[67] Specifically they envision three areas of activity for their enterprise. The first would involve defining the rules by which cultures produce texts and statements. By way of illustration they point to an important break or rupture in the latter part of the eighteenth century. Before this time, rhetoric, with its strong emphasis on *imitatio,* governed the production and reading of texts; after about 1770, with the disintegration of this tradition, literary texts start to be evaluated in terms of uniqueness and originality. The result of this new practice of reading and writing is both a hermeneutic that seeks the "inalienable truth" hidden in the text and the production of "the work" itself qua work. Through an investigation of the regularities and practices that underlie different kinds of texts, the authors envision a local history of text production marked by discontinuity, as opposed to the more usual, linear, monolithic historiography: "Such analyses could convert the singular writing of history, whose methodological principle is the identity of everything that is said—for instance in the form of 'world literature'—into many archaeologies that investigate the epochal specificities of speech itself."[68] As a prototype for the analysis of such a threshold phenomenon they cite Foucault's discussions in *The Order of Things,* especially his remarks on the differences in the discourses of General Grammar versus philology and of Natural History versus biology.

The second and third areas for the application of discursive analysis are also linked directly to Foucault's thought. Turk and Kittler suggest dealing with what traditional critics took to be themes and motifs in order to contribute to a history based on the transformation of cultural codes. For example, they point to the emergence of childhood around 1800 as an "effect of historical recoding."[69] In general, however, they seem to be interested here in a contribution to what Foucault calls "the genealogy of the modern soul."[70] Since Goethe, the "inner being," a new type of subject, the individual, begins to speak in and through literary texts. The formation and naming of individualized subjects and the "confessions" of these subjects become dominant "themes" in the literature of the modern era. A fruitful area for discursive analysis is thus the examination of connections between philosophical texts in which the self-formation of consciousness is described—for example, Hegel's *Phenomenology of the Spirit*—and literary works like *Faust* and *Antigone,* which are incorporated into the philosophical text and in which we witness the inner development of the hero or heroine. The object of such analysis is not knowledge in the traditional "objective" sense of the word, but rather the establishing of relationships between discourses, a kind of interdisciplinary intertextuality.[71] Finally, Turk and Kittler recommend employing discursive analysis to question notions of authorship. Proceeding from Foucault's thoughts in his celebrated talk "What Is an Author?"[72] they point out that the entity to whom we give this designation has many voices even in a single text. They do not content themselves with the traditional separation of author and narrator or persona, since all of these are similarly products of a cultural code. "The author that immanent interpretation brushed aside as an entity of empirical and constant stature is really just the opposite and just like the narrator a construct of discursive practices."[73] Here it seems to me that they are proposing an archeology of the author or authorship as a partial contribution to the archeology of the subject. For the author makes his or her appearance at about the time when the human being in Foucault's scheme becomes the subject and object of the "sciences of man."

These three Foucauldian tasks are undoubtedly worthwhile and formidable enterprises for German studies in the nineties. They suggest avenues for rethinking literary and cultural history as well as the unexamined vocabulary of literary scholarship. As we shall see, Kittler has conducted a research program during the eighties that draws heavily on these programmatic statements, although not many have followed him in Germany. With respect to the appropriation of Foucauldian thought, however, I would note two deficiencies in Turk and Kittler's tripartite suggestion. First, it seems to me that the authors focus too obdurately on the "early Foucault." Although *Discipline and Punish* and *The History of Sexuality* are acknowledged, the dependence on the pre-1970 works of Foucault is evident in the concentration on the notion of discursive analysis. By 1977, when *Urszenen* appeared, Foucault had long since abandoned the chimerical search for rules underlying discourse and had turned to other, more politically informed concerns. Closely connected with this reliance on Foucault the discursive analyst is the authors' adoption of what one might call the playful or "nonserious" Foucault. Turk and Kittler seem to revel in the epistemological relativity of poststructuralist thought, in the "Gay Science" that is content merely to subvert all other systems of knowledge. One could apply to the program sketched by Turk and Kittler in this introduction the same criticism of Foucault in his archeological period that was articulated by Dreyfus and Rabinow. In connection with the conclusion to *The Archaeology of Knowledge* they remark:

> Freeing oneself from the bureaucrats and the discursive police is surely exhilarating, but until one finds a new position from which to speak, and a new seriousness for one's words, there is no place in archaeology for a discourse

with social significance, no reason anyone should listen, and, in spite of Foucault's playful posturing, no reason anyone should write.[74]

What Turk and Kittler are missing is precisely the reintroduction of "seriousness," the concern for the place from which they speak, an analysis with social import and ramifications. In short, by assuming the complacent and distanced attitude of the archeologist, they present their readers with a "subversive" but depoliticized Foucauldian project. Although I recognize a value in what Turk and Kittler suggest, I would therefore suggest that we might also look beyond the theoretical aporias found in the early writings so that we might avoid the disturbing political indifference that they too readily support. Foucault has suggested how this might be done. Instead of remaining in the sphere of archeology—"the appropriate methodology" for "the analysis of local discursivities"—we should move toward a more emancipatory genealogy, "the tactics whereby, on the basis of the descriptions of these local discursivities, the subjected knowledges which were thus released would be brought into play."[75] To accomplish this dual theoretical task of description and application we might, with Foucault—Habermas and Honneth notwithstanding—turn from pure discursive analysis to the microphysics of power.

Foucault elaborated his notion of power during the last decade or so of his life. It is the concept that informs *Discipline and Punish,* but it is more satisfactorily explained in volume 1 of *The History of Sexuality,* as well as in essays and interviews from the late seventies and eighties. In general Foucault defines power as the multiplicity of relationships of forces that organize, individualize, and discipline a social body. This definition differs from traditional concepts in three areas.[76] First, it is not exclusively negative. Foucault exerts a great deal of his rhetorical skill in refuting what he calls the "repression hypothesis." What he means by this and what he opposes to it are most clearly illustrated in *The Will to Knowledge.* Most theorists who have examined the interplay of society and sexuality—from Freud to Reich or Marcuse—have concluded that capitalism, the family structure, culture, or some other entity represses our natural sexual drives. Foucault disputes this type of thesis, seeing instead the creation or production of sexuality itself through the continuous eliciting of "confessions" and the flourishing discourse about sex. The repression of sexuality—and on one level Foucault does not deny that this occurs—is thus only one moment in a larger strategy of power that seeks to control our bodies through our sex. Sexual liberation does not free us from being subjects of and to this power. Indeed, our becoming subjects—in all senses of the word—is partially due to the sexuality unleashed by power.[77] "Power reaches into the very grain of individuals, touches their bodies and inserts itself into their actions and attitudes, their discourses, learning processes and everyday lives."[78] It is, in short, active and productive, not merely negative and prohibitive. Second, power does not emanate from any single source. If Foucault is at pains to avoid naturalism in his critique of the repression hypothesis, here he is rejecting reductionism. We cannot locate the origin of power in economic relations, the patriarchal structure, or the exigencies of civilization. These are, rather, the products of power and the avenues through which it is distributed and takes effect.

Finally, Foucault maintains that power is not held by any one person, group, or class. It is not a possession, and it is not acquired. Rather, it is a relationship, or a network of relationships, distributed throughout society, affecting individuals in various and unequal ways. I think that this point is particularly important since it is open to a good deal of misunderstanding. I do not believe that Foucault is stating that because power is exercised on everyone, we are all, as it were, in the same boat. With this anti-possession hypothesis he is maintaining instead that power does not flow in any predetermined course and that no one stands completely outside its domain. He recognizes, however, that the effects of power ultimately support a certain social class, regime, and economic structure. In a discussion with Gilles Deleuze he stated the following: "It is often difficult to say who holds power in a precise sense, but it is easy to see who lacks power."[79] And further: "Power is exercised the way it is in order to maintain capitalist exploitation."[80] We should not be insensitive to the various criticisms leveled at Foucault's theory of power, particularly with respect to its neglect of class, sexual, and racial distinctions.[81] It has been called, among other things, "disturbingly circular," "overtotalized," "overblown," "Spinozist," "static," and "metaphysical," and these descriptions can frequently rely on evidence from incautious phrasings in Foucault's texts.[82] Nor should we disregard the objections of Habermas and Honneth that I cited above. But we might want to recognize that one of the main reasons for the cacophony of critical voices stems from Foucault's own exaggeration in order to correct previous one-sided truisms. For example, in his later work we often find that the ubiquity of power is emphasized more than its skewed distribution. A second serious problem, to which Habermas and Honneth allude as well, is that his notion of resistance to power is woefully inadequate and lacking in ethical substance. Still, we should not overlook that his rephrasing of the terms in which we conceive of power, particularly the microphysical plays of power, involves a potentially greater degree of differentiation and subtlety than has usually been the case in the past.

Perhaps most suggestive for cultural studies, however, is Foucault's insistence on the inseparability of power and knowledge, and it is in this area, as I have shown above, that he can most readily be considered an ally of the Frankfurt School. If it is true that "the exercise of power perpetually creates knowledge and, conversely, knowledge constantly induces effects of power,"[83] we will want to reexamine our own pedagogical and critical practices as mechanisms of power as well. Our discussions of individual texts, whether they are drawn from literature, philosophy, or social sciences, would then involve more than a mere exhibition of rhetoric and erudition; they could contribute to an analysis of the strategical paths on which power flows, the diverse and clandestine ways in which its effects are achieved. Along these same lines Leo Bersani has remarked: "Literature may not *have* much power, but it should certainly be read as a display of power; and it is a peculiarly instructive model of that play of complicity and resistance which characterizes the innumerable local confrontations of power in human life."[84] With this in mind, we might want to emend Turk and Kittler's threefold suggestion as follows: Instead of describing the pre- and postrhetorical text, we might want to examine how the interplay of individuating and globalizing strategies limits the force of the historical texts, and how this historical rupture redefines the role of culture and our involvement with it as a social practice. In lieu of cataloguing "themes" and "motifs," we might turn to the analysis of how we have been formed and informed by the introduction of a "soul" and what this change has suppressed, excluded, and protected. And in place of an archeology of authorship, we might propose a genealogy of authority, entailing an investigation of the mechanisms by which the subject as author becomes a relay for authorizing subjectivity. Indeed, for German scholars both here and abroad the relationship between power and knowledge is particularly suggestive. The very constitution of what we refer to as the "discipline" *Germanistik* is a prime area of study for the diverse networks through which power-knowledge, as Foucault calls it, induces effects.[85] In this connection we might want to adopt what Paul Bové has outlined as a task for criticism in general and apply it to our particular disciplines:

There is a demand to name the interchange of power, interest, and desire inherent in judging the value of poetry and criticism, in valorizing select critical terms...and in acquiring and teaching certain methods of reading and writing

> on the grounds that more subtly refined and detailed readings are cultural necessities.[86]

There is, Bové continues, a need to analyze the operations of power that "our most subtle and powerful criticism has extended and obscured." Viewed in this regard, a Foucauldian project would continue rather than abrogate the oppositional criticism most popular in Germany during the student movement of the late sixties and early seventies. Exposing and opposing the various techniques of power wherever they manifest themselves, this sort of analysis would more combatively and more effectively open new spaces for political struggles in the nineties.

In 1977 Jean Baudrillard published a rather long, sometimes obscure, and—in my view—misguided essay on Foucault. The details of Baudrillard's essay are not important for our present concerns; suffice it to say that he criticizes Foucault in general for holding an obsolete notion of power. The theoretician of power, he suggests, like Hegel's Owl of Minerva, appears on the scene only when a new age has already dawned. I do not agree with this evaluation of power, but I disagree even more strongly with the implications of the title of Baudrillard's piece: "Forgetting Foucault."[87] For it seems to me that today more than ever precisely the opposite activity is called for, especially in Germany and in German studies, where his border crossing has been so inhibited and where he has therefore been too easily and too quickly forgotten. In remembering him, however, we should be careful to treat his works in the same manner in which he treated Nietzsche's: "The only valid tribute to thought such as Nietzsche's," Foucault stated, "is precisely to use it, to deform it, to make it groan and protest."[88] Applying this to Foucault himself, we would not take his oeuvre as a blueprint or a road map, but as a series of diffuse and fruitful impulses. We would refrain from considering him the creator of a system, a theory, or a totality from which we can derive a method, and view him instead as a thinker who conveys local, criticizable, and revisable insights. We would thus conduct ourselves as co-workers in a larger, multileveled enterprise of cultural criticism, not as submissive disciples. For the realization of Foucault's project, as he himself states, lies in the future:

> Political analysis and criticism have in a large measure still to be invented—so too have the strategies which will make it possible to modify the relations of force, to co-ordinate them in such a way that such a modification is possible and can be inscribed in society. That is to say, the problem is not so much that of defining a political "position" (which is to choose from a preexisting set of

possibilities) but to imagine and to bring into being new schemes of politicization.[89]

By remembering Foucault in the manner I am suggesting, we might be in a better position to promote a more thorough understanding of his work in Germany and to contribute, however modestly, to the schemes he wanted realized.

5

Peter Szondi and the Missed Opportunity

IN my initial discussion of poststructuralism in Germany, I noted that one barrier to a more thoroughgoing reception was the lack of a prominent advocate with legitimacy in the establishment. Peter Szondi could have been just such an advocate. At his death in 1971 Szondi was on the verge of becoming the most respected literary scholar in the German-speaking world. Recently appointed as head of the newly established Institute for General and Comparative Literature at the Free University in Berlin, he was one of the few German professors of his generation who looked seriously to France, as well as to the Anglo-American world, for theoretical inspiration. Among the visitors to Berlin during Szondi's tenure there were Jean Starobinski, Lucien Goldmann, Pierre Bourdieu, and Jacques Derrida from France, René Wellek, Peter Demetz, Ulrich Weisstein, Paul de Man, and Geoffrey Hartman from the United States.[1] As far as I can ascertain, he was the first German literary theorist to call attention to poststructuralism; both Foucault and Derrida are cited in essays written in his last years. From the nature of his comments, and from an examination of his own interests, it is not unlikely that, had he not died, he would have become the very mediating force for French theory that Germany has so obviously lacked. I do not think it is an exaggeration to say that the entire critical landscape in West Germany during the seventies and eighties would have looked different if he had been alive. Perhaps only someone with Szondi's reputation could have obviated the almost allergic reaction that almost all recent French thought experienced at universities in the Federal Republic.

Yet despite his own interest in and active promotion of foreign theory, foreign theorists—especially theorists writing in English—have displayed scant interest in him. This is obviously true in the United States, where he is relatively unknown outside of German studies. Thus far only two of his books have appeared in English. One of these, his *Theorie des modernen Dramas* (Theory of the Modern Drama), is an early work that was extremely influential in Germany during the sixties, and although it does not represent his mature views, it is still well worth reading today.[2] It is a comparative study that begins by analyzing the crisis in dramatic form in late-nineteenth-century Europe, particularly as it manifested itself during the naturalist movement. After considering this crisis, Szondi turns to twentieth-century directions that tried to deal with it by discarding or revising old formal structures and developing new ones. Written early in the fifties and published in 1956, the *Theory of the Modern Drama* is a brilliant work whose theoretical basis is clearly Hegelian and influenced by Georg Lukács and Theodor Adorno. Because of these theoretical foundations, however, the study is apt to be of somewhat less interest for an American reading public today, especially in poststructuralist critical circles that have never dealt seriously or extensively with neomarxism or Hegelianized marxism. For these circles Szondi's *On Textual Understanding and Other Essays*, to which I would like to turn in a moment, will prove to be more familiar turf. This collection of essays on literary and theoretical topics is more typical of his concerns and demonstrates the breadth of his interests. Although drawn from various periods in his career, these pieces clearly indicate how he could have facilitated the entrance of poststructuralism into German critical life.[3]

Before we turn to Szondi's endeavor to reorient literary theory in Germany along lines receptive to poststructuralism, a brief biographical account is in order, not only because Szondi is unfamiliar to most English readers, but also because the stations of his life help to clarify his somewhat unusual relationship to the land in which he taught for over a decade. Born in 1929 in Budapest, Szondi fled Hungary at an early age; if he had not, it is quite possible he would never have written about literature at all. Although Hungarian Jews fared better than those in many other Eastern European countries, it is estimated that between 50 and 70 percent perished during the Second World War. His father, Leopold, a noted psychotherapist and psychological theorist, moved the family to Switzerland, where Szondi had to accustom himself to German as a foreign language. After an education at Zurich and Paris—he completed his dissertation, the volume on drama mentioned above, under the direction of Emil Staiger, a noted phenomenological critic—Szondi became a *Privatdozent* in Berlin in 1961, before obtaining a position at Göttingen the following year. In 1965 he was given a chair in Berlin; shortly before his death, he received an appointment in Zürich. Perhaps most important in this fairly uneventful career is the double alienation from Germany, first as a Jew and second as a non-native speaker. These differences explain in part his attraction to certain topics: the linguistically intricate verse of Friedrich Hölderlin and Paul Celan, and the essays of Walter Benjamin, an exiled Jewish intellectual who did not survive the war. Not coincidentally all three topics have been preferred concerns of German poststructuralists.

English readers interested in Szondi's thoughts on these topics can turn to several essays in *On Textual Understanding,* although Szondi has often treated them more extensively in his posthumously published lectures.[4] Two essays focus on the works of Benjamin, especially his writings on cities. Hölderlin's poetic craft is illuminated in "The Other Arrow," while his views on tragedy are juxtaposed with Schelling's and Hegel's in the following piece. And the final essay, a sensitive analysis of Celan's performative abilities in translating Shakespeare's Sonnet 105, is one of the most compelling interpretations of a Celan poem available. But if we want to get at the heart of Szondi's theoretical contribution and understand how his thought could have paved the way for a more sympathetic appropriation of poststructuralism in Germany, then we should look more closely at the title essay and the selection on the hermeneutics of Friedrich Schleiermacher. These two pieces capture best Szondi's seminal contribution to literary theory; for in both he is grappling with what was probably his central scholarly concern: establishing a literary hermeneutics.[5] Indeed, the other theoretical reflections in this collection and in his other works may be seen as contributing to the solution to this problem as well. His examination of Schlegel's aphorisms on the question of genre, for example, has a definite bearing on interpretive theory: must we know what genre a text belongs to before we can understand the text, or do we arrive at an understanding of the genre only through our reading of the text? This question, like many others implicitly posed in Szondi's oeuvre, relates to the hermeneutic circle which he thought essential in our confrontation with works of art. At the core of Szondi's interpretive praxis, whether he is dealing with theories of the tragic or the genesis of Hölderlin's hymnic style, is his endeavor to come to terms with what it means to understand a text. And it is in confronting this question that he reaches positions that open up the potential for a critical affiliation with contemporary theories in France.

That references to the hermeneutic theory of Schleiermacher continuously recur in these two essays may seem strange to an English audience. After all, Gadamer's magnum opus, *Truth and Method,* had appeared in 1960, prior to the publication of both "On Textual Understanding" in 1962 and "Schleiermacher's Hermeneutics Today" in 1970, and most commentators agree that it signaled a new era for hermeneutic theory. Schleiermacher, known more for his theological writings and concern for New Testament hermeneutics, seems at first glance both more distant and less adaptable for Szondi's purposes. Yet Szondi glimpsed in his work—and he was the first in the postwar era to do so—an untapped source for revitalizing philological interpretation. He recognized that Schleiermacher had advocated far more than the "psychological" hermeneutics for which he had been known for close to a century. This erroneous view was chiefly attributable to Wilhelm Dilthey; according to him Schleiermacher's contribution to hermeneutics consisted primarily in the insistence that we be able to empathize or identify with the author of a given text. The task of the interpreter would then be to recreate as accurately as possible an authorial state of mind, and the most accurate interpretation would be accomplished by scholars who could put themselves in place of the author to the greatest degree. Szondi pointed out that this was only part of Schleiermacher's significance. Relying on the notes and fragments published in 1959,[6] he demonstrated that Schleiermacher consistently referred to two levels of hermeneutic activity. The first is grammatical and has to do with understanding the text as part of a linguistic universe. The second is psychological or technical—Schleiermacher used both designations—and entails the individual contribution of the author as subject.

Dilthey and the hermeneutic tradition which followed him had thus been guilty of a significant distortion in reducing Schleiermacher's hermeneutics to a demand for empathy in accord with the notion of *Lebensphilosophie* (life philosophy). By viewing the hermeneutic task as the mere recreation of individual psychology, Dilthey removed hermeneutics from its essential linguistic foundation and thus destroyed the variant of the hermeneutic circle that could be best adapted to Ferdinand de Saussure, structuralism, and contemporary French thought. In Schleiermacher's theory the linguistic understanding of the text does not stand opposed to the psychology of its author; rather both are part of an ongoing process of interpretation. Perfect understanding—which Schleiermacher considered impossible—could be achieved only when either way of approaching the text would yield the same result, that is, when the individual and the general coincided. What Schleiermacher affirmed, therefore, was a dual approach to understanding. On the one hand, texts and utterances are dependent on a supra-individual structured system of signs. The interpreter must consider both the linguistic community of the original public and the particular combination of words in order to achieve grammatical understanding. As Szondi points out, Schleiermacher here anticipates Saussure's distinctions between *parole* and *langue* as well as between paradigmatic and syntagmatic relationships. On the other hand, the psychological or technical aspect of hermeneutics does not consist solely of a state of mind, as Dilthey had maintained, but also of the style or individuality of the text. Indeed, as Manfred Frank has shown in his work on Schleiermacher, this dimension of his hermeneutic theory provides a powerful tool for explaining how "subjectivity" asserts itself against anonymous and hegemonic structures.[7]

In "On Textual Understanding" Szondi has immediate recourse to Schleiermacher. He cites his contention that understanding "is an artistic achievement" to combat "scientific" and positivistic tendencies in German literary studies. The problem is, Szondi continues, that no one has ever endeavored to discover what precisely are the peculiarities of philological scholarship, as opposed to scholarship in the natural and social sciences. To a large extent Szondi's essay is a first attempt at drawing these necessary distinctions. While the reader will have no trouble agreeing with his specific criticism of German *Literaturwissenschaft* (literary scholarship; literally: literary science), it is not completely clear how the literary scholar is supposed to promote or further understanding. Szondi contends that philological knowledge is different from other kinds of knowledge because it is "perpetually renewed understanding" *(perpetuierte Erkenntnis)*. By this he means not only that it is altered by new points of view and new findings—for this would apply to all branches of knowledge—but also that its condition for existence is a constant reference back to understanding itself. The task of philological studies is not to convey knowledge about an object, which is what other disciplines do, but rather to refer the reader to the process of cognition itself, to the conditions of possibility for cognitive processes. But how the philological investigator does this, how this special task relates to the literary text, and why literary studies and no other field of knowledge (e.g., philosophy) is accorded such a unique place among the various disciplines are never explained adequately enough. Contemporary readers are apt to feel somewhat uncomfortable with this valorization of the literary even if they are sympathetic to Szondi's overall concerns.

What is clear is that Szondi has appreciated and adopted the reflexive model of hermeneutics as outlined in Schleiermacher's writings. In his analysis of the first strophe of Hölderlin's "Friedensfeier" (Celebration of Peace) he does not want to adjudicate between the various critical opinions concerning the existence of metaphoricity, but rather to examine the epistemological assumptions underlying claims to validity. In the process he shows that an adherence to facts as "givens" is impossible. This is so for two reasons. First, he points out that any fact presupposes a prior interpretation. Like Stanley Fish, who sees all interpretation as informed by a prior convention, Szondi contends that we have no unprejudiced and unmediated access to the reality of a literary text. But unlike Fish, whose neopragmatic stance remains one-sided in its insistence on a unidirectional process of subjective determination, he also recognizes the other side of the coin, namely, that we can have no interpretations without prior knowledge of the facts. Indeed, the strength of Szondi's position here is that he formulates this problem inside a fundamentally hermeneutic frame of reference:

> The evidential character of the facts is first revealed by the interpretation, while, conversely, the facts indicate the path that interpretation should pursue. The interdependence of proof and understanding is a manifestation of the hermeneutic circle.[8]

While Fish seems merely to reverse the positivist prejudice by placing the interpretation logically before the facts, Szondi, drawing on Schleiermacher, sees both dimensions as operative in our interaction with texts.

But facts are also useless for textual studies because of the very nature of philology. In contrast to other forms of knowledge, philology does not endeavor to formulate general laws inductively from individual occurrences. The "fact" that Hölderlin may never have used a particular description metaphorically in the remainder of his work is not sufficient reason to conclude that he did not employ it metaphorically in any single instance. To argue in this fashion, Szondi claims, is to confuse the procedures of the natural sciences with philological investigation. In the natural sciences anomalies are not allowed. If too many accumulate, as Thomas Kuhn argued at about the time of Szondi's essay, the laws or even the entire scientific paradigm is altered.[9] The essence of poetry, by contrast, is its individuality or uniqueness. Isolated occurrences do not violate norms since they are themselves the rule of the poetic process. Szondi, of course, concedes that one can make valid comparative observations about passages or individual works of art. But he argues that these generalizations are never conclusive for any specific text. A subtle dialectic, derived in part from Schleiermacher, but consonant with much contemporary French theory, informs Szondi's reasoning. While we must try to understand particular passages or poems against the background of a larger system, whether this be the other works of the writer or linguistic usage in general, the individuality of the poetic utterance—Schleiermacher would extend this to any utterance—demands that we not foreclose our interpretive activity too hastily. Only in this interplay of the general and the individual do we approximate understanding.

In the later essay on Schleiermacher's hermeneutics Szondi states the affinity with his own thought more succinctly. Again Schleiermacher is read against the grain. While Dilthey viewed him as the founder of a philosophical hermeneutics for his opposition to Enlightenment practices and his proclamation of the universality of the hermeneutic enterprise, Szondi wishes "to concentrate less on the philosophical intentions that Dilthey emphasized so strongly and more on both Schleiermacher's ideas about the practice of understanding and his project of a new hermeneutics founded upon the observation of linguistic materials." In a schematic sense one could say that Szondi advocates removing him from the universalist tradition in hermeneutics that culminated in the "existential" or "ontological" theories of Heidegger and Gadamer and situating him instead in a heritage that informs modern linguistics. If we do this, then Schleiermacher's oeuvre "can serve as a model for a new theory of interpretation."[10] In the ensuing discussion, in which he quotes liberally from Schleiermacher's works, Szondi repeatedly points to the hitherto undetected modernity of his interpretive theory. Schleiermacher's "decisive shift from writing back to speech"[11] is linked to both the phenomenology of Georges Poulet and more recent literary theories, deriving from Mallarmé, that focus on the notion of *écriture.*[12] But perhaps his most modern feature—and Frank underscores this as well—is his emphasis on a material hermeneutics. In contrast to most of his contemporaries, who saw words and language as a mere vehicle for the transmission of ideas, Schleiermacher stresses the constraints imposed by genre, poetic form, and the letter, and Szondi is quite correct to link this insight with Valéry and other views on modern poetics.

To this point I have pointed to Szondi's appropriation of Schleiermacher's hermeneutics to construct the foundations for a modern theory of interpretation. But we should not ignore totally the places where Szondi's project exists rather uneasily next to the theories of his idealist predecessor. One of these places occurs whenever the purview of interpretive theory is broached. Schleiermacher, we should recall, turned against the particularist hermeneutics of the preceding generations. He was not interested in developing a theory by which he could interpret the works of the classical world, as Friedrich Ast was, for example; nor was he solely concerned with using hermeneutics merely to perform biblical exegesis, although he writes at one point that he became involved with hermeneutics because of its inadequacy in precisely this area. He did not, in short, view hermeneutics as an art or science limited to one branch of interpretive endeavor, but rather claimed that it has universal applicability as a generalized theory of understanding. Szondi, on the other hand, although he never explicitly rejects the principle of universality, turns to Schleiermacher specifically for a grounding of philology or literary studies. His enterprise presupposes a distinction between the literary and the nonliterary text which Schleiermacher's denies. Indeed, it would appear that by accepting this kind of distinction, Szondi has violated the very sort of hermeneutical principles he is otherwise at pains to observe. For even if we assume that there is a difference between the literary and the nonliterary, or between literary and nonliterary language, the recognition of this difference would have to be the result of an interpretive endeavor, not its presupposition.[13] Szondi's partial appropriation of his idealist predecessor, it would appear, was not radical enough. If he had sought to expand Schleiermacher's insights into a general theory of textuality, rather than restrict them to a privileged domain, Szondi might have brought his reborn hermeneutics into closer proximity to trends in contemporary thought by stressing the ubiquity of textuality and structuration.

The second major failing of Szondi's revitalized literary hermeneutics concerns its relationship to history. While he admits that literary history has a legitimate function, and while he repeatedly affirms the historicity of all texts, he hedges enough to make this part of his theory problematical. He writes that the only approach which does full justice to a work of art is one which "allows us to see history in the work of art, not the one that shows us the work of art in history."[14] But at the same time his adherence to the hypothesis of individual occurrences compels him to conclude that every work of art contains "a certain monarchical strain," which demands "that it simply not be compared."[15] These two tendencies lead a precarious and contradictory existence in his theory: ultimately Schleiermacher's principles of stylistic and formal analysis, which seek "to grasp both the individuality and the historicity of literary phenomena,"[16] are never fully appreciated. This is perhaps most obvious in the individual analyses, in which Szondi's interpretive acumen does not always result in significant historical insight. Quite likely this neglect of historicity relates to the narrow textual bias for literary works mentioned above. An example can demonstrate how historical understanding suffers within the confines of literary textuality. Because there are only two basic types of understanding with regard to texts, in the early essay "On Textual Understanding" history is forcibly assimilated to the paradigm of the natural sciences in contradistinction to philological study. After citing Dilthey's distinction between the natural sciences (*Naturwissenschaften*) and the human sciences *(Geisteswissenschaften),* Szondi defends his revised division of human knowledge:

> This very reference to Dilthey's achievement, however, makes it necessary to point out that philological knowledge is fundamentally different from historical knowledge as well. The Thirty Years' War and a sonnet of Andreas Gryphius do not become objects of knowledge in the same way; indeed, in this regard the study of history appears to be closer to the exact sciences than it is to the study of literature.[17]

This is so, Szondi reasons, because the work of art is always present in a way that the historical event is not. This argument parallels one made several years later by Hans Robert Jauß, in which he sought to distinguish between the third crusade and Chrétien's *Perceval* on a similar basis.[18] Both Szondi and Jauß appear to go astray here because they ignore the textual basis for our understanding of literature *and* history. As Hayden White and Dominick LaCapra have shown in recent years, one can profitably examine historiography and historical documents as texts.[19] If we were to examine historical documents and literary works as part of a field of general textuality, the distinction between fact and interpretation, between explanation and understanding, between code and individuality, could be called into question. But Szondi, who appears intent on carving out a unique space for a literary hermeneutics, is obviously reluctant to apply "philological" rigor to nonliterary materials. As a result he cripples his ability to see the interpenetration of history and literature, to disclose "history in the work of art." By restricting his project in large measure to the most hermetic and "private" poets, Szondi winds up abandoning the larger enterprise of textual understanding as Schleiermacher conceived it, developing instead an incisive, but more limited, "hermeneutics of the avant-garde."[20]

The lectures and essays that comprise Szondi's collected works are perhaps a testimony to Szondi's genial revival and further development of romantic hermeneutics as well as to his narrowing of its interpretive potential. One might be tempted to speculate, in keeping with Paul de Man, that his full exegetical insight could have been unleashed only under the theoretical blindness he imposed on himself. Whether this is the case or not, however, one can scarcely overstate the importance of Szondi's work for both hermeneutic theory and interpretive practice in postwar Germany. In the former area he was the first to explore the implications of Schleiermacher's writings for modern criticism. His work therefore makes a necessary first step toward connecting the heritage of German idealism with the wealth of recent theory based on and superseding Saussurean linguistics. In this endeavor, in which too little research has been undertaken, he has found a most worthy successor in Manfred Frank, whose views on poststructuralism will be discussed shortly. In practical interpretation, he inaugurated a more nuanced and sophisticated manner of approaching the most difficult texts of the tradition. Perhaps nothing exemplifies the fecundity of his method more than his remarks on Celan's translation of Shakespeare's Sonnet 105 ("Let not my love be called idolatry"), which can be found in the final essay in *On Textual Understanding*. The theme of the poem is constancy, and Szondi is able to demonstrate deftly how Celan translates the argument into linguistic performance. In so doing, Celan implicitly rejects a traditional conception of language, "according to which different signifiers can correspond to the same signified,"[21] and affirms a performative principle, in which the poem "speaks about things and about language through its very manner of speaking."[22] Szondi, like the poet he so admired, was a pioneer in breaking with the interpretive tradition of his times, and his own constancy and rigor, which were unmatched by German critics of the postwar era, took him to the brink of theoretical breakthroughs that, on account of his untimely death, went undisseminated in Germany for almost a decade.

6

Manfred Frank as Mediator

WE have seen thus far that when a theory is imported into another country, it often assumes a different status than it had in its native land. In the first part of this study we observed that reception theory, hailed as a radical innovation in Germany, was largely ignored in the United States, and when it was recognized, it was considered a less daring variant of reader-response theory. Poststructuralism in France was obviously a challenge to the establishment at the academy, but in Germany, when it was discussed at all, it was viewed as a frivolous, irrational, and often politically suspect tendency in a misguided anti-Enlightenment heritage. One of the ways to make a foreign theory appear more acceptable in a strange theoretical environment is to assimilate it to a familiar tradition. Thus we have noted above that deconstruction could be appropriated as a *literary* theory in the United States because it extended, without totally subverting, tenets of textual criticism associated with the New Criticism. Similarly Iser's theory of reader response could attract more attention than Jauß's in the United States because it did not foreground its foundations in continental philosophy quite as much as the "aesthetics of reception" did. As we have witnessed in the reception of Foucault, in West Germany (post)structuralism was obviously unsuccessful on its own terms, in part because it conflicted with too many cherished notions in the native heritage. The more promising route for an understanding of contemporary French theory in Germany would therefore be by way of the hermeneutic tradition, and my point in the preceding discussion of Peter Szondi was to show how he was groping—perhaps unwittingly—toward a position that might have made such an understanding possible. For about a decade after his death, no similar endeavor was made, but in the early eighties, Szondi's implicit project found a most worthy advocate in the writings of Manfred Frank.

In contrast to Szondi, who never seemed completely aware of what was at stake in the importation of French theory, Frank (at least until 1985) was extremely conscious of his role as a mediator between two traditions. Born in 1945 and educated between 1964 and 1971 in Berlin and Heidelberg in the disciplines of philosophy, German, and English literature, Frank was perhaps most influenced in his studies by Hans-Georg Gadamer, the most influential advocate of hermeneutics in post-war Germany, and by Dieter Henrich, a specialist in German idealist philosophy. His earliest publications and first books followed from this training in the German heritage. His work on the concept of time in German romanticism[1] was followed by a book on Schelling that explored his impact on the critique of Hegel formulated by Feuerbach and Marx.[2] *Das individuelle Allgemeine* (The Individual General), to which we shall turn again in a moment, examined Schleiermacher's philosophy as a precursor of current debates in theory.[3] An edition of Schleiermacher's hermeneutic theory, an edition of Schelling's *Philosophie der Offenbarung* (Philosophy of Revelation), and a subsequent five-volume set of Schelling's works (with an accompanying introductory volume by Frank), as well as several books and essays on literary themes had all appeared by the early eighties.[4] Frank's preoccupation with the German heritage in his university training and his prolific publication record on German idealism, however, were supplemented rather early by a concern with structuralist and poststructuralist thought. By the mid-seventies he had already published an essay on Derrida—one of the first on the French philosopher to appear in Germany[5]—and selected essays and lectures from the second half of the seventies on matters pertaining to French theory appeared under the title *Das Sagebare und das Unsagbare* (The Speakable and the Unspeakable) in 1980.[6] At that point Frank was teaching at the University of Düsseldorf, where one of his chief aims was to introduce French thought to German students. In 1982, however, Frank was appointed to a chair in philosophy at the University of Geneva, where he was presumably able to continue his work of mediation by acquainting a French-speaking audience with German theory. Subsequently Frank has returned to the German academic world and is at present a professor of philosophy at the University of Tübingen.

Although Frank was concerned with mediation between French poststructuralism and German hermeneutics in much of his early work, undoubtedly the volume that had the most direct impact on legitimizing poststructuralism for a German public was *Was ist Neostrukturalismus? (What Is Neostructuralism?)*.[7] In this book much of

Frank's early philosophical training and analysis was brought to bear on tendencies in French thought that had hitherto been treated with disdain. Indeed, the title of this work is itself not insignificant. The question mark included in it gives another indication of the neglect of French theory in contemporary Germany. Frank obviously felt that he was providing a service to a German reading public by supplying them with information on a series of writers they had ignored. But the designation "neostructuralism" is also meaningful. Frank rejects the usual term "poststructuralism" because the temporal reference is too diffuse: many things occurred "after" structuralism; the prefix "post-" tells us only when this phenomenon happened and says nothing about its content. Frank makes it clear, however, that "neostructuralism" is also misleading to a certain extent. Most occurrences of the prefix "neo" (neomarxism, for example) indicate a school of thought that has reintroduced some tradition after a hiatus and begins to rethink this tradition using a similar basis. What he calls "neostructuralism" does not fulfill this paradigm since it comes into being not simply after "structuralism," but also, in Frank's view, as a movement or tendency that is intimately connected with the critique, radicalization, and overthrow of structuralism. What Frank seems to prefer in "neostructuralism" is the connection to the linguistic tradition of structuralist thought; what he dislikes is the implication that it renews a moribund school of thought. The term "neostructuralism" is thus a designation of compromise and convenience for Frank, slightly more felicitous than "poststructuralism," but not a totally accurate description for the phenomenon he wants to discuss.[8]

Most of the German version of the book is composed of twenty-seven lectures Frank delivered originally at Düsseldorf in 1981 and 1982 and then again in the following academic year in Geneva.[9] We would be wrong to conclude, however, that the lecture format makes this book casual or easy reading. There is no simplification or compromise in Frank's lectures, and the reader is apt to wonder how most auditors were able to follow these presentations when they were originally given. Not only does Frank insist on giving all citations in the language in which they were written (French, English, German, Latin, and Greek), but frequently the arguments take up extremely abstruse philosophical points. This intricacy and abstractness stem, of course, in part from Frank's topic, and it may have been for this reason that Frank introduces his readers to poststructuralism initially from its linguistic roots rather than from its philosophical predecessors. The first five lectures are accordingly devoted to a tentative exploration of the terrain occupied by neostructuralism as a critique of structuralist linguistics and anthropology. Ferdinand de Saussure's *Cours* and the writings of Lévi-Strauss are introduced as exemplary for the tendency opposed in more recent theory. After a short sketch of why neostructuralism takes exception to centered, closed structures and a brief explication of Lyotard's *La condition postmoderne* (1979), which Frank takes to be tone-setting for the entire movement, he moves on to a closer examination of issues. Fundamental for Frank is not only an answer to the question posed in the title, which is treated in excellent and detailed summaries of positions of major French contemporary thinkers, but another question that we will recognize as the key for a mediation between poststructuralist approaches and hermeneutics, between the French and German tradition, between the epistemological critique based on the linguistic turn and an ethical imperative that would allow us to avoid political nihilism:

> How can one, on the one hand, do justice to the fundamental fact that meaning, significance, and intention—the semantic foundations of every consciousness—can form themselves only in a language, in a social, cultural, and economic order (in a structure)? How can one, on the other hand, redeem the fundamental idea of modern humanism that links the dignity of human beings with their use of freedom, and which cannot tolerate that one morally applaud the factual threatening of human subjectivity by the totalitarianism of systems of rules and social codes.[10]

Frank does not take on this question directly, but instead divides his investigation into three subsidiary fields that deal with different aspects of the neostructuralist movement. The first of these concerns the intersection between neostructuralism and history. Not surprisingly Frank chooses to discusses this issue using the texts of Foucault, in particular *The Order of Things* and *The Archaeology of Knowledge*. The second major issue for Frank is how neostructuralism conceives subjectivity, and to approach this issue he examines Derrida's critique of Husserl, Lacan's rereading of Freud, Deleuze and Guattari's *Capitalisme et schizophrénie* (1972 and 1980), and Deleuze's early work *Différence et répetition* (1968). The final subquestion—how does neostructuralism explain the production of meaning—is elucidated chiefly through Derrida's readings of phenomenology and speech-act theory.

The scope of this undertaking is thus rather formidable. Although Frank ignores several figures in French theory—the absence of any concern with women and feminists is regrettable—and although he is compelled to deal selectively with even those writers he does select, he covers an enormous amount of ground. The importance of this volume, however, does not lie merely in its value as a mediator of French theory, although in my view it accomplishes this task far better than any other book in English or German. Amid the summaries and explanations Frank allows three themes to live, as it were, an underground existence, surfacing only occasionally, but often decisively, as a corrective or a supplement to neostructuralist thought. The first of these themes concerns the unacknowledged anticipatory role of German idealism for recent French theory. This theme is particularly important for the German reception of poststructuralism since it brings this body of thought closer to native concerns and makes it appear less "frivolous" and "perverse." Frank shows, for example, that it is not unlikely that Saussure's radical "innovation" in linguistics is actually a reformulation of bits and pieces of linguistic philosophy from Germany in the early nineteenth century. He contends, further, that Derrida's notorious neologism *différance* is not so very different from the Hegelian notion of "autonomous negation," despite Derrida's putative opposition to the Hegelian dialectic. Perhaps most important, however, is his recourse to the hermeneutic theory of Schleiermacher to explain, correct, and overcome the split between structure and hermeneutics. Frank's claim is that Schleiermacher's work evidences a unity of code and interpretation that was subsequently torn asunder. His twofold notion of hermeneutics, to which I alluded in connection with Peter Szondi, anticipates and grounds the very reconciliation he is trying to achieve. Frank's strategy in locating predecessors to the neostructuralists in the German tradition is not to discredit their thought or to show its obsolescence. On the contrary, at this point in his development Frank is attempting to convince a skeptical German public that neostructuralism represents "the current high point of a two-hundred-year tradition of thought."[11] Neostructuralism is not opposed to the German heritage; it is its logical and most stimulating consequence.

The second theme involves the concept of the subject and the related notions of subjectivity, consciousness, self-consciousness, and the individual. These matters have been constant concerns for Frank, and his best and most incisive discussions of these issues occur in works other than *What Is Neostructuralism*. In general, Frank calls into question the Heideggerian perspective on Western philosophy. Relying heavily on the work of Dieter Henrich, he criticizes the monolithic reconstruction of occidental philosophy as a gradual and unrelenting "'subjectivization' of Being."[12] He contends that Heidegger's views are a distortion and oversimplification of philosophical thinking over the past two centuries. Neither Fichte nor Schelling nor Sartre, whose philosophies Frank repeatedly cites as counterillustrations, can be recruited for this Heideggerian (and poststructuralist) schema. The problem is that Heidegger and his new French disciples fail to differentiate among various notions of the subject and of subjectivity. When they speak of the subject, they are referring to a Cartesian construct that did, indeed, entail total self-knowledge and self-presence. But even Kant hedged on this notion considerably. In the *Critique of Pure Reason* Kant did assert that the *cogito* must accompany all mental representations and affirmed a unity to self-consciousness. If this were not the case, then it would be impossible to speak of thoughts or representations of the world belonging to an individual or occurring within an individual. But the unity Kant postulated was transcendental, a condition of possibility for cognition itself. The dissatisfaction with Kant's discussion of self-consciousness arises from the fact that he describes it, at times, as a representation *(Vorstellung),* thus suggesting, as did Descartes, that consciousness can be an object of consciousness in the same way that the world is an object of consciousness. Kant's successors were keenly aware of the inadequacies of the master's discussion, and one could justifiably maintain that the entire course of German idealism should be understood as an endeavor to ground or to account for Kantian self-consciousness.

In Frank's short introduction to the Schelling edition, he gives us an idea of how we might conceive of German idealism in these terms.[13] Most important for him is not the existence of a subject or of an accompanying self-consciousness—to assert that we have no knowledge of ourselves or that we have no access to our own consciousness is as ludicrous as the assertion that we have perfect knowledge—but rather the contention that self-consciousness can be conceived according to the paradigm of reflection. That reflection is an inadequate model is obvious and was recognized by German philosophy at least since Fichte. The most simple objection can be formulated as follows: If we treat consciousness as the object of consciousness, then these two consciousnesses will never match since one always subsumes the other. Thus there can never be absolute consciousness of consciousness or self-consciousness (or a Kantian unity of self-consciousness) if it is framed within the reflection hypothesis. Fichte's *Wissenschaftslehre* (Science of Knowledge) in all its various forms was, as Henrich has shown, an attempt to come to terms with the issue of how to conceive self-consciousness and thus preserve that Kantian system that he felt was essentially correct.[14] As John Smith has shown, this was also Hegel's starting point, although his solution was different from Fichte's.[15] In general we could say that Fichte had recourse to various conceptions of the subject, but in each case it was absolute, logically prior to the world or nonsubject, and the active agent in asserting a material world opposed to it. Hegel rejected the subjective idealism of this view, as well as the "materialist" alternative found most prominently in Schelling's philosophy of nature, and postulated instead an identity of being and thought. He retains the model of reflection, therefore, and by including everything in the movement of self-consciousness from the very beginning, he tries—unsuccessfully according to both Frank and the poststructuralists—to eliminate the contradiction in the reflection hypothesis that had plagued it since Descartes.

Frank's reading of German philosophy is thus meant to correct and refine the way in which the subject has been thematized by various thinkers. His point is that it is not subjectivity that is ill conceived, but rather a model of the subject based on a contradictory notion of reflection. Indeed, Frank claims that many contemporary thinkers, writing long after Hegel—his work marks the point at which it became evident that "subject-philosophy" as traditionally conceived was untenable[16]—unwittingly succumb to the allures of reflection. Their putative rejection of the subject is simply a deferral; some form of reflexivity appears in their theorizing at another level:

> I am convinced that neither structuralism nor neostructuralism nor, for that matter, any other form of systems theory has truly succeeded in explaining the process of signification and of the alteration of signification without relying explicitly or implicitly on the category of the individual. Even the reified statement "Language speaks itself," or even the systems-theoretical statement about the "self-reflexivity of systems," has to employ reflexive pronouns that then hypostatize what was earlier considered a characteristic of the speaking subject as a characteristic of language or of the system itself.[17]

Neostructuralism simply postpones the argument for the constitution of subjectivity by attributing it to a "super-subject," i.e., some force not traditionally identified as a subject, but which is then given the attributes of a subject (language, code, system, structure). The result is an absolute determinism that negates precisely what Fichte also tried to defend: some notion of freedom or of free will that can preserve meaningful ethical (and political) action. Frank insists here and elsewhere that we should perhaps not wage war against the notion of the subject, but rather follow the lead of German idealists (as well as Kierkegaard and Sartre) by conceiving it in nonreflexive terms. He therefore suggests an alternative model, a prereflexive "familiarity of consciousness with itself," in order to avoid the obvious deficiencies of reflection as well as the absurd conclusions we are compelled to draw from the radical reduction of the subject to pure effect. The nonidentity of the self—a conception that Frank shares with the neostructuralists—is ultimately grounded, in a quasi-Heideggerian fashion, "in its ekstatic structure of projection [*in seiner ek-statischen Entwurf-Struktur*]....Ekstatically related to the object of its projections, the subject never coincides absolutely with its Being (i.e., with its having become Being); but it certainly has a consciousness of itself *as* a projection that does not coincide with itself."[18]

Another way to conceive of these issues—and this is the third of the "underground" themes that inform Frank's discussions of post-structuralism—is in terms of the necessity of supplementing any type of structuralist thought with some sort of hermeneutic principle. The nature of this supplementation was the chief theme of Frank's earlier book *Das individuelle Allgemeine.* Gerd Gemünden, who has written intelligently on Frank's project, correctly points to the importance of the subtitle of this volume for an understanding of the trajectory of Frank's thought.[19] *Textstrukturierung und -interpretation nach Schleiermacher* (Textual Structuration and Interpretation after/according to Schleiermacher) provides us with the two halves of Schleiermacher's hermeneutics that must be brought together again *in accord* with his theory of interpretation and over a century and a half *after* he originally articulated the project.[20] A supra-individual code or structure—the grammatical part of Schleiermacher's theory—cannot account for the generation of meaning without an interpretive moment, conceived perhaps infelicitously as a psychological or technical moment. Codes and structures are perpetually potential; Frank points out that no matter how we may think of a system of signs, even if we assume it to be a decentered and differential symbolic order, it remains "mute and unarticulated."[21] The concretization of meaning and—more important for the preservation of ethics and politics—the possibility of exceeding, breaking, or altering the meaning inhering in the structure are realized through acts of interpretation. If a structure is to "speak," to acquire meaning, then interpretive acts carried out by an individual consciousness are necessary.[22]

The importance of the subtitle, of course, should not obscure the centrality of the title. "The Individual General," another reference to Schleiermacher's hermeneutics, points to the synthesis of interpretation (individual moments) and structure (the general code or system) that is at the heart of Frank's neohermeneutic project. The more confusing term in this oxymoron is apt to be the "individual." Frank maintains that the subject contained in idealist philosophical systems (Kant and Fichte through Hegel) was a "radical general" *(radikal Allgemeines).*[23] Individuality must therefore be distinguished from traditional subjectivity (as well as from selfhood and ego, which are effects of individuality) as the element that escapes systematicity. It cannot be subsumed under general laws, as subjectivity is; nor can it be conceived as a result of or an element in reflection. When neostructuralists turn against the subject, following a tradition from Kierkegaard through Sartre, they are really attacking this generalized notion of the subject, not the individual. Conceived as an atomistic, irreducible core from which subjectivity emanates, the individual is related historically to the misunderstood notion of "divination" in Schleiermacher. Frank claims that we should consider divination not as a process of irrational guessing, but, in a more Gadamerian or Habermasian manner, as the entrance into a dialogic situation, where a give-and-take may result in agreement. In terms of contemporary manifestations, the "individual" is related to the series of Derridean anticoncepts, to "that which escapes the systematic interplay of identity and difference of any signifying structure even as it motivates the continuous synthesizing of identities and differences in order to produce meaning."[24] Language, then, correctly conceived, is not a general structure, a code, or a system, but rather itself an "individual general." As Frank explains, "it exists as universal code only on the basis of the principally instable agreements of its speakers."[25]

Frank's fundamental agreement and fundamental disagreement with neostructuralism, in particular with Derrida's deconstruction, should now be apparent. He too rejects the superannuated notions of the subject as a reflexive entity, present and transparent to itself. Likewise, his notion of the consciousness that is a prerequisite for language is void of presence and self-identity, and his view of interpretation is by no means the traditional search for the single determinate meaning of an utterance. Rather, consciousness should be considered in terms of a prereflexive, nonidentical "structure of projection" (*Entwurf-Struktur*) (which does not appear to be at odds with Derridean discussions), while interpretation would entail a never-ending, always already obsolete concretization of any particular *parole,* an infinitely differed and deferred determination of meaning that Derrida captured with the term "undecidability." What Frank objects to is the suggestion *at times* in Derrida's writings that we need not account for what Frank has called the "individual." He concedes to Derrida that without *différance* there is no meaning or change in meaning, but it does not follow for him that meaning *originates* only through and in linguistic differentiality. "Linguistic differentiality—the linguistic code, convention—forms the *condition* without which there could be neither speaking nor understanding. But the agency that sees to it *that* meaning can in each instance be produced and understood is subjectivity as individuality."[26] The radically anti-interpretive posture that Derrida and some of his followers occasionally assume leads only to a cancellation of all meaning. "If one were to take Derrida's antihermeneutics seriously in all its radicality, one would have to conclude that the disseminal character of signs—their total nonpresence—not only would make endurable signification impossible for them, but also would prohibit their signification at any point at all."[27] To avoid this absurdity Derrida, in his more cautious moments, writes of a "réstance non-présente de la marque," a notion that Frank feels brings him into the proximity of Lacan's postulate of a "true subject." Frank's preference for the designation "individual" for this "remainder" or "true subject" points in a slightly different, more German direction, preserving, or perhaps restoring, the connection to Schleiermacher and the hermeneutic tradition. His argumentation, therefore, is designed to include the implicit claim that a hermeneutic moment is furtively, always, and already inscribed in the best of neostructuralist theories.

From my previous remarks on the reception of poststructuralism in Germany, we can appreciate the complex strategy contained in Frank's work from the late seventies and the first half of the eighties. On one level it simply functioned as an introduction to the major theorists in contemporary France for a previously hostile or indifferent German, academic audience. But it accomplished this mediating function primarily by assimilating the French to a more familiar and acceptable tradition of German idealism. On a more important level, however, it also represented the beginnings of a dialogue between hermeneutics and poststructuralism. Frank's sympathies for French theory in the early eighties are unmistakable, and he possessed the philosophical training and the intellectual perspicuity to interject his own as well as differing views into his discussions. His call for a dialogue between German and French positions includes criticisms of both sides. In an essay written shortly after the publication of *What Is Neostructuralism?* for example, he points to the shortcomings of Gadamer's hermeneutics. Gadamer vacillates, Frank claims, between a refurbished notion of the Hegelian world spirit and a version of the individual subject as the bearer of tradition.[28] And his endorsement of the writings of Lacan, Derrida, and Foucault, as we have seen, carried with it misgivings with regard to the exclusion of the individual. What is still refreshing and worthwhile about his approach today (and what makes the English edition of *Was ist Neostrukturalismus* worth reading) is that it avoids the fatuous adulation of poststructuralism frequently encountered in the American academy, while at the same time refusing to succumb to a mindless conservative assault on "theory." Frank's discussion of deconstruction is a case in point. In contrast to Jonathan Culler in a book like *On Deconstruction*,[29] Frank does not simply parrot uncritically Derridean terminology and arguments. He is not awed by the use of foreign and philosophical terms like *pharmakon*, *ousia*, or *Aufhebung;* and he does not take Derrida's word on faith, as too many of his American disciples have done, particularly as deconstruction has degenerated into a cult-like existence in the past few years. Instead, he deploys the wide range of philosophical argument and analysis that is necessary for locating and criticizing Derrida's complex arguments. Perhaps this is also the reason that Frank has concentrated on Derrida's more "philosophically" oriented writings: his introduction to Husserl's *L'origine de la géométrie* (1962) and the book *La voix et le phénomène* (1967). Although Frank is not the only serious commentator on Derrida—we could cite Christopher Norris or Rodolphe Gasché as exemplary, although somewhat less distanced from his concerns[30]—his interest in philosophical roots and ramifications rather than *bons mots* distinguishes his readings from those of the majority of Derrida's American fans.

Equally significant is that Frank recognizes the political, as well as the philosophical, shortcomings of recent French theory. Indeed, from the question he poses at the outset of *What Is Neostructuralism*, Frank, like Jürgen Habermas (although in a much different vein), appears to be unwilling to conceive a separation of philosophy and politics. Most important, he has always refused to accept the easy "political" view that poststructuralist theory, because it fashions itself as an anti-establishment critique, is necessarily tied to political emancipation. Although direct references to political implications appear only occasionally, he does not fail to note, for example, the affinities between Nietzsche's thought and certain aspects of National Socialism,[31] nor does he refrain from mentioning the proximity of Foucault's rejection of all ordering disciplines to the "acte gratuit" of surrealism, "blind flailing (without principles) or running amok."[32] His most direct and severe political rebuke, however, occurs in connection with his discussion of Deleuze and Guattari's *Anti-Oedipe* (1972). Noting the similarities in some extreme neostructuralist positions, the views of the New Philosophers, and the outlook of the New Right, Frank again censures the fashionable opposition to all order for leveling in an abstract and undifferentiated fashion real political distinctions:

> The resigned leftist challengers of yesterday now take theoretical tranquilizers and spiritual analgesics (instead of working through their sorrow and returning to praxis). Because of their factual indifference (i.e., because of their unwillingness to take a position against the existing order and for an alternative order, one that would still be an order of intersubjective coexistence), they become the advance guard of a fatal integration of the individual into the dominant power. A kind of political and intellectual flipping-out, a spiritual Calibanism, a certain uncommon style that barely disguises its poverty of thought behind a flurry of images, and the limitless self-pity of many of our left intellectuals of yesterday: these are the characteristic features of this type of *imitatio* of Foucault.

Frank correctly sees that an abstract opposition does not necessarily define a desirable political practice. "To displease the bourgeois is not enough," he observes. "After all, even nazism was a 'completely unbourgeois adventure.'"[33]

In the second half of the eighties Frank extended his political reservations to other neostructuralist positions as well. In 1986 he linked the notion of the "death of man," a slogan drawn from Foucault but associated with almost all varieties of poststructuralist thought, with the irrationalist tradition in German philosophy during the first third of the twentieth century. Not Derrida, he pointed out, but Ludwig Klages, was the originator of the term "logocentrism," and it was he and other conservative thinkers who advocated the necessity to overcome it. By thus locating certain motifs of French thought in the proximity of right-wing German philosophy, Frank implies that neostructuralism may be unwittingly close to a fascist perspective.[34] This suggestion becomes a polemical and theoretical postulate two years later in a newspaper article that he composed to explain his philosophical goals as a new professor at Tübingen. After objecting to the contention—which he identifies with neostructuralism—that the evolutionary stronger, rather than the better, argument prevails, he recalls that a similar contention could be found in the work of Klages, Oswald Spengler, and Alfred Baeumler, all of whom are correctly considered prefascist thinkers. Most disturbing for him, it seems, is that students are beginning to appropriate neostructuralist thought without contemplating the political consequences:

New French theories are taken up by many students as if they were messages of salvation....I consider this phenomenon to be dangerous; for it seems to me that, under the pretext of an openness to French and international currents, younger Germans are here ingesting their own irrational tradition, which remains uninterrupted after the Third Reich, and which appears to be cleansed of all the nationalist detritus because it has gone through the hands of the French.[35]

If students have, indeed, turned to French theory in the latter part of the past decade, then this shift has probably been due in no small measure to the pioneering work done by Frank himself. His increasing skepticism toward the latest political ramifications of this border crossing is perhaps understandable in light of the conservative tendencies in German politics during the Kohl era. And we can also view sympathetically Frank's disappointment that his own work has not exerted a corrective and mediating influence on the younger generation. But these misgivings about the recent abuse of French thought should not detract from his immense service to German theory during the early eighties, at a time when he was more sanguine concerning the possibilities for combining the philosophical sophistication of neostructuralism with an ethically and politically responsible hermeneutic position.

7

Friedrich Kittler as Discursive Analyst

THE strategy pursued by Manfred Frank in the late seventies and early eighties was to integrate poststructuralism into German intellectual life by asserting its origins in a familiar tradition (German idealism) and by suggesting its amalgamation with acceptable approaches (hermeneutic theory). Another way to introduce poststructuralism to a skeptical German public is to present it as a rejection or as an overcoming of that same familiar tradition and those same acceptable approaches. The native proximity to poststructuralism would thereby appear less direct, and an appropriation would perhaps be less appealing. But this manner of presentation has the advantage of confirming Frank's positive evaluation of French theory without requiring that it be situated in a historical lineage with which it has obviously been somewhat uncomfortable. Most readers familiar with the central texts of Foucault, Lacan, and Derrida will have recognized that Frank's conciliatory gesture toward poststructuralism goes somewhat against the grain. The portrayal of poststructuralism as discontinuous with German idealism and hermeneutics is more consistent with certain tendencies in poststructuralism itself. The superannuated notion of history as a linear flowing or a one-dimensional passage of time has been a major target in many poststructuralist critiques. The postulate of a radical rupture with the past and with those theories that are obsolete extensions of the past thus follows a line of argumentation that by now has become extremely familiar. While Frank's careful analysis and reasoned contentions make sense, and while his plea for a "middle road" between poststructuralism and hermeneutics seems eminently reasonable, the depiction of French thought as the vanquisher of German theory preserves a potential appeal to the rebellious spirit often found in young students as well as the public image nurtured by most poststructuralists and their disciples.

This more confrontational route was the one traversed by Friedrich Kittler, possibly the most imaginative and original of the German poststructuralists. But perhaps more important than the antagonistic relationship between French and German thought in his works is the different way in which poststructuralism enters into his writings. In contrast to Frank, Kittler does not discuss French poststructuralist theory directly or extensively in any of his writings. He has not been interested in mediating the poststructuralists to a German public by explicating them or by rephrasing their views in more familiar terms, but rather by demonstrating in a practical way what poststructuralism can accomplish. We should recall that in 1977 Kittler was co-author of the programmatic introduction to *Urszenen* that promulgated a tripartite function for discursive analysis.[1] At that time he suggested implementing this Foucauldian project in order to describe events of traditional literary and cultural histories in a new, poststructuralist fashion. Although he did not detail his specific interests in this introductory piece, from the examples cited it was evident that he was particularly concerned with changes that had occurred around 1800 or, more generally, during what has become known as the "Age of Goethe." His first book, published in the same year as the introduction, did not really deal with these issues. Although there was some influence of poststructuralism, his study of dream and speech in the works of Conrad Ferdinand Meyer, a German-writing Swiss author from the second half of the nineteenth century, was more indebted to Lacan and psychoanalysis.[2] In the book he published jointly with Gerhard Kaiser the following year and in subsequent publications, however, his concern for isolating and analyzing the distinctiveness of discourse around 1800 became more apparent.[3] By the early eighties it must have been apparent to him that the best way to deal with the issues he had outlined in the late seventies was to present a contrast in distinctiveness between the "Age of Goethe" and what we might call for lack of a better description the "Age of Modernism."

The result of these considerations led to the publication of one of the most interesting monographs of the eighties: *Aufschreibesysteme 1800–1900* (literally "Notation Systems"), a book that has recently appeared in English with the title *Discourse Networks 1800/1900*.[4] Its project can be best understood as falling somewhere between the German and the English title. Kittler is definitely concerned on one level with notation systems, or more precisely, with how things become written down, recorded, and inscribed during the "Age of Goethe" and during the modern period, and one part of his book is bent on persuading the reader that two distinct and separate systems of writing were in effect during these periods. The first system, which is associated in general with classicism, romanticism, and idealism, views language as a conduit for an individual spirit or intellect. The human being is placed at the center in this conception of the production of the written word, as creator and controller of linguistic signs. The system which replaces it—Kittler does not deal with the messy business of how this transformation comes about—valorizes the written word over the human beings through whom it becomes recorded. Around 1900 language becomes a medium among other media. Its materiality is recognized, and the human being, who previously appeared to employ it for self-expression, recedes into oblivion. In its broadest outlines, therefore, the tale Kittler relates is not wholly unfamiliar, and the English title does a better job of capturing (or recapturing) one of his central preoccupations and of highlighting the major theoretical influence for the book. Although we encounter citations from Derrida and Lacan liberally sprinkled throughout this work, it is clear that Kittler draws more heavily on the work of Michel Foucault for his overall framework. Rather than the deconstruction of the text or the linguistic structuration of the unconscious, Kittler, like Foucault, is most interested in historical differences and the discourses that mark epochs.

The reliance on Foucault is perhaps most noticeable on the macrolevel of Kittler's thought. The division of the volume into two distinct time periods and the absence of a transition between them recalls the methodological procedures that Foucault employed in *The Order of Things* and justified in *The Archaeology of Knowledge.* Kittler is obviously also trying to discover discursive patterns for a particular age. Thus, like Foucault, he demonstrates a total indifference to the conflicts that occur within the confines of a certain era. As David Wellbery points out in his excellent and sympathetic introduction to the English version of the book, Kittler is not writing an ideological critique of specific utterances or subdiscourses, but endeavoring instead to delineate the regularities that underwrite even the apparent controversies. Like Foucault, therefore, Kittler employs a descriptive approach to establish discrete typologies. We will remember that Foucault's epistemes of the Renaissance, the classical, and (in a somewhat sketchier fashion) the modern were postulated by means of an examination of four disciplinary areas apparently unconnected with each other. The similiarity between them consisted in commonalities with regard to their relationship to and their constitution of their respective objects. In a similar fashion Kittler proceeds not by means of an interpretation or criticism of individual works or authors, but rather by observing "superficial" features. He is not interested in showing that an individual author was "right" or "wrong," or that a given text is "biased" or "accurate." His concern is instead with the conditions of possibility for utterance at all. This Foucauldian paradigm that Kittler shares leads to an array of unexpected connections between disparate phenomena. But it also evidences the central deficiencies found in Foucault's work of the late sixties: the absence of linkage or mediation between two epistemes or epochs, the relativistic implications of discursive configurations, and the impression that at times data are being forced into a framework that is more constrictive than it need be.

It would be wrong, however, to view Kittler solely as a German follower of Foucault. Although he definitely holds the late "professor of the history of systems of thought"[5] in high regard, his relationship to him is not one of simple discipleship. In the afterword to the second edition of his book Kittler describes most succinctly the limitations of Foucault's work. All the periods Foucault treats in *The Order of Things* are approached through written sentences. The archives he establishes for an epoch are based on documents that were all recorded in a fundamentally similar fashion. Foucault's hesitancy to describe the modern era, Kittler claims, derives from the trouble he had in coping with the altered methods that arose after the "second industrial revolution." In a word, what is missing in Foucault is an account of technology and the changes it brings with it for discursive analysis. "Archaeologists of the present must also take into account data storage, transmission, and calculation in technological media."[6] Foucault's "materialism" with regard to documents thus did not go far enough. It fell short of considering the changes wrought by modifications in the networks of discourse themselves. The consequences of this shortcoming can be seen in the equivocation associated with Foucault's discussion of certain disciplines in the modern era, in particular psychoanalysis, ethnology, and structural linguistics. Foucault views these fields with an uncertainty, Kittler claims, because he is unsure whether they "represented the last moraine of transcendental knowledge or a new beginning."[7] Foucault's error was not recognizing that these disciplines were themselves part of a discourse network that arose in conjunction with fundamental alterations in technology.

Accordingly Kittler focuses his own "order of things" not only on the discourse about writing, but also on the technology involved with writing, as well as on its implications for other areas of social life. In the first half of the volume, devoted to the " writing system" of 1800, he therefore finds it germane to consider the way in which reading and writing were taught, and to this end he cites extensively from various primers composed during the period. In particular he notes that there existed the tendency away from teaching language phonetically through nonsense syllables and toward the use of real monosyllabic words from the German language. Subsequently, at some point in the eighteenth century, Kittler hypothesizes, the sounds of the individual letters became more important than words for teaching literacy. His claim is that this methodological shift is part of a naturalizing trend; the arbitrariness of the linguistic sign, a hallmark of the previous epoch, is ignored, and language is thus incorporated into the sphere of nature. This reconstitution of the relationship between language and nature is connected, in turn, with alterations in familial and social structure. The mother, as nature and ideal, is the source for the mother tongue, entrusted with the pedagogical task of language instruction. It is her responsibility to educate her sons as civil servants for the state, which is responsible for enforcing the new literacy. Although I can give only the results of Kittler's various narrative strands, it should be evident to the reader that his concerns are broad. Throughout his initial discussion he is intent upon exploring the connections between such phenomena as the reduction of illiteracy, the socialization of the educational system, the rise of the concept of *Bildung* (education or acculturation), and the appearance of a particular notion of the human being. In the latter part of his consideration of the notation systems around 1800 he weaves other selected topics into his discursive mosaic; among these are translation theory, the reading public for *belles lettres,* and the close association of poetry and philosophy. A good portion of these latter themes are developed from an ingenious reading of E. T. A. Hoffmann's *Der goldene Topf* (The Golden Pot), which becomes something like the archetypical fairy tale for the "discourse network" of 1800.

One of the by-products of Kittler's analysis is the temporal displacement of the very traditions that Frank tried to make timely for a poststructuralist criticism. German idealism and the hermeneutic tradition that emanates from it are categorized not as wrong or deficient by Kittler, but simply as outmoded and therefore inapposite as partners for contemporary French thought. Hermeneutics, especially in its romantic form, is an interpretive enterprise that seeks the spirit behind the letter, that breathes life into the dead documents by insisting on a unique and vital source for utterances. The title to a collection of essays

Kittler edited in 1980 is instructive in this regard. *Die Austreibung des Geistes aus den Geisteswissenschaften* (The Expulsion of Spirit from the Spiritual [or Human] Sciences) indicates the direction in which Kittler is proceeding. His is an aspiritual approach, in contrast to a hermeneutically oriented procedure that, even in Frank's somewhat minimalist fashion, has recourse to a "spiritual" origin for textual production. As a practitioner of posthermeneutic criticism, Kittler "stops making sense."[8] He provides his own historical justification for doing so when he describes the analysis of the hermeneutic project as delimited by certain definable notions of language pedagogy, state interventions, maternal relationships to sons and daughters, and technologies of writing. The implicit message is that hermeneutics cannot be joined to an authentic poststructuralist enterprise because the two projects are themselves manifestations of radically different epochal practices. Hermeneutics belongs, for better or for worse, to the discarded archive from a previous era.

What, then, is the new network that Kittler detects at the beginning of our century, and how can one describe it in terms of technology and not merely in its discursive appearances? Perhaps Kittler's central claim in dealing with the modern era is that the logic associated with the materiality of language, a logic of "pure differentiality,"[9] also produces the typewriter, the phonograph, and film. The advent of these three machines destroys the "Gutenberg Galaxy" by splitting into different media the appropriate channels for words, sounds, and pictures.[10] Combining the analysis of statements made by the inventors and propagators of these technological innovations with the implications he derives from the technology itself, Kittler sketches for the reader a system in which the precepts and beliefs identified with the previous discourse network have been overturned. The distinction between sense and nonsense blurs;[11] the transcendental norm for language, formerly identified with a spoken ideal, "falls into an endless series";[12] the subject, who had previously been believed to use language, now disappears from the scene.[13] In short, "in the discourse network of 1900, discourse is produced by RANDOM GENERATORS. Psychophysics constructed such sources of noise; the new technological media stored their output."[14] The social manifestations accompanying the new technology are also radically different from what had established itself around 1800. The unity of culture, based on the mutual transparency of writing, reading, speaking, and hearing, disintegrates;[15] the role of the sexes is completely reversed since the "imaginary Mother's Mouth" is replaced by the man giving dictation to his secretary;[16] for the first time in a literate culture people are "reduced to the naked recognition of signs."[17] The "discourse network of writing"[18] evidences the victory of what Kittler refers to as psychophysics. Nietzsche is the inaugurator of this new system; Mallarmé its first poet; Freud the perhaps unwitting but exemplary proponent. The nation of "Poets and Thinkers" *(Dichter und Denker)* becomes one of writers and analysts.[19]

As in the first part of this book, Kittler explores these topics with materials from a number of unusual, as well as more conventional, sources. With the exception of brief remarks on Gottfried Benn, Arno Holz, and Stefan George, however, the traditional field of literature is less prominently represented. Rilke's *Die Aufzeichnungen des Malte Laurids Brigge (The Notebooks of Malte Laurids Brigge)* is the only literary work "interpreted" in any detail, and Kittler's suggestion for renaming it *Memoirs of My Simulations of Nervous Illness (Denkwürdigkeiten eines Nervenkrankheitssimulanten)*[20] gives some indication of the direction he wishes to take. His general observations about differences in literary production in the two epochs, however, provides some insight into both his method and his style. For readers unacquainted with them the following quote should give some inkling of what he is after:

Poetic works of 1800 belonged in the Kingdom of God. An Absolute Spirit, in which no member was sober, consumed all authors and works at the end of their earthly cycles. The authors turned in their civic names at the chalice of this realm of spirits, but only in order to attain the infinity of interpretation and the immortality of meaning.

A completely different God stands over the discourse network of 1900 and its inkwells. He has gone mad. In him the simulators of madness have their master. When the insane God drinks, it is not in order to sublate fantasies in a threefold sense. Where in 1800 there was a function of philosophical consumption, one hundred years later there is bare annihilation. Writers who drown in the inkwell of the insane God do not achieve the immortality of an author's name; they simply replace anonymous and paradoxical analphabets who are capable of writing down a whole discourse network from the outside. For that reason there are no authors and works, but only writers and writing.[21]

I have quoted at length here not only to allow Kittler to represent his own case but also to give the reader an idea of how he represents it. For I think that the single most disturbing factor for readers of this book, and, indeed, of much of Kittler's prose, will be the style in which it is written. Too often arguments seem obscure and private. One frequently has the impression that the author is writing not to communicate, but to amuse himself. His text consists of a tapestry of leitmotifs, puns, and cryptic pronouncements, which at times makes for fascinating reading, but too often resembles free association as much as it does serious scholarship. As in much of poststructuralist writing here and abroad, the often-cited rigor is more an assertion of the convinced than a fact of the prose: analysis frequently cedes to apodictic statement; logic repeatedly yields to rhetorical flourishes. Kittler goes out of his way to write genially, and although many connections he makes are both original and illuminating, his penchant for preferring *bons mots* to reasoned arguments is ultimately deleterious to his goals—assuming, that is, that at least one of his aims is for us to understand and to be persuaded by his presentation.

There is a related difficulty with Kittler's arguments. The incessant search for the witty phrasing, for the aperçu or pun, or for the semblance of profundity often means that he is willing to sacrifice philological accuracy in driving home his argument. Let me illustrate the shortcomings of Kittler's style and argumentation—for I believe they are inseparably linked—briefly with the very first sentence of the book. The initial statement reads as follows: "German Poetry begins with a sigh" *(Die Deutsche Dichtung hebt an mit einem Seufzer).* Kittler then quotes as "evidence" the initial verses from the first scene in *Faust I* ("Have, oh, studied philosophy" *[Hab nun, ach! Philosophie]*). His point here is, as I have explained above, that a spirit or intellect informs the written word in the discourse system of 1800; the *"ach,"* he maintains, is a sign of this "unique entity (the soul)."[22] Although this argument is neither uninteresting nor unfounded, the manner in which he seeks to demonstrate it asks readers to stretch their knowledge and their ability to read too much. Faust does not stand at the beginning of German literature; it is usually viewed as the culmination of Goethe's creative efforts and of German classicism in general. Even *Urfaust* was not Goethe's first work, and certainly no one would place it at the beginning of even the modern literary tradition. Nor does *Faust* actually begin with these verses; the authoritative version includes the poem "Zueignung" and two prologues before the scene in Faust's chamber. Finally, the *"ach"* does not start the line, much less German literature, but is embedded squarely in the middle. Now these objections can surely be seen as petty. They relate only to minor details, not to the thesis as a whole. Kittler could counter that his readers will understand what he means here, ignore the fudging of facts, and probably go along with his argument. The problem is that this sort of argumentation is not the exception, but the rule. The grand theses about the characteristics of discursive systems and technologies in 1800 and 1900 all too frequently govern the readings of passages, bending them out of shape, or rather, into the shape in which Kittler wants them to appear. At times his claims seem arbitrary; the examples he introduces, which are anyway the result of a selective process, seem to be read selectively and forced into a pigeonhole in which they fit uncomfortably. In short, even when we have managed to fight through the opaqueness of much of the text, we are asked to buy into the rhetorical strategy and hyperbole too much and too often, abjuring in the process obvious facts and counter-examples.[23]

In light of its style one would be justified in raising the question of what "writing system" Kittler's own work belongs to. On the one hand, Kittler is, for reasons I have enumerated above, a unique practitioner of poststructuralism in Germany, and his considerable intellect and originality are evident in all of his various writings. One might therefore be tempted to see his oeuvre as a throwback to the *"Geniezeit,"* or at least as the attempt to refashion this era for the present. On the other hand, Kittler himself obviously pays a great deal of attention to the materiality of the printed word. By this I mean not only those passages involving wordplays—he reminds us, for example, that *"ach"* is part of *Sprache* (language)—but also the manner in which he presents his materials. Here I am referring to more than just the style of writing. In the German version of *Discourse Networks* headings are supplemented by notes in the margins, a feature that was unfortunately omitted in the English edition; illustrations (reproduced in the English version) are frequent and carefully integrated into the text; the front cover of the German paperback shows us an austere, priestly figure pointing to a typewriter; the back cover depicts Goethe, as bureaucrat, answering a telephone. Kittler obviously feels that word and image in their material reality are as important as message, and his work is meant as both example and explanation of this materiality. Indeed, it is difficult to avoid the conclusion that Kittler believes he must operate under the "writing system" of 1900 since it is somehow more accurate to reality or at least more aware of the true function of the written word:

> The discourse network of 1800 played the game of not being a discourse network and pretended instead to be the inwardness and voice of Man; in 1900 a type of writing assumes power that does not conform to traditional writing systems but rather radicalizes the technology of writing in general.[24]

Kittler's lack of reflection on his own historical situatedness notwithstanding, from the remarks he does make about notation systems of two epochs his work can be viewed as obeying either the law of original spirit or the logic of differential materiality.

The uncertainty we encounter in trying to locate the force behind Kittler's own work is perhaps a consequence of the contamination of one system by another, a sign that the discreteness on which Kittler insists is less clear-cut than he imagines. But rather than having Kittler's work vacillate between these two epochs, we might want to consider that it participates in the beginnings of a new, as yet uncharted era. This new epoch is not even on the horizon in *Discourse Networks,* but in the introduction to *Grammophon Film Typewriter,* a book Kittler also published in 1985, he speculates on how we might begin to describe the notation system of the year 2000. It is characterized above all by the leveling of the distinctions among the various media. Glass-fiber optics has made the transmission of sound and sight, voice and text, a matter of fundamentally interchangeable electromagnetic impulses. On the basis of computer technology everything can be reduced to a binary basis, a choice between two numbers, zero or one, on or off. The differentiation that took place around 1900 is thereby canceled without bringing us back to the humanistic starting point. The age of media has become the epoch of microelectronics; "the compact disc digitalizes the gramophone, the videocamera, the movies."[25] Although it is impossible to name the writing system that will govern the year 2000 and under which Kittler composes his oeuvre, we might want to speculate nonetheless on what technological emblem to assign to it. If the "writing system" around 1800 employed pen and ink and "the Mouth of the Mother," if the subsequent system is identified with typewriter, phonograph, and film, we might see the "Discourse Network 2000" prefigured in the television, the computer, and above all the walkman, i.e., in hermetic, self-contained, privatized systems which use public media, channels, and data, but which, at least in their instantiation in modern industrial societies, do as much to defy as to promote communication.

When I listed the deficiencies common to Kittler and to Foucault's project in *The Order of Things,* I neglected to mention at least one item. In my previous discussion of Foucault's German reception I tried to show that the transition to his work of the seventies, the switch from archeology to genealogy and from epistemic structures to the microphysics of power, was accompanied by a marked politicization of his theory. Kittler's project, as I have also indicated in this previous chapter, fails to submit to this politicized regime. Although he supplements the notion of discourse analysis with a consideration of technology, he refrains from incorporating a notion of power that could possess political ramifications. What we find instead in his work is the antiseptic and distanced description of complicities. In *Grammophon Film Typewriter* the logic of the media is associated with strategies developed by the German High Command; and at the close of the same book Kittler implies that the National Security Agency is manipulating our future by appropriating and instrumentalizing the technology of the computerized epoch. But the "exteriority"[26] with which Kittler views these connections and, indeed, all the connections he describes leave him and his reader either on the outside gazing at a reified nexus of technologies and discourses, or caught in an infinite and immutable network of connections from which there is no escape. Unlike Frank, whose political criticism emanates from the insistence on an individual nondetermination that escapes structuration, Kittler is able to muster only a helpless and cynical political gesture. Thus we may admire his voluminous scholarship, his intuitive insights, and his stylistic bravado; and we may even want to affirm that his work has been a high point of the German appropriation of poststructuralism. But I suspect that while his postmodern readers are emitting spirited sighs of exhilaration and admiration, the "ach" uttered by those still adhering to political agendas will ultimately be one of exasperation and frustration.

Part Three

The Politics of American Deconstruction

8

Marxist Deconstruction

WHEN structuralism and poststructuralism burst almost simultaneously onto the American critical scene in the early seventies, they were greeted by left-leaning critics, who at that historical moment were far more numerous and vocal than today, with indifference or even hostility. Although there were rumors that poststructuralism had something to do with the events of May 1968 in Paris, there was no apparent claim to political legitimacy attached to it when it crossed the border into the United States. Indeed, its importation at the elite institutions of the eastern establishment did not seem to promise much in the way of political radicalism. The central works of both structuralists and poststructuralists seemed far removed from the type of criticism that had emerged among the most radical literary scholars of the Vietnam era, and their entire manner of procedure must have appeared obscure and detached from political reality.[1] Thus it is perhaps not surprising that as late as 1976 the Marxist Literary Group at the Modern Language Association contemplated staging a confrontation between structuralism or poststructuralism and marxism to demonstrate the superiority of the latter over the upstart French imports. The idea was to get two "big names" for this debate in order to attract a large audience; in the head-to-head combat the American marxists were obviously convinced that their side would have no trouble emerging victorious. If this agonistic suggestion appears medieval or foolish or simplistic today, it is not only because such a battle of the critical superstars would have most likely settled nothing. Subsequent developments have shown, moreover, that confrontation was a temporary and perhaps aberrant response to the perceived threat from the continent. The bellicose mood of the early seventies became considerably more conciliatory a few years later. Indeed, the project that was on the minds of many leftist literary theorists in the late seventies and early eighties was not to prove the preeminence of marxist criticism, but rather, after the student movement was laid to rest, to show the necessity of supplementing it, merging it, or correcting it with some variety of French thought. With regard to most French theorists the process of integration into leftist criticism in the States was accomplished without much difficulty. Aspects of the work of Foucault, Lacan, Barthes, and Althusser appeared with increasing regularity in politicized theories from the late seventies onward. Poststructuralism thus became the most significant development in American leftist criticism since the Frankfurt School was "rediscovered" in the sixties.

The integration of deconstruction into a leftist or marxist political agenda was a bit more problematic. It too originally appeared in this country at elite eastern universities and did not attract much attention from the traditional left. The initial translations of essays and the appearance in English of Derrida's *Of Grammatology* in 1976 did little to change this initial impression.[2] Although the book was certainly exhilarating reading and did make various gestures toward the political, its central themes and the direction of its analysis did not correspond at all with the concerns of the previous decade. It was only a matter of time, however, before an appropriation of deconstruction appeared on the agenda of the left as well. This endeavor to appropriate deconstruction for the left in the United States was undertaken largely in the work of Gayatri Spivak and Michael Ryan, as well as in a few "avant-garde" journals, most prominently *Diacritics*, which for a time reserved a prominent place for the topic of politics and deconstruction. The attempt to politicize deconstruction, of course, can more properly be considered a repoliticization of deconstruction for American criticism, since the affinity with radical and marxist thought had existed in France from its very inception. Still the project is philosophically remarkable. Deconstruction, it would seem, does not lend itself readily to political analysis in any traditional sense of the word simply because it refuses to accept the traditional vocabulary of political discourse at face value. Although Derrida reminds us, as did Marx before him, that the space of philosophy is not a neutral arena,[3] it is never quite clear how this alleged lack of neutrality translates into political terms. Moreover, Derrida and those who identify with deconstruction would seem to claim a privileged status for their own discourse, at least implicitly, while simultaneously denying the possibility of such a status. What this means for the politics of resulting analyses is not clear; but at the very least this paradoxical stance suggests an ambivalent relationship to the political tradition of marxism. In asserting its privileged perspective, the result of an at least implicit claim of superior analysis, deconstruction appears to place itself outside of all traditional political theory. From this position it is able to assist in the deconstruction of the texts inside the tradition. In admitting the impossibility of a privileged outside to the tradition, however, it seems to partake in the very process it deconstructs. Although it may temporarily find a common ground with some forms of marxist analysis, in general it would appear to deny the validity of a marxist political discourse.

In fact, as many commentators at the time noted, a prima facie argument for linking deconstruction with conservative politics can be just as easily constructed (and perhaps deconstructed) as one that merges the projects of Marx and Derrida. One section of such an argument could consist of an examination of the heritage most frequently cited by deconstructors, an issue that forced itself on deconstruction only in the late eighties in the Heidegger affair. Among the most frequently cited authorities we quite often find thinkers whose philosophical insights were not at all at odds with conservative social and political theory. Nietzsche and Heidegger, to name the most prominent and obvious sources of deconstructive thought, exemplify this ability to combine philosophical prowess with questionable political affiliations. Nietzsche's occasional remarks concerning democracy (in particular working-class participation in governance), women, socialism, racial breeding, and a host of other social and political topics are notorious enough that they do not need repetition here. Although Nietzsche was never aligned with the nationalist conservatives of his era, his views reflected in many ways the worst aspects of the elitist mandarin caste to which he belonged. Heidegger's involvement with National Socialism, which will be discussed in more detail in the following chapter, is by now, thanks to Victor Farias, also common knowledge. The most frequently invoked objection to this argument of deconstructive lineage is that it is biographical and simplistic: One could even admit that the political views found in certain passages by Nietzsche or Heidegger were foolish, offensive, or reactionary, yet still find a more important discourse in their works than in those who apparently propounded the right, that is, a left, ideology. One could continue this objection by noting that placing so much weight on a superficial reading of these philosophical texts misses the point entirely: the importance of Nietzsche and Heidegger lies not in their political views, but in their insights into the workings of the Western metaphysical tradition.

There is no doubt some merit to such an objection, although we might want to question the insistence on a strictly "New Critical," antibiographical reading of philosophers, one that separates the activity of putting words in texts from activities in other realms of life. I believe, however, that even if we concede that these are superficial readings, we would still have to admit the potential compatibility of reprehensible political positions and philosophically interesting or even protodeconstructive writing. Indeed, the liabilities of the tradition on which deconstruction most heavily draws have been consistently thematized by Derrida himself. In contrast to many of his American followers he has always been sensitive to the politics of tradition. In an essay from the late seventies he quite correctly observes that although it would be simplistic and crude to see in Nietzsche's use of the word *Führer* merely a prefiguration of Hitler, it would be just as myopic to deny any connection at all. It is not totally coincidental, Derrida notes, that the discourse that bears Nietzsche's name served as a legitimizing reference for Nazi ideologues and that the only political cause that really elevated him to its highest and official standard was National Socialism. Derrida, of course, makes it clear that the future of Nietzsche's text is not closed; there always exists a potential for a different political functioning in his or in any text. But at the same time he cautions that with respect to politics both Heidegger and Nietzsche, as complex as their cases may be, should not be completely and precipitously extricated from their former political affiliations.[4]

Since the point I am making is apt to be misunderstood, let me reiterate here. I am not arguing that the philosophies of Nietzsche and Heidegger are in and of themselves conservative, that they are conservative in essence. I do think that an argument could be constructed concerning their affiliations with conservative politics of their time, and this has been done often enough by others. My point here is rather to point out some potential and perhaps obvious difficulties with a merger of deconstruction and progressive politics. Those German philosophers who have played and who still play a major role in deconstructive theory have often written texts that, at least from a "superficial" reading, supported, in their historical context, conservative, antifeminist, antisocialist, and at times even profascist positions. I am certainly not contending that the philosophies of Nietzsche and Heidegger are irreconcilable with marxism or with leftist politics: while some critics may have presented persuasive arguments to that effect, we could point to many leftists who have been influenced by both philosophers. Instead I am arguing the much weaker proposition that there has not been a necessary connection between these philosophically seminal texts and leftist or marxist positions in the heritage most often cited with favor by deconstruction. In reading the works of some deconstructive critics in the United States one has the impression that a reference to Nietzsche or Heidegger is itself a sign of radicality. I am simply restating here Derrida's caution concerning the natural and hasty assignment of a political valence to complex philosophical positions.

To construct an argument for a nonprogressive, conservative, or a potentially conservative reading of deconstruction one would not have to rely solely on tradition. Fairly early in its American appropriation Maria Ruegg, for example, argued that deconstruction evidences conservative tendencies because it fails to call into question the system of values that accompanies deconstructed oppositions.[5] By excluding systematically the realm of ethics (choice, interest, values), Ruegg claims that deconstruction unwittingly winds up reinforcing existing values. Although Ruegg at times simplifies Derrida's arguments—her objections deal primarily with his texts—I think that her observation on the apparent absence of a deconstructive ethics identifies nonetheless a major problem in connecting deconstruction with leftist politics. Political theory cannot be conceived without ethics, and this is particularly true of marxism. A perspective that advocates changing the world instead of simply interpreting it cannot do without standards of political conduct and a connection between understanding the world and acting in it. A philosophy that excludes the issue of appropriate action may thus function as an indirect support for the status quo. Indeed, if we reduce ethics to a willful participation in the teleologically based tendencies of history, as some forms of marxism do, deconstruction is even less likely to be an ally. It would seem that a philosophy that avoids ethics—at least in the traditional use of this word—and spurns teleology, as deconstruction seems to do, denies all progressive praxis by eliminating both politics and progress. Furthermore, no matter how we understand deconstructive textuality, it would seem to be difficult to reconcile it with marxist theory. By situating all texts in a metaphysical prison from which no escape is conceivable, deconstruction not only homogenizes, in a Heideggerian fashion, the history of Western thought, but also proclaims the ineffectuality of the text. If the force of a text lies primarily in its undecidability, its inability to be grasped, then a political affiliation, whether ethically based or informed by a telos, is difficult to imagine. We can easily grant the trivial insight that all texts have some ethical and political effect, and that in a given context—France in 1968, the United States in the late seventies and eighties—deconstruction too has had a political valence. But the notion of textuality as it has been discussed by deconstruction often suggests not a close association with political theory, but rather an alienation from political praxis.

Indeed, at just about the time that Spivak, Ryan, and others were asserting a necessary linkage between marxism and deconstruction, Vincent B. Leitch, one of the foremost American authorities on deconstruction, was maintaining precisely the opposite view. In an essay in *Critical Inquiry* discussing the critical peregrinations of J. Hillis Miller,[6] Leitch registers deconstructive conservatism in several areas. Deconstruction, he contends, "ultimately renews and preserves culture," depending on repetition rather than revolution. "All the deconstructors," Leitch writes in a rather ill-advised generalization,

> are conservative in that they work primarily with the established texts of the great tradition and in that they aim mainly to foreground the hitherto unrevealed dark underside of the tradition. Since our literary traditions are not undergoing massive revision, the deconstructors only seem to be discontented sandhogs attempting to sandbag the glorious past.[7]

Although this may be judged a rather narrow way to determine political affiliation—in terms of support for or rejection of the canon—it is no doubt a trenchant observation on the function of deconstruction in the American academy. Miller himself, who was perhaps more responsible for popularizing deconstruction in the seventies than any other critic, concurs for the most part with this political evaluation.[8] Although he does claim that deconstruction will promote "more or less radical changes within the institution," he asserts further that "the changes that matter...will take place within the minds of the teachers of literature, and then in their students." It is worth remarking in passing that Miller's characterization of deconstructive dissemination reinforces the traditional model of a hierarchical, nonparticipatory relationship between the English professor as mentor and willing student disciples—an image that is reinforced perhaps unintentionally by Miller's reference to "minds" only with regard to the teachers of literature. More important for deconstructive politics is Miller's rather dim view of its compatibility with marxism:

> I do think that the conservative aspect of deconstruction needs to be stressed. Its difference from Marxism, which is likely to become more sharply visible as time goes on, is that it views as naive the millennial or revolutionary hopes still in one way or another present even in sophisticated Marxism. This millenarianism believes that a change in the material base or in the class structure would transform our situation in relation to language or change the human condition

generally. Deconstruction, on the other hand, sees the notion of a determining material base as one element in the traditional metaphysical system it wants to put in question.[9]

Certainly we can object to the rather vulgar version of marxism Miller presents here. His gesture toward the religious is gratuitous; and no marxist of any sophistication sees a mechanistic relationship between the "material base" and "language" or the "human condition generally." Yet Miller's remarks in reply to Leitch are not unimportant. They advance the notion of a conservatism in the deconstructive project and correctly question, therefore, the viability of a merger between deconstruction and leftist or revolutionary politics.

Four Arguments for a Marxist-Deconstructive Merger

To confront the difficulties of the favored deconstructive political heritage and the apparent indifference or even hostility to leftist praxis, the marxist deconstructors of the late seventies and early eighties adopted a number of linkage strategies. One of these, which we might term the "historical-continuity argument," places the German revolutionary in the role of a precursor to the French deconstructor. The argument runs approximately as follows: Marx should be considered one of the first to challenge the myth of the autonomous subject. He did this by pointing to the fact that individuals do not make their own world, as most previous bourgeois philosophers would have us believe; rather, individuals act within sets of relationships whose terms and conditions have (always) already been established. Freedom of choice, originality, free will, and the philosophies connected with subjectivity are disclosed by Marx as bourgeois obfuscations that serve to perpetuate the logos of capitalism. Marx's contribution, however, was only one stage in the attack on the autonomy of subjectivity. Subsequent thinkers, in particular Nietzsche, Freud, and Heidegger, continued the assault in the areas of epistemology, psychology, and metaphysics. Derrida's writings should therefore be considered a continuator (as well as a deconstructor) of this philosophical heritage. His analyses serve to confirm Marx's insight into the already structured nature of our existence. Deconstruction, then, belongs to the same family tree as marxism; although the line of descent is not clearly linear, the physiognomic similarities prove beyond a doubt a familial relationship. Or, to put the relationship into another metaphor, deconstruction is an exponential marxism. The most useful passages from Marx for this merger with deconstruction are those in which he has traditionally been judged most deterministic. The famous statement from the preface to *A Contribution to the Critique of Political Economy* (1859) concerning relations that are "indispensable and independent" of the will of those who enter into them and tasks that arise only when the conditions for their solution already exist[10] can be cited as a good illustration of the marxist-deconstructive affiliation. With these observations from 1859—which Marx, incidently, felt were the result of scientific investigation—Marx, according to this argument, contributed to the critique of "humanism" that Derrida would continue with a more rigorously philosophical and linguistic urgency.

A second strategy, which might be called "the completion thesis," views deconstruction as a necessity for completing the marxist project. The argument here is in some respects similar to the "continuity hypothesis" except that the emphasis in this case is on the partial nature of both marxism and deconstruction, rather than the developmental nature of the critique of the bourgeois/metaphysical/humanist heritage. Marxism is considered an adequate method to employ for the analysis of the political economy. Since this is the field to which Marx devoted most of his attention, however, he was forced to ignore other areas of human activity, and the work of Engels in these areas falls far short of that of his collaborator in sophistication. Most notable among the deficiencies in marxism is the lack of an extensive theory of language. The few offhand remarks that Marx made on this and related topics, like those on art and literature, are unsatisfactory for explaining such a complex and fundamental human activity. Deconstruction, therefore, as the most sophisticated linguistically oriented philosophy available, can be helpful in two respects: Either it can be used as a plug to fill in the gap (or one of the gaps) in an otherwise adequate theory, or it can be used as a cleansing fluid to remove the residual idealism in marxist theory, deposited there presumably due to Marx's failure to pay sufficient attention to language. In either case, as a plug or as a polish, deconstruction serves to finish the marxist project. The advantage of this argument, compared with the "continuity thesis," is that one does not have to select carefully the deterministic passages and texts or consider the "humanist" Marx an aberration from a fundamentally deconstructive core. With the "completion theory" the bulk of Marx's writings can be accepted; the only emargination necessary is in connection with remarks outside the true center of Marx's concerns, i.e., in areas other than political economy. These passages or texts can be eliminated from consideration because they are either nonessential to Marx's authentic project, casual remarks insufficiently developed and nonserious in nature, or vestiges of bourgeois thought that linger in the marxian text. The disadvantage of this approach, and I shall return to this in a moment, is that it compartmentalizes not only marxism, but also its completer, deconstruction.

A third argument postulates a similar task for marxism and deconstruction. This "functional hypothesis" identifies Marx with Derrida on the basis of a common enemy. The essential link between the two discourses is evidenced in the way in which they function with respect to the philosophical tradition. Both are demystifying in the sense that they help us to see through the obnubilation of conventional thought. In contrast to the "continuity thesis" a demonstration of descent is unnecessary here; in contradistinction to the "completion argument" one does not need to establish separate domains of competence for the two theoretical perspectives. What is important for the "functional hypothesis" is that marxism and deconstruction have the same "other," and that their manner of dealing with this "other" be similarly oppositional. They are complementary and never exclusory strategies of critique. There are several variations to this argument depending on what one takes to be the object of marxist and deconstructive analysis. The most frequent candidates for the role of "other" are the bourgeois tradition, Western metaphysics, and idealism (which seems to include aspects of both). By their ability to critique or to deconstruct these traditions marxism and deconstruction demonstrate that they are made of the same stuff, and the Derridean strategy is thus legitimated as a leftist practice by association. In other words, instead of contending that there is something essential that unites marxism and deconstruction, some necessary link in their respective views or values, the functional thesis argues that the common negating function indicates natural affiliation. If one can agree upon the general makeup of the "other," the functional argument has the advantage of being the most simple to demonstrate. The oppositional status of the marxian and deconstructive discourse is thematized, indeed, foregrounded, in both. But this relatively facile verification of the functional hypothesis points to the most telling weakness as well. The possession of a common ideological opponent and the possession of a common ideology, politics, and purpose are two separable, if not separate, matters. Marxism and deconstruction may oppose the same tradition and want to further the most radical critique possible, but it is far from certain that the revolutions that they could underwrite are of the same kind.

A fourth and final argument, which we could term the "personal politics hypothesis," associates Derrida himself with leftist political activity and then views this activity as logically derivative from his deconstructive practices. One could cite a number of items in this regard, from the role of Derrida and deconstruction in May of 1968 to Derrida's *engagement* for Nelson Mandela and an end to apartheid.[11] Around 1980 we find proponents of this argument frequently citing deconstruction's institutional critique, in particular the organization GREPH (Groupe de Recherches sur l'Enseignement Philosophique), in which Derrida evidently played a formative and guiding role. Neither Derrida's support for leftist causes nor his institutional commitment can be denied. With regard to the latter his notes on the occasion of a meeting of GREPH, published under the title "Où commence et comment finit un corps enseignant," evidence a good deal more in the way of openly political statements than are usually encountered in his more rigorously "philosophical" writings. He writes that there is no neutral or natural place in the educational process and that his own place is not and cannot be one of indifference.[12] The program or "avant-projet" of GREPH, included as an appendix to the essay, also contains important projects for research, which resemble tasks undertaken by leftists at European and American universities during the sixties and seventies. Derrida's overt political commitment appears to confirm Christopher Fynsk's argument (which is a corollary to the "personal politics hypothesis") that it is not Derrida or his deconstruction that is politically suspect, but rather several of his more important, albeit conservative or apolitical, disciples in the American academy.[13] Derrida's leftist political stance, while perhaps obscured because most of his texts do not evidence a direct and unequivocal advocacy of political positions, and because his reception in the United States has been incomplete and deforming, is clearly manifested in his institutional politics and in his less "philosophical" writings. The flaw in the "personal politics hypothesis" is simply that it does not address the issue at hand in the leftist appropriation of deconstruction. It certainly does not say anything about the compatibility of marxism and deconstruction. GREPH may be a radical leftist organization and Derrida may be leading the charge to the philosophical barricades in France, but he certainly has not had the same impact on American institutions, even after he was hired at the University of California at Irvine. The problem here may not be just that the message—or at least its political content—had trouble getting through in the altered environment. Derrida assigns philosophy the task of deconstructing "phallogocentrisme" and of attacking the root of the university; he writes of a "positive transformation"—although he quickly qualifies this wording by adding the more Nietzschean and ambiguous modifiers "affirmative" and "audacious." He also assaults most thoroughly and consistently the conservatism of traditional philosophical instruction.[14] But what deconstruction contributes politically besides an "interesting" critique, and, more important, what its positive political position is, what it affirms, and why one should consider the "new logic" to be more leftist, more democratic, or more emancipatory than what it replaces are never clearly argued in Derrida's texts. His political appeal lacks the concreteness usually associated with politics. Perhaps this is why Fynsk has a much easier time criticizing the domestic (mis)appropriation of deconstruction than delineating its own political positions. "A deconstructive logic might seem to make any decision, critical or ethical...untenable," Fynsk concedes. But he assures his readers that although "the ground grows unstable, a stance will impose itself and always be taken." This process of ethical and political decision making is apt to be unattractive to a large body of politically active people. Fynsk, like Derrida, is silent concerning what the stance consists of. Fynsk laments that "little is said of the possible ethics implied by the deconstructive posture," yet he himself immediately drops the topic and gives the reader no hint of where to turn in order to follow up on this pivotal issue.[15] In short, the "personal politics argument" fails, not because there are any doubts concerning Derrida's institutional commitments or political worldview, but because the logic of deconstruction does not appear to allow for any concretely identifiable political position.

If we turn back to the first three arguments, however, we fare no better. In each the intent was to establish a necessary political position for deconstruction, to assert a deconstructive politics that is definable in leftist or marxist terms. I have already indicated one of the central weaknesses with the "historical continuity hypothesis." Any argument that reduces marxism to its determinist component abrogates at the same time the marxist notion of political praxis. If we are no more than an ensemble of social forces, if there is no possibility of transcending social, political, economic, and linguistic determination, then political action resulting from ethical decisions or intellectual insight is either eliminated or made arbitrary. In order for individuals and groups to work on and in the world, there must be some notion of an escape from determination. One does not have to be so naive as to conceive of this escape as a total autonomy of subjectivity, but some portion of the subject must be more than epiphenomenal; otherwise, political actions and the arguments that accompany them would be pointless. The "historical continuity argument" also contains a strange teleological assumption that is troubling. With deconstruction considered the end of philosophy, one proceeds to read the tradition backward to discover the origins or at least the contributors to the enlightened path. Such a view of philosophical history should trouble both halves of the marxist-deconstructive partnership: the former, because it locks marxism into a heritage whose only claim to legitimate leftist politics comes with the "correct" interpretation of Marx by French structuralism (Althusser) or American deconstructors in the postwar era; the latter, because admitting a telos into philosophical history, even if it identifies itself with or as deconstruction, reintroduces an illicit center into speculative activity. Deconstruction cannot claim marxism for an ancestor because from the marxist perspective there is no necessary and exclusive genetic continuity, and from the deconstructive perspective postulating descent itself repeats an inadmissible, though perhaps inevitable, metaphysical line.

To circumvent the infelicities of lineage, descent, and all familial metaphors, one could embrace the second strategy that I outlined above. The "completion hypothesis" severs the historical linkage and reestablishes a connection on an altered theoretical basis. But this argument also evidences weaknesses. Although one is no longer compelled to ignore praxis-oriented passages in Marx, the compartmentalization resulting from assigning areas of competence emarginates other aspects of Marx's work. If one begins ignoring or polishing away Marx's comments on noneconomic matters, how can one be certain that the genuine finish will not also be rubbed off in the process? By whose authority can one decide what lies outside the area of competence and what lies within it? An analogous problem would present itself with regard to Derrida's texts. Where is one to draw the line between the critique of language and the critique of language used in discussing political economy? Can deconstruction, in other words, be denied a politics by reducing it to the role of linguistic corrective or complement and then supplied with a new one by surrounding it with marxism? A more troublesome difficulty, however, is that compartmentalizing these two discourses obstructs or negates their critical authority. The strength of marxist theory is that it posits the primacy of the material in explaining ideas, ideals, and ideologies. Presumably, then, deconstruction would be itself subject to marxist analysis as well. Since marxism appears to claim, especially in its Althusserian variant, scientific or metahistorical validity, allowing deconstruction to occupy the space of completer (or allowing a completer to intrude on an equal theoretical basis) would disqualify its explanatory power. An analogous argument can be made for deconstruction and its claim to general competence. If deconstruction has anything to teach us, it is that no text is immune from the "metaphysical tradition" (including deconstructive texts). To use deconstruction to fill in gaps rather than to expose them, to finish rather than to forestall all finishing, to detect and correct idealistic residue, rather than to disclose the inevitable traces inhering in discourse, undermines the analytical power of this philosophical strategy. Neither marxism nor deconstruction can compromise the area of human activity they respectively privilege without self-destructing. A compartmentalization of these theories deprives them of the possibility of theorizing.

To avoid the pitfalls of compartmentalization and the completion argument, one might resort to the third alternative I presented, the "functional hypothesis." With this argument, however, we would encounter two major obstacles, both of which I referred to in my brief description above. The first concerns the status of a relationship based on a mutual opposition to other theories. That both marxism and deconstruction have attacked and appear capable of challenging identical ideological opponents seems to be a secure proposition. That this common focus implies either a similarity in political perspective or an overlap in leftist persuasion, however, is a false and illogical conclusion. Marxism and anarchism, for example, have often fought against the same repressive features of bourgeois society, yet the history of their relationship is far from amiable; structuralism and deconstruction both pose as an alternative to an outmoded French academic tradition in scholarship, yet one frequently detects an incompatibility of views in the works of representatives of these two directions. Nietzsche and Engels, Heidegger and Lukács, Derrida and Goldman—each of these pairs has at one time or another opposed the same philosophical school or the identical theorist. Yet the political views and strategies of the two halves of these odd couples are hardly comparable. The problem with the "functional hypothesis," then, is that unless one considers why and how the critique is developed, the similarity based on common ideological opponents remains a formal, unessential abstraction. And when one goes beyond this superficial understanding of commonality and tries to locate a commonality of approach, intent, or purpose, then one sees clearly another weakness in the argument. Despite the apparent similarity in function, marxism and deconstruction operate quite differently with texts. To cite only the most apparent discrepancy: the marxian interpretation of a text posits the primacy of a world outside the text; deconstructive readings call into question this opposition of inside and outside. Indeed, the celebrated Derridean quip "il n'y a pas d'hors texte," which is rather a textualization of the world than an exclusion of it, is a critique of the very outside/inside dichotomy on which marxist readings are normally based. The gulf between these two approaches does not preclude, of course, the possibility of occasional similarities in interpretation; both marxism and deconstruction may be able to expose identical contradictions or aporias in an argument or an ideology. But the manner in which these contradictions are revealed and the consequences drawn from the analysis diverge enormously. Indeed, the difference in method and conclusions can be just as persuasively considered antagonistic. As I have argued above in regard to disputed privilege, marxism and deconstruction tend to undermine the status of each other's argument. The "functional hypothesis" keeps marxism and deconstruction at bay by turning them loose on an unsuspecting third party, but refuses to consider what would occur if the two were made to confront each other.

Arguing Political Deconstruction

The four arguments I have presented for a merger of marxism and deconstruction are abstractions drawn from various essays, conference papers, and discussions. These arguments did not appear when deconstruction was initially imported into the United States in the late sixties and early seventies. At that point, which was also the time of the greatest political activity on university campuses, there was no concerted endeavor, as far as I can tell, to make deconstruction relevant for the antiwar or the civil rights struggles. Rather the notion that marxism and deconstruction could be compatible, or that deconstruction is inherently leftist, occurs only in the late seventies and early eighties. The original context into which deconstruction was appropriated in the United States was literary and secondarily philosophical, not political and institutional. Along these lines Art Berman argues that the political optimism that accompanied the student movement had exhausted itself by the late seventies and was replaced with a general skepticism toward social action. Widespread disillusionment with the possibilities for promoting change led to a "retreat from the arena of political action and social thought into the primacy of mind, into the potentiality of artistic creativity, and into poetic speculation as a source of knowledge and achievement."[16] This was the climate in which deconstruction thrived in the United States. But not every adherent of deconstruction was content to acquiesce to the changed situation. The politicization of deconstruction around 1980 must be seen therefore as a struggle on two fronts. First it was a battle against the historical exigencies of the deconstructive reception in the American academy. Marxist deconstruction was an endeavor to recreate what was perceived as the original force of Derrida's work and in this way to preserve its oppositional status. Therefore it was simultaneously a struggle against the dominant, literary, and elitist reception of Derrida's writings. Not coincidentally none of the critics who took up this fight were core members of the Yale School; they did not teach at a prestigious Ivy League institution, nor did they confine their deconstructive practice to exclusively canonical texts. Their work, therefore, presents a marked contrast to the fashionable and yuppified profile deconstruction acquired at many institutions during the eighties.

The argument for a marxist deconstruction was articulated most trenchantly and persistently in several essays that appeared in consecutive issues of *Diacritics* in 1980. Since Michael Ryan's essay "Self-Evidence" appeared first, and since he has subsequently done the most to follow up on this line of thought, I would like to begin by considering his arguments.[17] Ryan's goal is stated directly as an attempt to bring marxism and deconstruction together, and he employs several strategies to that end. Deconstruction, he contends, provides the marxist with "a sophisticated instrument for the critique of ideology" and "a means of detecting and correcting residual idealism in marxist theory itself." Marxism, for its part, supplies "the broad political and socio-historical outlines" that deconstruction lacks, "the framework of a broader revolutionary theory." In sum, if deconstruction "is not to remain an academic sub-discipline, a philosophical critique of philosophy and of its institutions or an elitist critical method, it must be joined to a Marxist critique of race, class, and sex exploitation."[18] Ryan here comes very close to arguing that the joining is a necessity. If marxism requires deconstruction to become really materialistic and if deconstruction without marxism would be condemned to the status of an academic subdiscipline, then the case for a merger involves more than mutual benefit. What remains uncertain, however, is how this joining is to be accomplished. This uncertainty is reflected in a number of ways, one of which is Ryan's inability to settle on a term or metaphor for the partnership. At times he writes of an "overlap" between the two discourses; sometimes, as we have just witnessed, deconstruction is placed within marxism, recalling the plug metaphor of the "completion hypothesis." In other cases marxism and deconstruction are simply "put together" to yield one result, or seen as collaborating, or combined to produce a "lesson." At one point Ryan seems to identify deconstruction with a microstructure (presumably on the level of text and discourse) and marxism with a macrostructure ("in terms of class conflict, ideologies, etc."), each of which informs the other. Finally, in what I take to be a variation on the "functional theory," we read that the fact that "macrostructural ideology" is derived from and sustained by "microstructural idealism should tell us something about the necessity of supplementing the dialectic of contradiction in the Marxist critique with deconstruction's dialectic of undecidability."[19]

The relationship between two bodies of thought, philosophies, or discourses is certainly not an easy matter to define, and the problem of relationship can only be compounded when one is dealing with discourses as fecund and varied as marxism and deconstruction. Nevertheless, the use of so many and such diverse metaphors to describe the relationship or desired relationship reflects, I believe, more than just a concern to do justice to the complexity of the commonalities. That Ryan resorts to them suggests, in addition, that the most difficult questions about the relationship may have remained unposed and unexplored. For example, how can these two discourses overlap when one is situated within the other? How does one "put the two critiques together" when they are shown to operate on two (a microstructural and a macrostructural) levels? But perhaps more important are the unanswered questions concerning the status of the union. Are deconstruction and marxism natural and necessary allies in the sense that one cannot do without the other? Is the overlap morally incumbent upon a deconstructor or a marxist in order to perform an adequate critique? Or is the status of the merger optional for the critic, something that would enhance an argument by doubling its force? Although Ryan never discusses these issues—and his wording at different points leaves open the possibilities of all of these readings—he does seem to be aware of the difficulties in the merger that he is attempting. Twice, in fact, he admonishes the reader not to confuse marxism with deconstruction; the overall effect of these admonitions, however, either undercuts the desired "overlap" by emphasizing the dissimilarities, or underscores the difficulties of a union by again leaving the difficult questions unanswered.

The first warning is found in the footnote to a passage in which Ryan has already weakened the force of the postulated union. At issue is the notion of "self-evidence," which has been the object of deconstructive critique in the form of Cartesian self-certainty, and which has been subjected to a marxist critique in the form of the self-evidence of property rights in the eighteenth century. In the body of the text Ryan writes that the marxist and deconstructive critiques of self-evidence "might intersect" in some respect, but the footnote to this sentence weakens the possible commonality: "I want to make it clear that I am not suggesting that the two critiques are the same. The two discourses can be articulated, but it would be a mistake to identify them."[20] This is a curious statement. That the two critiques cannot be the same or identical is obvious; one does not have to delve into deconstructive dealings with identity and difference to concur. We might wonder, then, what the purpose of this footnote is. It purports to clarify something for the reader that she or he could have erroneously inferred from the preceding text—presumably the identity or sameness of the marxist and deconstructive critiques. But the text to which this footnote is appended, though in desperate need of clarification (it is not clear, for example, what "in this respect" refers to—and this unclarity obscures the entire meaning of the sentence), relates only to the possibility of an intersection: the two critiques "*might* intersect." Furthermore, in the main body of the text Ryan proceeds to sketch the differences between the critiques, how they complement each other. What is needed more than the reaffirmation of nonidentity is an elucidation of the status of the intersection or a rationale for the footnote. What precisely is the same or identical or overlapping or similar in the philosophical and the political critique? And why does Ryan make such an effort to remind us to distinguish two critiques that "*might* intersect," that is, might have one point in common?

In the second instance of exhortation to the reader, which occurs toward the end of the essay, we are again confronted with some irregularities. Ryan argues that

> just as the free exchange of the bourgeois legal contract is attenuated by its situation within a field of economic-political force, social power, and material production, so also free exchange of truth in autobiography would be problematized by its situation in a larger historical space where it is shaped and determined by forces that are structural and unconscious, that is, beyond the conscious control of the "free" participants.

He continues in the next paragraph: "Although in this case, an idealist abstraction from real history on the macrostructural level coincides with an abstraction from the microstructural forces of rhetoric, it would be a mistake to conflate deconstructive undecidability and Marxist contradiction."[21] However, the following sentence goes on to postulate that there is "something" nonetheless that insists on the supplementing of marxism by deconstruction. Again a series of queries needs to be posed and answered. How do the macrostructural and microstructural levels "coincide"? How is the problematizing of free exchange in autobiography "just" like the attenuation of free exchange in the legal contract? And why should one conflate marxism's concept of contradiction with deconstruction's notion of undecidability if the former is relegated to macrostructural criticism while the latter is assigned to microstructural analysis? We are again tossed to and fro, told first that the two discourses "coincide," then warned not to conflate them, and finally informed that we should have, nevertheless, learned "something" about the necessity of supplementing one with the other.

The various metaphors of joining and the denials of identity are signs for a furtive discomfort in the project of merging marxism and deconstruction. A further sign of this discomfort involves the technique of slippage of concepts. By this I mean that Ryan often uses a term from one discourse and allows it to slip into synonymity with a term from the other discourse. This slippage is facilitated somewhat—or at least made less noticeable—by the manner in which marxism and deconstruction are defined. Practitioners of the latter are for Ryan "those critics who try to maintain and broaden the critical forces (political, ethical, social) of Derrida's work and to avoid reducing it to yet another new critical, literary critical method." Marxism is considered a "strain" that extends from the writings of Marx himself to the work of Louis Althusser.[22] These two descriptions of the two discourses assist in slippage because deconstruction is already defined in terms of characteristics that Ryan would like it to possess (and against its dominant practice both here and abroad), while marxism is brought closer to deconstruction by valorizing the Althusserian, structuralist variety: it is the line through which and to which marxism runs. The slippage is furthered as well by the pre-text for the essay, a volume by Philip Lejeune on autobiography; concepts of personal autonomy, which are introduced due to the themes of self, selfhood, and self-presentation, are easy targets for both marxist and deconstructive critique. With the territory for the "overlap" so favorably charted it is a simple matter to slide terms from one discourse into the other and thus reinforce the metaphors of unity. One of the prime illustrations of this slippage involves the word "idealist," which Ryan frequently employs to describe the objects of deconstructive analysis. We find references to the reversal and displacement of "idealist hierarchies," to "idealist philosophy" as a necessary component of capitalist class rule, and to "idealist truth" that needs to be deconstructed.[23] What is immediately conspicuous in these formulations is that "idealist" seems to have replaced the more commonly encountered, neo-Heideggerian term "metaphysical" in Ryan's discourse. The use of "idealist" allows Ryan, via the functional argument, to homogenize the critiques of marxism and deconstruction: both are conceived as an anti-idealism. Derrida, it may be noted, is much more circumspect in his discussion of similar issues. When pressed in an interview about his avoidance of marxism, about the relationship of deconstruction to the "materialist text," and about the marxist concept of ideology, he carefully replied: "If one wanted to be schematic,...what I have attempted can also be recorded as a 'critique of idealism.'" And later in answer to the same question he states: "It goes without saying that if, and to the extent to which, in this general economy, matter designates, as you were saying, radical otherness (I will specify: with respect to the philosophical opposition), what I write could be considered 'materialist.'"[24] Derrida is evidently as suspicious of the conventional opposition idealism/materialism as he is of other putatively antithetical pairs. Ryan, on the other hand, by never questioning the opposition, by allowing the substitution of metaphysical for idealism to stand without comment, and by causing the marxist critique of idealism to slip onto a deconstruction site, obscures the issue of a possible foundation for merger.

Two other examples of what I have called slippage are noteworthy in Ryan's essay. In contrast to the (ab)use of idealism they both involve terms normally associated with deconstruction that are then smuggled into marxist vocabulary. In the first case Ryan tries to relate the word "difference"—and by extension, of course, *différance* as well—to the marxist concept of history. "The Marxist dialectician," he writes, "would note that the repetition which allows sameness to be defined always contains a difference, a difference or process of differentiation which is history."[25] I confess that I am not quite certain that I understand this sentence. Why "difference" is repeated and how repetition can contain a difference that is history (which implies that this repetition contains history) are unclear to me. What I do comprehend, however, is that here and in the following sentences, where the movement of differentiality is equated with history, a Derridean terminology is being forced upon marxism. This is not mere translation of and with a difference, but rather a misrepresentation of the marxist notion of history. Even if one conceives of the "process of differentiation" and the "movement of differentiality" as deconstructive equivalents of the dialectic, the materialism of Marx's notion of history is lost in the slippage.

The second instance of slippage occurs with the term "absence." After Ryan correctly notes the primacy of historical class contradictions for marxist analysis of textual mediations and contradictions, he writes the following:

> If the text is ideological, those contradictions will appear in foreclosed form—by their absence. The mark of their absent presence will either be the excessive balance or homogeneity of a text (the self-evidence or non-contradiction in Lejeune) or else the taken-for-granted one-sidedness of the representation (only men, only white, only first world, etc.). Deciphering these contradictions for recent Marxist critics (Macherey, Eagleton) consists of locating the unsaid of a text, that ensemble of absences within a text which do not correspond to the author's conscious meaning, a sub-text which can say something different or else entirely contradict the author's intention or ideology.[26]

Ryan confuses here two kinds of absences and makes them appear to be identical. The first is related to choice of themes for a text and what one might call ideological blinders: authors who exclude characters from the working class in a social novel, for example, can be accused of evading the most pressing social problems. This "absence" is the opposite of presence. The second or Derridean "absence" is, as I understand it, a word of convenience for a concept that cannot be properly described in terms of traditional oppositions. This is the "absence" that is marked by a trace, the "absence" already inscribed in nonopposition to presence, an "absence" that could not be filled by simply naming the proletariat, or African Americans, or the "third world." It is the "absence" that is appropriate perhaps to the latter part of the passage that I have quoted—one that Ryan then reads and writes into a marxist critique of ideology. Once again, therefore, we encounter a case of slippage fostering the illusion of overlap or collusion.

I should note here that Ryan employs similar strategies in his subsequent monograph *Marxism and Deconstruction: A Critical Articulation.* Most attentive readers will not fail to notice how often he rephrases marxist terms in deconstructive language and vice versa. In this fashion the dialectic slides into *différance,* and Marx's descriptions of social phenomena become variants of a more generalized textual deconstruction. Let me cite here only one specific example, which will have to stand for many. When Ryan examines Marx's analysis of credit, he reproduces a rather lengthy quotation from the third volume of *Capital* that delineates two characteristics of the credit system in a capitalist economy. On the one hand, it gives incentive to capitalist production by accelerating "the material development of the productive forces and the establishment of the world market." On the other hand, it also accelerates the contradictions inherent in capitalism by increasing the concentration of capital: hence, it constitutes "the form of transition to a new mode of production." Marx thus elucidates the "ambiguous nature" *(Doppelseitigkeit)* of credit under capitalism. Ryan's comment on this passage is then typical of his attempts to reduce one discourse to the terms of the other without respecting the difference in the level of abstraction or meaning. We read: "Instead of 'ambiguous nature,' a deconstructionist might have said that credit constitutes a structure of 'undecidability' or 'radical alterity.'"[27] But in what sense is the two-sidedness (a more literal translation of *Doppelseitigkeit)* that Marx discovers in credit the same as "undecidability" and "radical alterity"? Marx's view is clearly dialectical: the two-sidedness of credit persists only as long as it is embedded in a capitalist economy. The contradiction inherent in credit under capitalism will be overcome or sublated *(aufgehoben)* in a higher stage, which Marx calls socialism. Can one say the same about notions Derrida has labeled "undecidable"? Do they cease to be undecidable because of sublation *(Aufhebung)*? Since Derrida and other deconstructors have made no secret of their criticism of dialectical thought, it is difficult to see how this could be the case. Furthermore, the term "radical alterity," like "absence" above, is abused. Derrida's most famous illustration of it occurs when he analyzes the "trace." But in what sense is this anticoncept—this mark for something prior to and different from all binary oppositions, this radical "absence"—similar to credit? We are not dealing here with the conditions of possibility for credit, that absent unnameable that allows credit-for-capitalism and credit-against-capitalism to come into being. We are simply looking at two contradictory aspects of one phenomenon that, inside of a given systemic context, reinforce opposing tendencies: the support and destruction of capitalism. Ryan is forced here, as in his essay, to dedialecticize Marx's analysis or to remove the truly radical philosophical force from Derrida's deconstructive (anti)terminology. Even if we could reconcile ourselves to the violations of the respective discourses, however, we would still want to ask what is the status of an analogy between capitalism, a network of economic and political relations, and philosophical systems produced under capitalism, for example, Edmund Husserl's phenomenology. Can one legitimately slide back and forth between these two areas, pretending that difference in their constructs and claims (if capitalism can be said to make implicit claims) are negligible?

Let me give only one further example from *Marxism and Deconstruc-*

tion to demonstrate how the radical philosophical critique associated with the writings of Derrida is blunted in order to preserve a marxist conceptual system. At the close of the initial chapter of the book Ryan discusses various readings of the historical text of World War II, and, in particular, of the entry of the United States into the global conflict following the bombing of Pearl Harbor. He argues that the "causal instance" of the Japanese attack is inadequate for a deconstructive reading:

> Political interests are served by this limitation of causality to the presence of an observable event. To deconstruct that privilege of presence and to find the nonpresentable, nonobservable root system of the event would necessitate tracing the history of trade relations between Japan and the United States during the 1930s. One could even reach the conclusion that Japan was at least in part provoked into launching its attack by protectionist trade sanctions and the cutting off of access to raw materials and markets.[28]

Ryan's criticism of a simplistic monocausal reading of history is undoubtedly valid, although the manner in which it is presented here is not unproblematic. Would deconstructing the historical text also lead us to see that the National Socialists were "at least in part provoked" into slaughtering Jews, gypsies, communists, socialists, Slavs, and homosexuals?[29] Who is going to let us know when we have arrived at the "root system" of the event? No matter what the answer to these questions might be, it is nonetheless difficult to see the rejection of monocausality as deconstructive. Very few serious historians would adhere to a simplistic explanation of our entry into the war. One does not have to be a deconstructor to explore Japanese motives or to find provocations on the part of the United States. And in any case these factors are hardly "nonpresentable" or "nonobservable." By setting up a vulgar straw man, Ryan has an easy time criticizing views that no knowledgeable historian would entertain, but he does not really show how these views of history are deconstructive, or how they bring deconstruction closer to marxist perspectives.

Let me be clear about one thing. Although I do not believe that marxism and deconstruction can be merged in any meaningful manner, and although I am skeptical about ascribing to deconstruction any inherent and progressive political value, I am not in the least questioning Ryan's motives. His endeavor to engage deconstruction in progressive politics is understandable for several reasons. Like the Nietzschean critique for previous generations, Derrida's works have had an almost irresistible attraction for many progressive humanists in the academy. To infuse intellectual fascination with an ethical commitment for social justice is obviously a laudable goal, and, like Ryan, I can validate a "deconstruction" (although I probably would name it differently) that is socially, politically, and ethically responsible. A second reason for desiring a more leftist profile for American deconstruction is a justified dissatisfaction with tendencies in the Western world and its treatment of the rest of the globe. Deconstruction, because it purports to be opposed (radically) to all that is detestable in the Western heritage, is often defended by leftists because it is apparently against the accepted practices of interpretation, whether these be New Critical, phenomenological, old left, or historicist. As an advanced form of Heideggerianism, however, it has unfortunately promoted the totalized and facile view that the entire Occident, including all "traditional" alternatives, is implicated in the maintenance of the hegemonic political, economic, social, and philosophical systems. Therefore what we frequently encounter in the writings of deconstructors, especially those who engage in political discussion, is a tendency to divide all of modern theory into two camps, which we might call "poststructuralist" and "the establishment," and this dichotomization then serves to foster the iconoclastic and oppositional image of their own endeavors. The step to overtly political categories is a short one indeed. The "establishment" in scholarship (and the extent to which poststructuralists and deconstructors control and influence the "establishment" is usually downplayed by leftist deconstructors), resorting to neo-McCarthyist tactics to defame the critical rebels, is compelled to enact suppressive measures against this guerrilla insurgency in the form of discrimination in hiring and promotion, unfavorable reviews, and, above all, a stepped-up production of "counterrevolutionary" propaganda. Even when and even though deconstruction is not at the margins of academic criticism, it wants to appear as an outsider to promote its oppositional image. As we shall see in the discussions of the de Man and the Heidegger controversies, this insistence on marginality and the paranoia of persecution persevere well into the eighties. The unfortunate by-product of the dichotomization of criticism, however, is that political attitudes, as they relate to real issues of local, national, and international (rather than literary and philosophical) import, are often considered less significant than whether a colleague is a practicing Derridean. Thus in his 1980 essay Ryan obviously feels justified in calling Gerald Graff a member of the "class police," even though

Graff's views on political matters are probably closer to Ryan's than the views held by deconstructors at the various elitist institutions on the East Coast.[30]

It is this context of mistaken dichotomization that explains the tenor of the second essay from *Diacritics* that I wish to consider, Michael Sprinker's review of Gerald Graff's *Literature against Itself* (1979) entitled "Criticism as Reaction."[31] Like Ryan, Sprinker seems to approve of deconstruction as much for what it is not as for what it is. Although he claims that he would not defend "deconstruction as a critical method against any and all attacks," his review does argue that an assault on Derrida's work has to be "more than a critique of its ideology."[32] On how he would proceed to criticize deconstruction (the only objection he cites to a deconstructive text is the lack of "precise and lucid thinking"[33] in Geoffrey Hartman's review of *Glas*—a judgment Graff would probably endorse), and why an ideological critique is inadequate (after all, one can argue that Sprinker's review of Graff amounts to an ideological critique), he remains silent. Most of his comments on Graff's presentation of deconstruction consist of rebukes for Graff's alleged inability or unwillingness to appreciate the subtlety of deconstructive discourse,[34] and they are therefore of little direct interest for the issue of the politics of deconstruction. Toward the beginning of this essay, however, we do encounter a rather noteworthy passage dealing with the politics of criticism:

> Just as in political and cultural criticism, where the climate of opinion has shifted from most favored status for Marcuse, Roszak, and Chomsky to Moynihan, Daniel Bell, and the Friedmans, so in literary criticism the wave of structuralism and post-structuralism that has swept, somewhat belatedly, through the American academy finds barriers in the recent work of E. D. Hirsch, M. H. Abrams, and now Gerald Graff.

In the following sentence Sprinker writes of his perception of "a larger shift within the world of literary studies from more open and more self-consciously ironic styles of criticism toward traditional claims for the 'determinacy of meaning'...in literary texts."[35] The lament of political discrimination, which I alluded to above, is evident in this passage as well. But two other aspects are also troubling. The first concerns the rather facile and somewhat deceptive identifications that are posited by the first sentence that I quoted. The grammatical parallelism of leftist cultural and political commentators (Marcuse, Roszak, Chomsky) and structuralism/poststructuralism is used evidently to suggest a similarity in political perspective, although Sprinker relies here totally on sentence structure to make his point, eschewing "precise and lucid" argumentation. That the crest of the domestic reception of the French "wave" did not coincide with the heyday of the student movement likewise fails to move Sprinker to argument; this infelicity is taken care of with the casual qualifying remark "somewhat belatedly." What Sprinker avoids, then, is both a consideration of the effects of "crossing borders" and a cohesive argument for associating poststructuralism in the United States with leftist thought. The hard questions—how is the traditional/poststructuralist opposition "just" like the radical/conservative political groupings, and why did the reception of French criticism coincide with the growth of conservatism and the beginnings of the Reagan era—remain unanswered.

The second curious aspect of Sprinker's essay is the assumption that poststructuralism is a "more open" style of criticism. Obviously Sprinker is responding to a particular situation when he makes this claim. He no doubt has in mind the stifling atmosphere in some traditional English departments during the years of his own education and the dogmatically conventional and antitheoretical attitudes of the faculty. Given the fact that poststructuralism has its own theoretical underpinnings, however, we are entitled to pose the question: more open to what and for what purpose? Throughout Sprinker's review of Graff he argues implicitly or explicitly that literary criticism should not be open to certain traditional concerns: "reason," "determinacy of meaning," and "realism." That critics can possibly churn out more interpretations using what is mistakenly taken for poststructuralist freedoms does not mean that this criticism is necessarily more open, and certainly not more liberating in its politics. What is going on here is another case of slippage. The "undecidability" of meaning, used with philosophical precision by Derrida, is translated erroneously into greater openness, which then slips unnoticed into a better or a more progressive or simply leftist politics. This error is perhaps enhanced by another widespread and unmentioned assumption on the part of leftist deconstructors, namely, that the "avant-garde" in theory or philosophy must hold views that are "avant-garde" in politics. Only this unstated presumption can explain why a critic like Edward Said, who is among the most politically astute, could be surprised in 1976 that contemporary critical discourse was "disturbingly quietistic," and why he would wonder at "the ideological and evaluational silence of criticism" in the mid seventies.[36] Sprinker counters Said's perceptive remark about the absence of a radical deconstructive or poststructuralist politics by simply asserting their progressiveness. This is probably the greatest irony in the review. The work he is presumably evaluating,[37] despite its shortcomings in its dealings with deconstruction, frequently thematizes the topic of adversariness in literature and criticism. Graff indicates that the issue for him is still open and arguable. Sprinker, who presumably subscribes to openness, closes off debate. He, like Ryan, accepts in 1980 the familiar but debatable view claiming "traditional bourgeois values" cannot be used to oppose the status quo since they belong to the ideology of the status quo.[38] One could argue, however, that the chaos and uncertainty of late capitalist society are actually mirrored in the affirmation of deconstructive "undecidability" and in the debunking of reason, determinacy of meaning, and realism; in short, that deconstruction and not (or perhaps as well as) the tradition of bourgeois freedom, tolerance, humanism, reason, and realism is implicated in the political and ideological hegemony of capitalist relations. This hypothesis, in any case, should be taken as seriously as those that assert the contrary, although it is my view that both arguments make the issue too simple. The real point is that openness is indeed a desired quality in political criticism, but that in the name of a putatively greater openness one must not precipitously disqualify any theory that does not conform to deconstructive standards.

Gayatri Spivak presents a third alternative for linking deconstruction with leftist politics (she does not use the term marxist) in her essay "Revolutions That As Yet Have No Model."[39] Ryan confronted the project of marxism and deconstruction directly, but encountered difficulties with this slippery enterprise. Sprinker suggests the possibility of a politicized deconstruction because of its oppositional and open nature. Spivak embarks on a somewhat different and more cautious course, and this is signaled by the fact that her remarks on the political possibilities of deconstruction are attached to the end of her review of Derrida's *Limited Inc.* I mention the position of her comments because I think that this location underscores a number of roles that politics plays in her treatment of deconstruction. One can see these remarks on the politics of deconstruction as a *continuation* of thoughts developed beforehand. According to this reading Spivak has picked up threads of her earlier arguments and extended them into the realm of politics and society. The comments, however, can also be viewed as a *conclusion*, both logical and formal, to a philosophical discussion: philosophy leads necessarily to the topic of the uses of philosophy; theory finds its end in praxis. From this angle the positing of a politics for deconstruction can be considered a strategy for confining the scope of the playfulness and undecidability in philosophical discourse. Politics brings an end to and pins down what otherwise might be judged elusive and infinitely regressive. Finally, the concluding comments may be seen as an *appendix* or *appendage* to a philosophical review; the space or rupture in the text signifies that this is the place for afterthoughts to philosophy, or for a new but belated beginning, or, in any case, for something that has escaped philosophy proper.

Before continuing and to avoid misunderstanding I should perhaps make two comments of my own here. First, I recognize that Spivak's discussion of politics and deconstruction in this essay is not limited to the final seven paragraphs of her essay. I shall focus on these paragraphs, nonetheless, because they contain the most sustained and conclusive account of the problem. Second, the first eighteen pages of the essay are a perceptive and intelligent presentation of Derrida's arguments against Searle, and, with minor exceptions, I have no quarrel with her discussion or with Derrida's playful rejoinder to the advocate of speech-act theory. The excellence of the first ninety percent of the essay is, however, not matched by the final pages, and this is not due to my difference with Spivak's political views, or, as she phrases it, "regional commitments." The reason for my disappointment in her discussion is rather that, after it becomes clear that Spivak is going to write directly about the politics of deconstruction, the sustained and persuasive argumentation that characterizes the discussion of "pure" philosophy becomes marked and marred by a series of partial and unfinished arguments, each of which breaks off whenever the subject of deconstructive politics is broached. I am suggesting, then, that although one may view Spivak's concluding remarks in each of the four ways I have described, my feeling is that my ordering of these options is inversely related to the strength of the argument that can be made for each option: the strongest case can be made for a rupture between the philosophical and the political discussion. Indeed, there are four pivotal points in Spivak's argument, and at each one can note a turning away from a potential argument, a failure to carry through a particular line of thought to its conclusion. The result in each case is an evasion of or swerve from the topic of deconstructive politics.

Spivak begins concluding by summarizing in phrases selective ideas that she has developed elsewhere in the essay, what she terms "enabling principles for more than a constant cleaning-up (or messing-up) of the language of philosophy." What these principles enable can be perhaps best understood by an examination of what Spivak adds to one of them. One of the "enabling principles" is recorded as "a call to figure out and *act* upon 'something like a relationship' between 'ideology' and 'social production' which, ever non-self-identical, will not keep us locked in varieties of isomorphism" (my italics).[40] Neither Derrida's text (from which the internal quotations come) nor Spivak's original discussion of that text mentions *acting* upon this enigmatic "something." Derrida writes of the *existence* of "something like a relation," and Spivak, after quoting herself from another essay, reminds us that theory "is also a practice."[41] It is soon apparent, however, that this seemingly insignificant switch of verbs is meant to bridge the gap between the deconstructive "lesson" and a possible ethics or philosophy of action. The final sentence in this paragraph—the key sentence for both this bridge and the title of the piece—reads as follows: "If the 'other that is not quite the other' were to be conceived of as political practice, pedagogy, or feminism—simply to mention *my* regional commitments—one might indeed look for '"revolutions" that as yet have no model.'"[42] The problem, as in the essay by Ryan, is highlighted by the use of the conditional. If the "other" could be named as "political practice," "pedagogy," or "feminism," would it still be the radically "other" of deconstruction? In any case, Spivak proceeds to restore part of the context for this modified citation from Derrida by informing the reader that "'literatures' or" preceded the word "revolutions" in the original text. If she had restored the entire context, it would have been clear that *her* new context for "revolutions" (a possible philosophy of action, political practices, pedagogy, and feminism) and Derrida's context (iterability, fictionality, parasitism, and a supplementary code) have little in common. Spivak simply leaps from philosophical discourse to political discourse although Derrida's text does not even vaguely suggest this possibility. When she partially restores the context by citing the word "literatures," Spivak commits her initial evasion. Instead of clarifying her jump from Derrida's reference to "'literatures' or 'revolutions'" and sustaining an argument for its political relevance, Spivak decides to explain herself "by way of" another topic: Walter Benjamin writing on Brechtian theater. She thus swerves away from Derrida to the more readily identifiable leftist Benjamin and from deconstruction to political theater.

Spivak soon returns to Derrida, however. After exploring some of the facets of the Brechtian critique of identity as outlined by Benjamin, she argues that Benjamin's emphasis on the ideology of identity in his discussion of epic theater "reminds us of citationality or iterability." Then, in what by now has become a familiar structure in the argumentation of political deconstruction, we find the "just as..., so" construction used to link Derrida's and Benjamin's text.

Just as Derrida insists that no speech act is, even originarily, tied to its appropriate context; and that thus iterability disrupts the so-called unity of voice and intention even as it remains the condition of possibility of form; so also Benjamin writes: "Interruption is one of the fundamental methods of all form-giving. It reaches far beyond the domain of art. It is, to mention just one of its aspects, the origin of the quotation. Quoting a text implies interrupting its context.... 'Making gestures quotable' is one of the essential elements of epic theatre. The actor must be able to space his gestures as the compositor produces spaced type."[43]

The distinction between Derrida's discussion and the use of quotation according to Benjamin/Brecht is not unimportant, for we are once again dealing with different levels of analysis. Derrida is writing about the realm of conditions of possibility for citation; Benjamin and Brecht are thematizing the effect of epic devices on consciousness, the making conscious of context through quotation. Derrida's discussion is therefore again focused on the realm of the radical other, the nonpresent absence, the trace. Benjamin/Brecht are more firmly planted in the "logocentric" arena of politics and political consciousness. Spivak, however, does not persevere with this analogy, which I would insist is riddled with differences of level and purpose, but instead suggests that the matter could be pursued if we would read Derrida's early essay on Artaud. She does not do this, however, and so we are again left with an aborted endeavor to establish leftist credentials for deconstruction.

Spivak does not continue with the topic of "iterability" and "identity" because she is "more interested in the contrast that Benjamin exposes between Brecht's practice, which can be pedagogic, and Romantic irony, which it superficially resembles." Her thesis is that Derrida can be "placed with Brecht in Benjamin's discussion," while American deconstruction (she cites only de Man) "resembles what Benjamin writes of Romantic Irony."[44] We should note again that this type of contrast between French and American deconstruction is not at all unusual: the Americans are accused of subduing and depoliticizing an original radical impulse from France. In Spivak's argument the purified and original notion of deconstruction is then connected with Brechtian theater and, by implication, with marxist politics by the following statement: "It seems to me that Derrida's position is to grasp iterability as the condition of the possibility of the positive which will, however asymmetrically and unrigorously, result in the remains of a consensus; it therefore behooves us to forge theories (practices) of practice (theory), to whatever degree both are 'normed' by the minutest detail of their structuration."[45] This is a difficult sentence that refers us back to several points in the "philosophical" discussion, and my commentary will not do justice to it here. Let me circumvent detailed philosophical argument by translating it into the core of its political meaning. Spivak argues that Derrida's position does not exclude practice or action or even ethics. Rather, on some "normal" level, communication, consensus, and everyday life must go on. Formulating guidelines for our actions, carrying them out, and reflecting on these guidelines are unavoidable activities on this "normal" level. A connection between Brecht and Derrida can be made because Brecht, too, affirms theory, practice, and pedagogy. Again, however, the difference is one of level. Even if we agree with Spivak here and judge Derrida's position to be "affirmative" and "positive" (in the enabling sense), she has still distorted slightly the commonalities. Brecht's theory, practice, and pedagogy are not only "affirmative" in the Derridean (or Nietzschean) sense; Brecht (even as interpreted by Benjamin) would never feel that he had to argue the *possibility* of pedagogy. His affirmative attitude, rather, entails both a teleology and an ethics, direction or guidelines for actions (theory and practice); his pedagogy teaches us to act with specific goals in mind. Derrida, in contrast, even if one grants the leap from "undecidability" of texts to inevitability of acts, still must deny that there can be any final or even advisory arbitrator, in the form of a telos or ethos, for these unavoidable actions. One cannot not choose, one cannot not act, but the choice cannot not be beyond good and evil. His pedagogy may demand action, but without the imperative that we engage in a determinative struggle, for example, for socialism, or on the side of the proletariat. Spivak's essay evades the consideration of this point, however. After asserting the Brecht (via Benjamin) connection to Derrida, she takes up the task of demonstrating the affiliation between romantic irony and American deconstruction. For the third time, then, she abandons the politics of deconstruction, this time having argued the necessity of action, but with nothing more than the hope that it might resemble something Brechtian.

If I am correct in my assessment of Derrida's "call to action," then the distinction that Spivak draws between American and authentic Derridean deconstruction collapses. Neither variety of deconstruction would, as Searle claims Derrida does, privilege fictionality by entertaining the notion that "the world may, after all, be just a stage." Both would (along with Nietzsche) hail the necessity of something positive and affirmative despite and because of the repetition of an aberration in the text; and Reading, which Spivak blames for the deficiencies in de

Man's deconstructive strategy, would become just another term in the series of named unnameables. The "itinerary of skepticism" that "critics from the left and the right tend to see in deconstruction" will remain, however, despite Spivak's efforts to overcome it. It may no longer be understood, however, as a skepticism "on the part of deconstruction to disturb the status quo of theory,"[46] but rather as a skepticism about determining how to disturb the status quo of theory, or, once it is disturbed, how to determine the politics, the left or right, of this disturbance. Perhaps even Spivak senses that she has neither refuted skepticism nor established a persuasive "positive" politics for deconstruction; for she immediately and cautiously suggests after her protest against the skeptical reading of deconstruction that if we want to examine "a more specifically (if not in every detail) deconstructive practice," we would "perhaps turn to the 'life' and 'works' of Antonio Negri." At this point we reach the fourth and final evasion of the conclusion with the deflection from Derrida to Negri. Spivak does not pursue a consideration of the Italian philosopher, however, but turns instead to a discussion of the "humble pedagogic benefit" she receives from Derrida's text.

This discussion, a personal conclusion to the conclusion, a private appendage, is not uninteresting for us because it again approaches the brink of an argument concerning deconstructive politics. The fragmentation and decentralization of the individual's control over his or her life paradoxically generates an ideology of individual centrality, according to Spivak. This individualism paralyzes "collective practice toward social justice" and precludes our recognition of "the ethico-politically repressive construction of what presents itself as theoretical, legal, benign, free, or natural."[47] While this argument has much merit, it ignores the not insignificant previous endeavors of leftist theorists to promote collective action and to demystify the repressive structures of the modern world. Spivak minimizes the extent of previous opposition, I believe, in order to extol the political benefits of the "deconstructive 'lesson'" in *Limited Inc.* The list of things it can teach us is impressive indeed: It can

> teach student and teacher alike a method of analysis that would fix its glance upon the itinerary of the ethico-political in authoritarian fictions; call into question the complacent apathy of self-centralization; undermine the bigoted elitism (theoretical and practical) conversely possible in collective practice; while disclosing in such gestures the condition of possibility of the positive.[48]

No doubt deconstruction can serve us in doing all these things. But in no way does it have to be used for these purposes. Deconstruction is treated by Spivak—and to some extent by Ryan and Sprinker as well—rather like a tool with which one may accomplish certain progressive tasks provided one has already acquired the "correct" political views. Indeed, Spivak shows an awareness of this difficulty when she adds parenthetically that the examples of this "morphology" cannot match its discourse. But if we can conceive of politics only in terms of a "normal," deconstructable discourse, one that can never match the discourse of deconstruction, why should leftists or marxists feel compelled to embrace deconstruction, and why should deconstructors feel compelled to embrace a leftist political position? Spivak is silent on this point, and we are left with the uneasy sensation that we may have encountered a fifth and final evasion of an argument for political deconstruction.

Problems of a Politicized Deconstruction

In the early eighties the endeavor to forge an alliance between leftist political theory and deconstruction in the United States was perhaps destined to fail. The oppositional impulse that deconstruction had demonstrated in the French context in 1968 was unsuited for the American academy, particularly at the start of the Reagan presidency. In part this failure was due to the manner in which it was appropriated and employed at American universities. Conceived primarily as a method for interpreting literary texts, it lacked a general appeal outside of English and French departments. Because the analytical tradition so thoroughly dominated—and continues to dominate—philosophy departments, and because philosophy is considered more of a technical, exclusively college-level field of study in the United States than it is in France, deconstruction lacked the intellectual basis as well as the institutional framework for a more pervasive political impact. Indeed, the central figures of deconstruction in the eighties have been almost exclusively professors of literature, many of whom understand their central task to be the interpretation of literary texts. Deconstructive strategies may have occasionally found their way out of the literature department and ventured into legal studies, historiography, and social sciences. But in the United States, it seems, literature is viewed as its proper place. Thus at the Modern Language Association convention in December of 1990, in a session on "the fall of deconstruction," J. Hillis Miller described the trajectory of deconstruction as from literature to other fields and back to literature. Such a perspective is not likely to attract those who are interested in progressive social and political causes, and it is probably not coincidental that the authors of the essays I have discussed in the last section have moved into other areas. Ryan has done a good deal of work in analyzing Hollywood films; Sprinker has taken an active interest in social and political issues; and Spivak has been a major force in the discussion of colonialism and feminism.[49] None has abandoned deconstruction entirely, but I do not see in their more recent work the insistence that deconstruction be fused with marxism, or that deconstruction form the core of a progressive political critique.[50]

It may have been more than just the infelicity of the Reagan era that prevented a convincing and widespread politicization of deconstruction, however. As I have indicated in commenting on the essays of Ryan, Sprinker, and Spivak, their arguments make manifest various problems in leftist deconstruction. To conclude this chapter I would therefore like to summarize briefly three obstacles to a merger or "articulation" of philosophical deconstruction and oppositional political positions, particularly as they relate to marxism. The first arises from what I perceive to be claims for primacy or privilege. Marxist political theory cannot explain social or textual phenomena without assuming the primacy of the material world, labor, or praxis. Deconstructive strategies posit, by contrast, a textual universe whose outside is inconceivable and meaningless. These two disparate starting points raise a series of dilemmas for a prospective marxist deconstructor. Can we think of textuality as material or as praxis without abandoning the marxist meaning of the latter concepts? Or, alternatively, can we define labor as textual without compromising the deconstructive process? The most common solution to these implicit dilemmas is to stop short of their most disturbing implications. By relinquishing the condition of mutuality, marxism (or any political theory) or deconstruction serves as an aid or adjunct to the primary critique. If one were to privilege deconstruction, marxism would become a political corrective to the philosophical critique, a non-dogmatic, infinitely correctable (through deconstruction) guide to revolutionary positions that would stop deconstruction whenever it threatened to turn into skepticism or nihilism. If one started from marxism, deconstruction could fulfill the role of a safeguard against sclerosis of categories, as well as serve as a tool with which to dissect and expose the minutest instances of bourgeois ideology. There is, of course, nothing wrong with employing the theories hierarchically in this manner. This is what has been done effectively in the best marxist-deconstructive (or deconstructive-marxist) analyses, and the use of the "secondary theory" strengthens the persuasive force of the primary claims. But this sort of strategic implementation of theory highlights indirectly the difficulties and perhaps the ultimate incompatibility of a merger that would retain the full force of the two discourses. As I have stated above, denying a primacy of the material as it is inscribed in marxist theory—and here I do not mean the reinscribed "material" about which a deconstructor might speak—robs it of its power to theorize. Positing an outside to textuality would likewise annul the deconstructive analysis. Marxism and deconstruction, therefore, if either is allowed to operate without restraint, annul the theoretical assumptions of the other's most powerful arguments. A marxist deconstructor or deconstructive marxist appears to be something of an oxymoron.

A related area of difficulty has to do with epistemological matters, especially the thorny issue of reference. This topic is important for a number of reasons, not the least of which is that to make statements about history or oppression or classes or a wide range of topics at the center of political discourse there will have to exist some agreement about the status of these statements. Unfortunately both marxist and deconstructive positions have been distorted to the point that clichés have often been regarded as substantive arguments. Detractors from deconstruction—and occasionally less sophisticated advocates as well—have portrayed it as a nonsensical theory of total textual self-referentiality. The truth in this absurd assertion comes only when one adds that the "text" that is totally "self-referential" is not restricted to words printed on the pages of books. Opponents of marxism, as well as vulgar proponents, have frequently reduced its epistemological stance to a simplistically conceived reflection theory, and from this conception of cause-and-effect mirroring, it is not difficult to dismiss "marxist" referentiality as another metaphysical longing for presence. Neither deconstruction nor marxism, at least not the best theorists involved with these discourses, propounds the reduced positions polemically ascribed to them. Deconstruction does not do away with reference—indeed, it is difficult to imagine how it could do this and what this would entail—but rather problematizes simple and simplistic notions of how and why words, sentences, and texts acquire meanings. We should acknowledge that deconstruction has often facilitated a more thorough understanding of what reference is, by repeatedly cautioning us about the pitfalls of epistemological theory. Marxism, for its part, has never been comfortable with a simple theory of reflection, although there is seldom an abandonment of some form of representation in various complex models. The problem should not be whether texts "refer," but rather how and with what force they relate to and in the world. Intelligent proponents of the political left, both marxists and nonmarxists, as well as poststructuralists, including deconstructors, should all have something to say about this important issue.

The epistemological contribution of deconstruction to a sophisticated notion of marxism was explored in the mid-eighties briefly in an essay by Christopher Norris.[51] Claiming that the incompatibility of marxism and deconstruction was overstated, Norris contends that deconstruction can supply marxism with an epistemology that would render it more suitable for a radical critique of societal powers and practices, and more resistant to the premature totalizations, than most previous marxist endeavors. His thesis is stated succinctly in the final sentence of his essay: "If Marxism is currently searching for a counter-epistemology purged of totalising concepts, deconstruction is the critical path it needs to follow."[52] The problem with this attractive claim is that it is not clear to me that deconstruction supplies any sort of "epistemological grounding" at all. Indeed, Norris himself correctly notes that deconstruction participates in the contemporary assault "on notions of a grounding epistemology."[53] The best one can obtain from deconstruction's radical critique of the unavoidable metaphysical bias of epistemology is the notion that speculation in this area is ultimately futile, a tack taken by pragmatists like Richard Rorty, or that epistemologies are relative systems inscribed in a particular set of social and political relations. Both of these paths leave political theory in somewhat of a quandary. While it is true that either alternative could then actively challenge "relations of power" found in and bearing upon texts,[54] neither says anything about how to find one's way in taking sides on political issues. We are again up against a familiar problem in the politicization of deconstruction; the "destructive," diagnostic, or critical side of the strategy is fairly well delineated, but the practical, ethical, and affirmative side, associated with the inserted syllable "con," never comes into focus.

A final area in which I detect problems for a politicized or marxist deconstruction in the United States involves the broader realm of political activity. Certainly we can again affirm the notion that no action is without some political significance, and that therefore the very act of deconstructing texts has a necessarily political valence. Indeed, my contention throughout this book has been that there is always a political dimension to theory, but that this dimension changes in different cultural contexts (although I do not think that the resulting politics are totally determined by context). Here, however, I am referring more specifically to activities where we take sides on issues of local, national, or international importance. In this area I fail to understand how deconstruction can assume the role of advocacy of any position. Marxism, by contrast, appears to provide some guidelines for action in terms of ethical principles or a teleology that informs action. At least one can debate about appropriate action by referring to such principles. Deconstruction, however, appears to admit action only because there is no alternative. Thus even if we are inclined to accept Spivak's contention that deconstruction somehow "behooves us to forge theories (practices) of practice (theory)," there is nothing in the deconstructive "lesson" that would argue against bringing deconstruction to bear on putatively progressive causes. The speeches of Martin Luther King and Nelson Mandela are riddled with "metaphysical" assumptions and binary oppositions, sometimes the very assumptions and oppositions that inform the writings of their adversaries. In the world in which we live the choices are not between a metaphysical/logocentric/humanist and an antimetaphysical/antilogocentric/antihumanist position, but usually between two equally deconstructible statements or texts. Deconstructors who propose a more politicized agenda have failed to show why conservative political views (and actions that support them) are any less consonant with deconstruction than traditionally leftist views. The homogenization of Western tradition into one inescapable metaphysical prison suggests an essential equality and deconstructability of positions. As we have seen before, the bridge between the deconstructive "lesson" and a leftist politics appears to be at best an arbitrary construction, and certainly not a necessary connection.

Again Derrida initially showed more insight into this problem than some of his American followers. In an interview from 1975 he suggested an insurmountable discrepancy between politics or praxis and deconstructive theory:

> if this deconstructive politics is indispensable, it is necessary to take into account certain deviations or differences [*écarts*] and to try to reduce them, even if, for essential reasons, they are impossible to efface: for example, between discourse or practices of this immediately political deconstruction and a deconstruction of a theoretical or philosophical mode.[55]

If I understand Derrida correctly here, he is affirming the unavoidably political nature of deconstructive procedures, but cautioning that the political and the philosophical in deconstruction cannot be brought together for essential reasons. Although Derrida, as we shall see in his discussion of de Man, appears to have revised this position when he ascribes an inherent political antifascism to deconstruction, here he expresses reservations about precisely the type of project that was undertaken in the United States around 1980. The gap that he located between philosophical theory and oppositional practice poses the foremost challenge to politicizing deconstruction. If the revolution for which we are expected to struggle has "no model"—as Spivak citing Derrida reminds us—if goals can be stated only obliquely or negatively, and if, finally the elusion of authoritarian fictions may ultimately be only another illusion of metaphysics, then the practice of this theory is indeed a risky proposition. Undoubtedly inherent theoretical considerations and liabilities, as much as the general climate of the Reagan years, inhibited development of leftist deconstruction in the eighties and contributed to its declining popularity in politicized theoretical circles in the United States.

9

The Uncomfortable Heritage

THE decline of deconstruction as a theoretical force in the United States has been evident since the mid-eighties. Although I will concentrate on the political aspects of its demise, this decline also had institutional and cultural dimensions. On one level, deconstruction simply lost its novelty for native critics. The general feeling pervading the academy was that the "deconstructive movement" had exhausted itself. The seminal works had appeared during the late sixties in France and had been made accessible to the American public about a decade later; new impulses from abroad and novel adaptations domestically were lacking. Derrida had been read with interest in the late seventies, but his influence peaked at some point in the early eighties, and his more recent texts seemed to contain nothing radically new. Derrida's French disciples, critics such as Philippe Lacoue-Labarth and Jean-Luc Nancy, appeared to be more or less clones of their mentor. The Yale School, which had always been a relatively heterogeneous group, lost any coherency it had possessed by the middle of the decade. J. Hillis Miller moved to Irvine; Paul de Man died in 1983; Geoffrey Hartman became involved with the Holocaust archives at Yale and with Jewish mysticism; and Harold Bloom produced almost nothing in the way of theory (and his criticism had been only tangentially related to deconstruction anyway). But deconstructors themselves contributed to their own self-deconstruction in the late eighties by persisting with their cliquish ways. They became increasingly intolerant of criticism.[1] Even well-meant and intelligent questioning became anathema, and often writers perceived to be "opponents" were simply dismissed as theoretical dinosaurs, unintelligent trespassers on a sublime critical turf, or reactionaries bent on persecuting an oppressed minority.[2] The references and footnotes in their writings became increasingly hermetic, and the conferences they sponsored and attended began to resemble religious revival meetings at which no principled objections could be raised. Indeed, the penchant toward private seminars and closed lectures fostered the cultist image. During the eighties the discourse of deconstruction became increasingly exclusive and defensive. It no longer emanated excitement and novelty, but rather too often had the air of dogmatism and ritual.

The Defense of Paul de Man

No doubt a major contributing factor to the demise of deconstruction has been its uneasy relationship to politics. We have just examined in some detail the largely unsuccessful attempt to politicize (or repoliticize for the United States) deconstruction during the Reagan era, but in the late eighties a different kind of political challenge presented itself. It was not the politicization of theory itself that was foregrounded, but rather the way in which adherents to deconstruction responded to political challenges. In particular two events thrust the topic of the connection between deconstructive theory and politics more urgently into the limelight than had been the case since its advent in the late sixties. The first of these was the revelation in the fall of 1987 that the late Paul de Man, one of the most respected critics in American letters during the past three decades and perhaps the leading American advocate of deconstruction, had contributed articles to newspapers, *Le Soir* and *Het Vlaamsche Land,* which harbored pro-Nazi sympathies. Even his strongest defenders do not pretend that these articles do not contain repugnant passages which implicate him in a discourse of racist and nationalist stereotypes. Since he composed them as a young man in Belgium during the early forties, however, there are not many serious critics who would claim that theoretical pronouncements he made after the completion of his graduate studies in the early 1950s are necessarily tainted by fascism or racism. Those who, for example, would simplistically view deconstruction, which can be identified with only the last decade and a half of de Man's critical work, as a late mutation of National Socialist ideology are wholly ignorant of both the philosophical diversity and complexity of the deconstructive enterprise and the historical forms in which German fascism proliferated. Anyone with even a cursory knowledge of philosophy under National Socialism knows that the relationship between this discipline and the state was rarely direct and unproblematic; only the most crude philosophical hacks were open propagandists for the fascist cause. Even the worst of de Man's early essays do not fall into this category. Although he does make more than occasional use of a vocabulary that is tainted by fascism, and although he does praise authors who were celebrated by the National Socialist regime, he appears more consistently interested in aesthetics than in politics.[3]

Still there are several troubling aspects to de Man's newly discovered political activities. First and foremost among these is his total silence about any involvement with journalism and politics during these crucial years. From all the public testimony that has emerged thus far it seems that he was not candid with even his closest friends, and certainly this behavior must strike those of us who are not quite beyond good and evil as morally reprehensible. Indeed, some evidence has surfaced that indicates that he either attempted to cover up his actual involvement in right-wing circles, or, when compelled to comment on these activities, sought to minimize the extent of his participation.[4] It is therefore perhaps inevitable that his wartime journalism will cast a shadow on his later theoretical work, and even the past few years have seen critics beginning to read him somewhat differently than they have in the past. In essence two extreme camps have formed around the issue of deconstruction and de Man's deconstructive activities. The first views deconstruction as a philosophical subterfuge employed to evade responsibility for past works and deeds. Deconstructive strategies, this camp claims, by negating the subject as moral agent and by declaring a fundamental undecidability in all linguistic utterance, provide the perfect theoretical alibi for precisely the type of activities in which the young de Man was involved. Critics of this persuasion, who are relatively few in number and who in most cases have preconceived notions concerning the perniciousness of deconstruction, claim that de Man's theoretical proclivities toward relativism or nihilism amount to a program of self-exoneration. Deconstruction, one might then conclude, was adopted and developed by de Man to justify his past deeds and later silence.[5]

What is of greater importance for my concerns in this book is the response of deconstructors themselves to the revelations about de Man. As far as I can tell, very few of de Man's students and even fewer adherents to deconstruction have even entertained the possibility that his later theoretical positions could be related in any but an antithetical manner to his early journalism. Indeed, the deconstructive party line was established rather early on, almost immediately after the extent of his wartime writings was known at the beginning of 1988, and it has changed very little since that time. The immediate reactions from de Man's supporters differ only in nuances. With regard to the early journalism each defender admits the undeniable fact that de Man wrote reprehensible passages about the Jews in the early forties, although an effort is usually made to minimize his involvement with actual fascist propaganda or the most virulent forms of antisemitic diatribes. With respect to theory, on the other hand, de Man's defenders insist that his later work must be seen as an attempt to deal theoretically with the very "mistakes" he committed in his youth. In one of the first essays to appear on this issue, Christopher Norris, who has had a rather large stake in deconstruction in general and who had just completed a book-length study of de Man's criticism,[6] argues that the thrust of de Man's critical work after he reached the United States can be understood as an implicit rejection of the very type of essentialist philosophical stance associated with both Heidegger and with the political position de Man himself formerly advocated in print.[7] In this line of argument Heidegger becomes the heavy, and Norris' playing off of de Man against the German philosopher of *Dasein* makes the former a champion of philosophical progressiveness and an enemy of all retrograde theoretical undertakings. A month later Geoffrey Hartman, de Man's friend and colleague at Yale, took a similar approach in his essay in the *New Republic*.[8] When de Man speaks of "killing the original" and of "essential failure," Hartman maintains, he is referring to "the mediated and compromised idiom of his early, journalistic writings."[9] And Werner Hamacher, who was mentioned previously as one of the few German adherents to poststructuralism, was even so bold as to assert that de Man's writings are an immense "work of mourning" *(Trauerarbeit)*, a term reserved almost exclusively in the German context for coming to terms with the National Socialist past.[10]

There is, of course, much prima facie evidence that speaks against such claims. Norris' notion that de Man's highly sympathetic readings of Heidegger contain the seed of a political opposition is at best an odd interpretation of these texts. If de Man had really been so concerned about Heidegger's association with National Socialism—as he indeed should have been—a much more likely step for him would have been simply to write about it, as many others, including Derrida, have done. But de Man avoided this topic, just as he shunned almost all overtly political topics as a professor of literature. During his tenure on the Yale campus he was not known as a political personality, and his hiring in the French department at that university was uncontroversial from a political perspective.[11] He was most definitely not appointed as a representative of the revolutionary spirit of May 1968. It is surely not coincidental that no one appears to have hailed him as a political beacon in the various short speeches given at his memorial celebration,[12] and until his early right-wing proclivities came to light, it is difficult to find anyone among his supporters or detractors connecting him with progressive political positions. But the political perspective Norris and others suddenly imputed to de Man when confronted with his past is also not apparent in the writings he left behind. From all indications de Man seems to have avoided rather obstinately the endeavor to discuss anything recognizable as a direct political stance. Let me cite only one illustration of how obdurately de Man circumvents political discourse. I take this example purposely from his later work, since all recent defenders of de Man appear convinced that his deconstructive efforts shortly before his death were deeply political. De Man had just delivered the last of six Messenger Lectures at Cornell in March of 1983 on Benjamin's essay "The Task of the Translator." The audience then engaged him in discussion, and we are fortunate enough to possess the transcript of this exchange.[13] Of particular interest is the question posed by Dominick LaCapra, who sees Benjamin as a thinker combining the subtlety of contemporary French criticism with a "political dimension that's very much identified with messianic hope and utopianism."[14] But de Man swerves away from this potential political issue and pushes Benjamin into a less dangerous Nietzschean camp, even though he is compelled to admit that Benjamin admired the leftist philosopher Ernst Bloch. His answer here, as in his discussion of Benjamin in his introduction to a collection by Hans Robert Jauß,[15] has the effect of severing Benjamin from marxism, Brecht, and perhaps most important, from Benjamin's opposition to and fate in fascism. I am not arguing, of course, that de Man's deconstructive writings cannot be interpreted as political. The early responses by Norris, Hartman, and Hamacher, as well as the various essays that have appeared since, make it apparent that such an argument can be constructed.[16] What seems odd, however, is that de Man himself never referred to politics or antifascism in any direct or open fashion. Thus his supporters are forced to strained interpretations and pious hopes. Although Hartman evaluates the subversion of hope that was so central for Benjamin's revolutionary politics as de Man's confrontation with his own past, this move can be more directly read as an indication of how de Man evaded or, indeed, subverted political implications in many of his later essays. It is hard to believe, as Norris maintains, that de Man envisioned a thoroughgoing investigation of Marx, Adorno, Althusser, and other marxist thinkers—except perhaps to undermine their political value—and wishful thinking probably plays a large role in his claim that "on the basis of those writings we do possess it is clear that his work had long been directed toward problems in exactly this area."[17] As strange and forced as these contentions may appear, they are relatively inoffensive when compared with Hartman's transparent excuses for his former colleague. The early defense of de Man reached an apologetic low point when he accounted for racist remarks by asserting that in the early 1940s de Man "had been trapped by an effect of language."[18]

The contorted reasoning and exegetical maneuvering of de Man's early supporters served only to reinforce the view that they had something to hide. Instead of admitting in a candid and unequivocal fashion that de Man had acted reprehensibly for a short period during the war and then stating the obvious fact that people change and mature, and that his later work must be judged on its critical merits, they wound up damaging both deconstruction and their own credibility by composing such contrived defenses. The major discourse events that took place in print around de Man's politics only made the consensus position of deconstruction appear more foolish and farfetched. In 1988 and 1989 a series of conferences and talks dealt with the de Man case in minute detail. Essays on de Man appeared not only in scholarly journals, but also in the *New York Times, Newsweek*, the *Nation*, and other popular periodicals. In 1988 the public was treated to a complete edition of de Man's wartime journalism, and soon thereafter Hamacher, Neil Hertz, and Thomas Keenan edited a lengthy volume containing thirty-seven essays and additional documentation. To their credit the editors asked not only supporters of de Man, but also persons who were apt to be critical of deconstruction and link it with his wartime journalism, although the collection consists primarily of contributions by friends, colleagues, and former students of de Man.[19]

Perhaps the most interesting discourse event on de Man, however, appeared in the pages of *Critical Inquiry*. It featured two lengthy contributions by Jacques Derrida, one published in the spring of 1988 (which was also included in the *Responses* volume), the other a rebuttal to six short responses to his original article, all of which appeared in the summer of 1989. Included in this latter issue of *Critical Inquiry* is also an essay by Shoshana Felman, a colleague of de Man's at Yale, and it is to this apology for "Paul de Man's silence" that I turn first.[20] It is an important essay, not because it provides an insightful analysis of de Man's actions or writings, but because it is representative for the contorted reasoning that has so discredited so many of those who were formerly taken seriously as theoreticians. Near the beginning of the essay Felman sets up what has become the accepted narrative for de

Man's apologists. The early de Man, like his uncle, who was a leading political figure in Belgium and who supported collaboration with the Germans, was "captivated by the Nazis' seeming revolutionary promise."[21] Paul de Man started work for *Le Soir,* Felman informs us, in December of 1940, "at a point when the Second World War seemed to many to have been definitively won by Germany, five months after the publication of his uncle's manifesto [urging cooperation with the invaders], and one month before the birth of his first son."[22] Only one article strikes her as offensive, "Les Juifs dans la littérature actuelle," in which openly antisemitic sentiments are contained.[23] But Felman softens the effect of this essay by producing evidence from Edouard Colinet, who maintains that de Man wrote this essay only under pressure and the fear of losing his position. After the tightening of censorship and the recognition that the National Socialists were exterminating Jews, de Man resigned his position. After a brief stint at a publishing house, de Man was fired and turned to translating Melville's *Moby Dick*.

One of the few meritorious remarks one can make about de Man's silence about his past is that he never succumbed to the temptation of constructing such a masterfully apologetic autobiographical narrative. Evidently blinded by her fidelity to de Man, Felman misses the point on a number of issues. The nature of National Socialism was obvious to any European well before 1940. It was well known that it was a regime without regard for human dignity, that it was aggressive toward its neighbors, that it denied fundamental rights to its own citizens and to the citizens in the territories it occupied, and that it propagated racist doctrines that it then enshrined in law. Indeed, de Man had firsthand knowledge of how Germany treated the Jewish minority in occupied countries. On 28 October 1940, not quite two months *before* de Man's first article appeared in *Le Soir,* the German military command in Belgium banned all Jews from the Belgium civil service, effective at the end of that year. If de Man was "captivated by the Nazis' seeming revolutionary promise," then we have to wonder how he could accept a promise that so blatantly discriminated against so many innocent people. It is much more likely that de Man, like so many of his contemporaries, opportunistically overlooked the many crimes of the Germans for the sake of an easy paycheck and because he could reconcile some parts of Nazi dogma with his own elitist positions. De Man, like Heidegger, Ernst Jünger, Gottfried Benn, and a host of other conservative European thinkers, tolerated or propagated fascism and its many injustices because they had no fundamental commitment to democracy or to individual liberties. Fascism was not the monolithic ideological system that de Man's defenders construct, so that they can show how their hero deviated from it or opposed it. Especially in the occupied countries, but even in Germany itself, conservative thinkers supported National Socialism selectively. Only the most ignorant believed the biological foundations of racist theory and the outlandish antisemitic propaganda. The support de Man lent to the fascist regime was not unusual in its deviation from the official party line, but it is obviously not excusable simply because others followed the same course.[24]

Felman's explanation for the composition of an antisemitic article on 4 March 1941 is likewise unconvincing. Left unanswered are why he could not resign in 1941, but could at the end of 1942, and how he could manage to survive after relinquishing all apparent collaborationist activities in 1943, but could not risk losing his position in 1941. She also leaves unmentioned and unexamined his partisanship for German authors, many of whom were supporters of Nazism or right-wing ideologues closely allied with the regime. Furthermore, Felman, like so many of de Man's defenders,[25] conveniently passes over another article with antisemitic content. Over a year after his supposedly singular slip into racist propaganda, de Man published a piece entitled "Blik op de huidige Duitsche romanliteratuur" (A View of Contemporary German Fiction) in *Het Vlaamsche Land*.[26] In this article he divides postwar German literature into two groups: one that produced a cerebral art based on abstract principles that came into conflict with the "proper traditions of German art." This group is specifically identified with the Dutch word "ontaarding," a translation of the German "Entartung," which was reserved for degenerate art and largely identified with non-Aryans. De Man follows the National Socialist propaganda machine precisely when he states that "mainly non-Germans, and specifically Jews," produced this art. Would such an occasional contributor as de Man—he wrote only ten articles for *Het Vlaamsche Land*—have been compelled to compose an antisemitic article? Is there any testimony that he was pressured to censure a Jewish, degenerate art while lauding a properly German art, whose representatives he moreover praised individually in other articles during his journalistic activities?[27] The evidence we have at hand, if it is not treated selectively and interpreted in a contrived fashion, certainly indicates that de Man's commitment is much larger than Felman cares to admit. The issue for me here, of course, is not really what that commitment was in all its dirty details. This has been the subject of scrutiny in several excellent contributions to the *Responses* volume. Rather what concerns me is why a large portion of the most respected part of the literary establishment, including Felman, the Thomas E. Donnelley Professor of French and Comparative Literature at Yale, would want to participate in such blatant apologetics.

Felman's account of de Man's wartime activities is not the real point of her essay, however. Like most of de Man's fanatically loyal following, her real purpose is to rescue the late writings—although, as I have already pointed out, there is really no reason to do so. Instead of simply condemning his understandable silence as a human weakness and regarding his theoretical work since the sixties as an apolitical but interesting (for some critics) attempt to deal with rhetoric, language, figures, and their philosophical implications, Felman insists on presenting an interpretation in which de Man's silence was more integral and heroic than any discussion or confession could have been. Proceeding to lionize de Man with a series of literary identifications, she likens her former colleague to Ahab in *Moby Dick,* who, similar to de Man, left his wife and children to fight the great whale as a kind of ersatz suicide. "Might both de Man's eleven-year-old silence and his radical departure be viewed as substitutes for suicide?" she queries.[28] But de Man is also Ishmael from the same novel, the self-imposed exile who has survived and learned a lesson from survival. (The difference here, which Felman omits, is that de Man never tells us his story.) Like Ishmael, de Man is plagued or perhaps blessed with the "doubleness of vision" that enables him to recognize "the bankruptcy of all conventional historical divisions and the blurring of boundaries."[29] But according to Felman, in perhaps her most insidious comparison, de Man is also Primo Levi since his theories "inscribe the testimony of the muted witness and...address the lesson of historical events, not...as a cover-up or a dissimulation of the past, but as an ongoing, active *transformation of the very act of bearing witness.*"[30] (Once again Felman seems to forget the slight difference that de Man refused to bear witness.) De Man is also and perhaps most importantly Rousseau, whose confessions he showed to be lies and from whom he learned (rather conveniently) that "excuses generate the very guilt they exonerate."[31] And in a final distasteful gesture Felman compares de Man to Benjamin, the German Jewish writer who committed suicide rather than be captured by the Nazis. Both men

> experience the war essentially as a mistake, as an impossibility of reading (or of witnessing), as a historical misreading that leads both men to a misguided action. The one dies as a consequence of his misreading of the war whereas the other survives in spite of it and constructs his later life as a relentless struggle

with the powers of historical deception, including his own former historical misreading.[32]

Even if we assume, as Felman does, that Benjamin's suicide was precipitated by a false report of capture, it is unconscionable that the two men should be juxtaposed in this fashion. Any person not under the spell of deconstructive unreason can see that Benjamin's death is intimately linked with the same Nazi racism that de Man supported, for whatever reason, at least twice in print. Benjamin's life was cut short because of a regime dedicated to exterminating the Jewish population of Europe; de Man, who collaborated publicly with this regime, lived the comfortable life of a Yale professor in his postwar years by suppressing his involvement.

While Felman's aesthetic analogies may be the occasion for disbelief on the part of the reader, her ethical arguments are suspect for their inability to deal with distinctions that really matter in life. Typical for the illogic of her argument is the following series of odd statements: "It is judged unethical, of course, to engage in acts that lent support to Germany's wartime position, but it is also judged unethical to forget; and unethical, furthermore, to keep silent in relation to the war and to the Holocaust."[33] We can assume that everyone agrees with the first statement, and this is precisely the reason that de Man's involvement should not be excused as Felman does in her short biographical account. But no one would judge it unethical to forget; if de Man forgot his umbrella one day, or the name of his wife's cousin, no one would care. The issue is not forgetting, but repressing and covering up behavior that almost everyone would agree is "unethical." Similarly it is not necessarily reprehensible to keep silent about the Holocaust and the war. If one were born in 1972, then such a silence could not be judged unethical. But it may be considered unethical if one's actions lent support to the nation that perpetrated both the war and the Holocaust, particularly if one wrote publicly for collaborationist newspapers at a time when the criminal nature of Germany was evident. Felman's strange and illogical framing of these issues is apparently related to what I take to be her central ethical statement: we are all implicated in "de Man's forgetting, and in his silence," "in de Man's ordeal and in his incapacity to tell more about it."[34] The message is that we are all guilty, that none of us have the right to exonerate ourselves from complicity, and on some level Felman is no doubt correct. In the metaphysical sense Jaspers outlines in the *Question of German Guilt*, we are all guilty whenever another human being suffers and we do nothing about it.[35]

But such a global framework serves only to vitiate distinctions that are necessary for moral and political responsibility in the real world. Today, as in Nazi Germany, there are some people who inflict punishment, some who are forced to accept it; some who oppress people and deny their rights, others who are oppressed and whose rights are denied; some who kill, maim, and torture, while others are killed, maimed, and tortured. And it is precisely these distinctions that matter in both our daily conduct and in evaluating de Man's actions. We do not condemn him because we are "outside these moral and historical implications,"[36] but precisely because we recognize that we are always inside of these implications, because we recognize that only by distinguishing ethical from unethical conduct can we gain some amount of insight into our own values and actions. Felman, blinded by her image of de Man as a "liberator,"[37] escapes into a realm of moral relativity that effaces rather than questions the distinction between ethical and unethical behavior.

What could be the authority on which Felman's essay rests? How could she commit such fundamental errors in argument and have drawn such reprehensible parallels? How could she misread the case of de Man? Part of the answer to this lies in the essays of Derrida, to which I referred above. For although the initial journalistic responses of Norris, Hartman, and Hamacher set the tone for the entire and massive defense, it is not difficult to detect the influence of Derrida's essay, written in January of 1988 and published in the spring issue of *Critical Inquiry.*[38] Derrida sets the tone for the debate by rejecting all "journalistic haste,"[39] which leads inevitably to errors of oversimplification. In stating this, Derrida obviously does not have in mind the apologetic texts of Hartman, Norris, and Hamacher, but rather the writings of those who have reported on the discovery of de Man's wartime journalism in the press, in particular the article Jon Wiener wrote for the *Nation* in early January of 1988.[40] But Derrida's reference to "journalistic haste" also includes implicitly de Man's own wartime articles, the inference being that these were not representative of his thought, but occasional and hurried products of a person pressed for deadlines. This reference, therefore, is only one in a series of rhetorical strategies Derrida employs to make his apology appear to be a balanced, objective, and thoughtful account.

Since many of these strategies figure prominently in the replies to Derrida's essay, I will mention only those that are most relevant. Derrida fosters the appearance of fairness by conceding at various points what detractors have argued or will inevitably argue. He condemns de Man's journalistic activities in several places, although he never calls them "collaborationist." But these concessions are included only to set up an opposition whose logic governs almost the entire essay. Derrida employs "on the one hand" and "on the other hand" as two poles of argument or two possibilities of argument. The initial phrase always points to the most apparent aspects of de Man's texts: "the massive, immediate, and dominant effect"[41] of his journalism. The second phrase then presents itself as a deeper reading, a more profound and considered understanding of strategies that de Man practiced. The first corresponds to the hasty journalism that has caused so much trouble; the second to a careful and reasoned position. Obviously Derrida places more emphasis on this second level, on the contradictory, ambivalent messages in de Man's texts, which he refers to throughout as "a double edge and a double bind."[42] The effect of such a rhetorical ploy is to deemphasize the force of the statements following "on the one hand," and to attach the most significance to the interpretations that are usually the end product of the "other hand."

The implications of this sort of reading, which does not resemble Derrida's previous deconstructive strategies, are most evident in the third series of examples, in the discussion of the article "Les Juifs dans la littérature actuelle." Derrida devotes two pages to the obvious antisemitism and eight pages to the ambiguities and complexities of this text. This unevenhandedness in pure quantity is coupled with a transparent and ultimately futile endeavor to extricate de Man from the consequences of his racist phrasings. At the outset Derrida announces triumphantly that "the whole article is organized as an indictment of 'vulgar antisemitism,'"[43] and he allows this unproven, and I dare say unprovable, claim to guide his entire argument. The contorted nature of his reasoning, which was the subject of comments by several responses, is most apparent in his interpretation of de Man's initial sentence. De Man wrote: "Vulgar antisemitism readily takes pleasure in considering postwar cultural phenomena as degenerate and decadent because they are *enjuivés* [infected with a Jewish spirit]."[44] Derrida's interpretation hinges on the first two words: "to condemn 'vulgar antisemitism,' *especially if one makes no mention of the other kind,* is to condemn antisemitism itself *inasmuch* as it is vulgar, always and essentially vulgar."[45] This reading is nonsensical, and in fact the mention of "vulgar antisemitism" has precisely the opposite effect: it affirms antisemitism by implying a nonvulgar variety. If in a book discussing marxism, I would refer to "vulgar marxism," or if on a page in a newspaper devoted to a discussion of deconstruction, I would refer to "vulgar deconstruction," I would not be asserting the nonexistence of a true or authentic variety of marxism or deconstruction, but in fact claiming that such a variety exists. Having explained away this obvious affirmation of antisemitism, Derrida proceeds to read the essay as a clandestine criticism of the very page on which the article appeared. Only the last paragraph, "the only one that can be suspected of antisemitism,"[46] still presents a few minor difficulties. In order to account for the blatant racism here—de Man writes that "the solution to the Jewish problem," the "creation of a Jewish colony isolated from Europe," would not be detrimental to the "literary life of the West"[47]—Derrida suggests that the editors may have intervened. Since the other damaging essay from *Het Vlaamsche Land* was not available to Derrida when he composed his initial response, he is perhaps justified in regarding this essay as an isolated instance that could have been doctored by editorial interference. But why, we are entitled to ask, after the entire record was accessible to him, did he not alter his analysis in the least for the *Responses* volume? Why does he continue to maintain that the article "Les Juifs dans la littérature actuelle" was unique in the wartime journalism? Derrida may indeed be correct in stating that de Man was opposing the very sort of crude antisemitism that surrounded him on this page in *Le Soir,* but only the most perverse reading can turn this racist complicity into a furtive resistance to all notions of the antisemitic.

The other rhetorical strategy Derrida employs to argue his case is to set the stakes at a point where no one would want to counter him. His contention that critics of de Man want to prevent us from reading his works or want to burn his writings is ludicrous, and I have found not even the hint of such a statement in any of the scholarly or journalistic accounts of the affair. Derrida's intent is obvious and malicious. If those who have criticized de Man are made to look like fascist book-burners, then they are the fascists and not de Man. By going on the offensive, Derrida's role of self-appointed defense attorney is that much easier. And there is no doubt that Derrida conceives of his essay as a court brief. The early articles criticizing de Man did of course present "evidence" and gathered "testimony" from "experts," but this is a commonplace procedure for journalism. The aspect of a trial was strongly introduced, however, only when Derrida and his various cohorts began to write like pseudo-lawyers. But the deconstructive courtroom Derrida would have us enter is a strange place. It is not an arena in which the notions of critical legal theory, much of which has been influenced by deconstruction, are put into practice. Rather, it is a legal setting in which the defense establishes the ground rules for appropriate definitions, admissible evidence, valid testimony, and juridical procedure, and we, as readers, are supposed to submit to the authority of the court's readings.

With regard to the first issue, definitions of terms, Derrida would have us believe that de Man did not maintain silence about his wartime collaboration because he explained himself *publicly* in "a public act."[48] He is referring to a letter that de Man composed when he was evidently denounced to the Society of Fellows at Harvard in 1955.[49] But this letter was not "public" in any commonly used sense of the word. It was addressed to Renato Poggioli, Director of the Society of Fellows at the time, and was possibly seen by others involved in the society, although we have no evidence that anyone except Poggioli actually had access to it. Before 1989 this letter was in no way promulgated in a public and open fashion, neither for the Harvard community, nor for the general public at large. It is not at all commensurate with the articles de Man published in *Le Soir* and in *Het Vlaamsche Land,* which were public documents accessible to all citizens, excepts perhaps to those who were being carted away to concentration camps, or who were forced to go underground to avoid this fate. As either a public or a private document, however, this letter is hardly a document on which the defense should rest its case, since it contains a number of rather glaring evasions of truth. De Man admits that he stated his profession was "professeur" when he was not employed in this position; he clearly underplays his involvement with *Le Soir,* stating only that he wrote "some literary articles" for the journal in 1940 and 1941 (he actually wrote 170 articles and continued writing until almost the end of 1942); he totally ignores his work for *Het Vlaamsche Land* and for the *Bibliographie Dechenne* (from February 1942 until March of 1943), which was the bulletin of a publishing house also under German control; and he identifies his uncle, Hendrik de Man, as his father. It is difficult to know why or how he could misidentify his own father, but it is not unlikely that de Man felt such a close identification with Henrik de Man would provide an explanation for why he, Paul de Man, was being accused of collaboration.[50] Knowing that these errors crept into the record of his (deconstructively conceived) "public" confession, we have a right to be suspicious of other claims in the letter: e.g., that he ceased working for *Le Soir* when "nazi thought-control did no longer allow freedom of statement." After all, he continued to work for Dechenne under the same thought control until March of 1943. De Man's final contention about his activities cannot but have a hollow ring to it: "During the rest of the occupation, I did what was the duty of any decent person."[51] If this letter had been made public during de Man's lifetime, we have to wonder how he would have explained the various prevarications it contains.

The criterion for admissible evidence is similarly unusual. Derrida's claim is the following: "a statement can never be taken as a presumption of guilt or evidence in a trial, even less as proof, as long as one has not demonstrated that it has only an idiomatic value and that no one else, besides Paul de Man or a Paul de Man signatory of the 1940–42 texts, could have either produced the statement or subscribed to it."[52] Derrida is here referring to statements taken from de Man's later work that would be used to make a case for covering up his earlier journalism. But again the absoluteness of his prohibition is baffling and ultimately dogmatic. In legal terms, at least in the United States, one does not have to demonstrate that a statement made by an individual is either unique or could be subscribed to by no one else in order to introduce it as evidence. Indeed, such a restriction, if actually introduced as juridical practice, would effectively paralyze all legal proceedings. What Derrida apparently wants to prohibit is claiming that there is a collusive relationship between the early writings and the later work, what he calls "compulsive and confusionist practices—amalgam, continuism, analogism, teleologism, hasty totalization, reduction, and derivation."[53] The stakes, however, are much too extremely stated. Derrida conceives of a procedure connecting de Man's deconstructive strategies with his early journalism as a claim that "everything is already there in the 'early writings,' everything derives from them or comes down to them, the rest was nothing but their pacifying and diplomatic translation."[54] But no one has really claimed this at all. At most some critics view deconstruction as a strategy that enabled de Man to avoid confronting his past and admitting his errors, and there is no reason why this hypothesis should not be treated seriously. By setting up such a straw man, Derrida seeks to disallow and to prejudice statements that may lead to an understanding of the personal appeal deconstruction may have had for de Man.

For this reason he rails against those who are the "hurried detectives."[55] Those who look at de Man's work without the proper circumspection fall into two types of error. One of these, referred to above, is making de Man's work a continuum in order to condemn the later work on the basis of the wartime journalism. The other is the opposite error: enforcing "an interdiction against any contamination, analogy, translation."[56] These two contradictory errors would appear to leave little room for critical discussion. If we cannot affirm a rupture between the early and late de Man, and if we cannot assert a continuity, then how are we to conceive of his oeuvre? Derrida's answer to this conundrum would appear to be contained in two rules he lays down for all further commentary on this matter. The first is that we show respect for the other. No humanistically inclined person would object to this as a guideline, and Derrida is certainly right to insist that we pay careful attention to what de Man himself wrote, both in the journalism from 1940–42 and in his later works. His second rule, however, shows that he does not desire simply careful attention to de Man's oeuvre, but rather "attention" that takes as its premise precisely what this careful attention would have to demonstrate. The "regulating ideal" of the second rule is for critics "to avoid reproducing, if only virtually, the *logic* of the discourse thus incriminated."[57] But for Derrida what does this amount to? Nothing short of disqualifying anything but a deconstructive discourse as legitimate for analyzing and evaluating de Man's works. Indeed, deconstruction is defined in this essay as a program "to uncover the statements, the philosophical, ideological, or political behaviors that derive from it [a formalizing, saturating totalization] and wherever they may be found." Deconstruction, and deconstruction alone, rids us of the pernicious logic of "purification, purge, totalization, reappropriation, homogenization, rapid objectification, good conscience, stereotyping and nonreading, *immediate* politicization or depoliticization..., *immediate* historicization or dehistoricization..., immediate ideologizing moralization...of all the texts and all the problems, expedited trial, condemnations, or acquittals, summary executions or sublimations."[58] What Derrida is autocratically asserting here is that only his philosophical analysis can be employed as an antidote to totalitarian discourse. "To put it in a word, deconstructions have always represented, as I see it, the least necessary condition for identifying and combating the totalitarian risk in all the forms already mentioned."[59]

The consequence of this dogmatic assertion of rules, of this hegemonic and *totalized* disqualification of any discourse but one's own, is to make de Man the best source for evaluating his own earlier involvement with fascism. Indeed, Derrida proclaims without bothering to provide evidence—it is his court after all—that de Man's critics exhibit a closer proximity to totalitarianism than de Man in his later writings. We must therefore exclude their criticisms of de Man and especially their views on his later theoretical work because only through deconstruction(s) can we ever come to an understanding of the essence of National Socialism. We will have occasion to return to this claim of exclusive political correctness in observing the deconstructive interventions in the Heidegger controversy. For now it is sufficient to note that the incessant plea that we read de Man, as well as Derrida's reply to his critics that they have not read him (Derrida), should be understood not as a demand that those holding differing opinions read texts, but rather as a demand that they cede any opinion that does not correspond to what have unfortunately become the dogmas of deconstruction. Derrida's poignant statement toward the close of his essay reaffirms this desire to exert hegemonic control over the reading process. "Having just reread my text, I imagine that for some it will seem I have tried, when all is said and done and despite all the protests or precautions, to protect, save, justify what does not deserve to be saved. I ask these readers, if they still have some concern for justice and rigor, to take the time to reread, as closely as possible."[60] When we consider Derrida's reading of a phrase like "vulgar antisemitism," we have to ask what Derrida's own concern for justice and rigor has been, and why our reading of de Man and of Derrida should not be allowed to differ from what Derrida wants it to be. Derrida is not asking his readers to reason with and against him, to test his interpretations against other evidence (he ignores the new evidence of the essay in *Het Vlaamsche Land*), and to suggest better methods of analysis and strategies for coming to agreement. Rather, he is foreclosing the validity of any reading that does not agree with his own. Playing by his own rules in his own court of justice, Derrida demands absolute assent.

He did not receive this absolute assent, of course. Five of the six replies printed in *Critical Inquiry* were openly critical of his reasoning, his facts, and his method of dealing with the issues.[61] Most concentrated on matters related to the composition of the wartime journalism and the situation in Belgium during the Second World War. They correct and supplement the historical record, add new information that Derrida left out, or provide criticism of Derrida's exegetical techniques. Nowhere is the main target deconstruction; nowhere is the central concern contemporary literary theory. Only one response, the remarks by Jonathan Culler, objected to the *severity* Derrida exhibited toward de Man. Not coincidentally Culler himself has built a rather large part of his reputation on his books dealing with deconstruction.[62] Thus it is not surprising that he, like most other deconstructors, winds up parroting the party line: The policy of racism under National Socialism, he tells us, is the clearest case of "the deadly functioning of a culturally constructed binary opposition." We are urged to draw "on the resources of de Man's works" to combat Nazi totalitarianism. "His later writings offer some of the most powerful tools for combating ideologies with which he had earlier been complicitous."[63] Culler, like Norris and others, is particularly attracted to the later essays on aesthetic ideology, which now resonate, he claims, "also as a critique of the fascist tendencies he had known."[64] As I have stated above, the absence of any direct political reference speaks against this contention. But even if we are inclined to entertain this generous interpretation of de Man's "antifascist" phase, it may strike us as strange that it took him over thirty years to get around to dealing with such issues.

In his rebuttal Derrida finds only Culler's remarks "an honest reading."[65] All the other critics are dismissed by a venomous and abusive procedure that is at points disingenuous and condescending. Those who dared to criticize Derrida's interpretation, those who venture to object to his procedures and rhetoric, are termed, variously, "behind the times," "frightened," or "confused and dishonest"; their texts are "diatribes" written "with a pen dipped in venom," "monolithic," beyond "dishonesty and bad faith," characterized by "violence and mediocrity."[66] Derrida, having failed to bludgeon the critical community into concurring with his kangaroo court, resorts now to name-calling and undifferentiated hysterics. He compares his critics to "someone who says to you 'beat me so at least people see me or hear me crying and don't forget me.'"[67] He feigns concern for their psychological well-being: "I would even like (if only in order to avoid this spectacle) to help them free themselves from this frightened, painful, and truly excessive hatred."[68] He claims that he has "rarely read more abstract and logocentered texts, more enclosed within the prison house of language, then these."[69] And he maintains, against all evidence (has he read the work of all these critics?) that, without exception, they "understand nothing" about deconstruction. "I mean nothing, and this goes equally for them all."[70] One has the impression that Derrida has come unhinged in the heat of what he construes to be a life-and-death struggle. Paul de Man's war has become Derrida's war.

Two themes predominate in this vituperative rebuttal. The first is that the five critics (Culler is always an exception) have not bothered to read him. For this reason Derrida evidently does not feel obliged to reply to their individual objections. Instead he compiles what he labels a "Table of Concor(redun)dances" and a "Table of Discordances,"[71] which consist of page numbers from the "Critical Responses" and from his original text "Paul de Man's War." He does this, so he claims, because he does not want to repeat himself; if his critics had bothered to read his essay, then he would not need to reply at all. But the suggestion that he has anticipated all his critics' additional information as well as their objections is simply wrong. Particularly with regard to the alleged "Discordances" one finds that most of the passages he cites as answers to an allegedly careless critic's objections contain only the original contention that he or she objected to in the first place. For example, when Jon Wiener remarks that the phrase "vulgar antisemitism" cannot be interpreted as a criticism of antisemitism as vulgar, something both W. Wolfgang Holdheim and John Brenkman/Jules David Law note as well,[72] Derrida simply refers us to the place in his text where he originally postulated this absurd interpretation. At the place where Wiener questions Derrida's statement that the letter to Renato Poggioli was public and points out that several statements were misleading, Derrida counters by referring us to the clause "whether or not this letter speaks the whole truth" and to his farfetched argument that de Man's "modesty" prevented him from bringing up his wartime journalism. Almost every item on Derrida's list is not an anticipated answer to a careless critic, but in fact merely the citation of the passage to which this critic objected in the first place. Again Derrida seems to believe that if one reads what he has written, then there must be total agreement. The exhortation to "read me" translates into the imperative: "Agree with me!"

Actually it is Derrida, and not his critics, who commits obvious errors in reading. Since his failures to read are numerous, I will cite only three instances. (1) He asserts that Holdheim "takes aim" at a "standard deconstructionist practice."[73] What Holdheim considers a "standard deconstructionist practice" may or may not be one. Since Derrida apparently now claims to be the final arbiter of what is deconstruction and what is not, of what is a "deconstructionist practice" and what is not, of who understands deconstruction and who does not, I will not challenge his authority here. In fact, however, Holdheim does not "take aim at" the practice he considers deconstructionist; he does not object to it at all, but merely wonders why it could not be applied to the case of Paul de Man. He is simply asking why it should be illicit, simply because Derrida declares it illicit, to apply de Man's later reflections on "memory, mourning, and autobiography" to his earlier journalism. He does not "take aim" at this practice; on the contrary, he wants to adopt it for his own argument.[74] (2) Derrida objects to a conditional statement at the beginning of the essay by Brenkman and Law. They noted correctly that Derrida considers the "mode of philosophical and literary analysis embodied in his own and the later de Man's work" to be "a bulwark against totalitarianism, including fascism itself." They then wrote the following:

With these claims Derrida puts the prestige of deconstruction on the line: its political significance, its power to explain political and cultural conjunctures, and its capacity for self-understanding. If these remain staked on the procedures and outcomes of his account of "Paul de Man's War," the wager will be lost.[75]

Derrida makes the wager a quite different one:

Another respondent concentrates his [*sic*] whole argumentation around what is derisively called "the prestige of deconstruction"...and announces clearly that if one fails to clear de Man..., deconstruction would be definitively compromised and "the wager would be lost"(!).[76]

There is nothing derisive in Brenkman/Law's reference to "the prestige of deconstruction." Moreover, Brenkman and Law do not state anything about "clearing de Man" and about a compromise that would result from "failing to clear" him. Rather their statement can be read in two ways: as a simple condemnation of Derrida's procedures in the essay "Paul de Man's War" (their final sentence would mean something like "if this is the best result deconstruction can bring to these matters, then it is not worth much"), or as a true conditional (meaning something like "if we find in our analysis that the procedures of deconstruction have not been able to account for de Man in a fashion that is adequate, and the reader is persuaded by our account, then we may conclude that the contention of political superiority for deconstruction, claimed by Derrida, is disproven"). In neither case does it matter whether de Man is cleared, unless Derrida claims that this should have been the outcome of his own analysis, which he explicitly denies. Brenkman and Law demand simply that deconstruction be able to live up to the political claim Derrida has attributed to it. Derrida misreads this as a necessity to exculpate de Man. (3) Derrida misconstrues the following statement in Marjorie Perloff's response: "Derrida's own 'exercice du silence' on such issues [historical context of Belgium in 1942] raises some hard questions, not only about this particular text but about the turn the deconstructive project, originally so liberating, is now taking."[77] Derrida's comment: "For another respondent, the stakes are even more precise. It is a question of nothing less, *in conclusion and to conclude,* than of handing down a verdict while pretending to deplore 'the turn the deconstructive project, originally so liberating, is now taking.' As if what happened to de Man in 1940–42 could constitute a 'turn' or a 'turning' of the 'deconstructive project' in 1988!"[78] Again Derrida does not understand the words on the page. Perloff is attributing the "turn" not to de Man in the forties, but to Derrida's contrived defense of de Man in the eighties. She is concerned that Derrida's project, which she conceived as originally so liberating, has now degenerated into something else. Derrida is apparently as inept at understanding Perloff's criticism as he is at recognizing her compliment.

The second major theme of this rebuttal is the paranoid fear that all the respondents are really attacking deconstruction. Near the start of the essay we read "'deconstruction' is for them the threat, the common and public enemy. *This* war is the most urgent in their view." And twenty-five pages later Derrida is still repeating his wild claim: "the actual stakes, the enemy to be destroyed in these simulacra of trial proceedings, is doubtless not only and not principally the de Man of 1940–42, but 'the Deconstruction' of 1989."[79] No doubt a few of the six writers find deconstruction objectionable, unpersuasive, or uninteresting, just as a number of de Man's critics, before and after the revelations concerning his wartime journalism, found his procedures ahistorical, apolitical, and obscure.[80] But it is ludicrous for Derrida to maintain that opposition to deconstruction is behind these responses since repeatedly and almost exclusively they refer to logical and informational inadequacies in Derrida's arguments in "Paul de Man's War," and since the writers of these response rarely mention and never discuss the larger issues that surround the place of deconstruction in contemporary American criticism. Indeed, this aspect of Derrida's frenzied rebuttal redounds to his discredit. The irrationality and error of his remarks might be mitigated somewhat if we could read them as the heartfelt reaction of someone endeavoring to protect a dear and deceased friend whom he feels is being unfairly maligned in public. But it turns out that Derrida is more concerned, or at least just as concerned, with a petty defense of *his* school, of *his* philosophy, of *his* academic turf. Derrida frames his remarks with musings on how this affair might be read by a future investigator, an Ortwin de Graef reexamining the forgotten archives for his generation. He speculates that the hypothetical researcher will have trouble understanding the accusations. But it is just as likely that a future scholar, if she or he proves to be a more accurate reader than Derrida, will judge this a pathetic and disgraceful tirade by an arrogant and condescending man who feels that his cult of interpretation is on the wane. It is a pity that Derrida, whose deconstructive project was one of the most challenging and exciting academic events of the postwar years, found it necessary to debase himself and his project by engaging in such dubious tactics.[81]

Heidegger and the Anti-Humanist Argument

The second event that compelled deconstruction to consider more carefully its politics was the publication of Victor Farias' *Heidegger et le nazisme* in late 1987.[82] This book, which caused such a stir in French intellectual circles,[83] contains nothing startlingly new about Heidegger's relationship with National Socialism, but it does demonstrate that his involvement was more sustained and more enthusiastic than was previously thought. Heidegger's case, of course, is slightly different from de Man's. There has never been any dispute that he was a member of the party, that he lent his considerable prestige to the fascist cause when he became rector of the University of Freiburg in 1933, that he supported various principles of Nazi ideology in public speeches, and that he praised the "Führer" as the "Existenzprinzip" (principle of existence) and as the highest law. That the French were apparently so shocked by this information, all of which had been documented and discussed for decades, shows perhaps the political oblivion and the ideological naiveté in which supposedly sophisticated avant-garde theory has thrived for the past two-and-a-half decades. Where de Man and Heidegger were most similar, besides apparently in their basic political views for a time, was in their inability or unwillingness to come to terms with their rather dubious past activities. De Man, as we have learned, was not exactly forthcoming about his wartime journalism. Heidegger, for whom concealment was no longer a possibility, simply ignored the topic completely. His only sustained discussion of these controversial issues came in an interview that he gave on the condition it be published posthumously. In it he is obviously defensive and prevaricating.[84] These are neither the actions nor the words of a man with a clear conscience.

Heidegger, like de Man, avoided overtly political topics in his published works after the war. He exhibited no feelings of remorse or guilt for personal actions and, like most German intellectuals—Karl Jaspers is the great exception here—he evidently did not feel at all compelled to account for the horrific occurrences on the battlefield or in the concentration camps in terms of philosophical reflection. At the very least we can say that the war and the Holocaust were never the focus of sustained and direct attention in his postwar writings. One of the few documents we possess that gives an indication of his views on undoubtedly the most shocking aspect of National Socialist barbarity—the endeavor to annihilate European Jewry—is the correspondence with Herbert Marcuse in 1947 and 1948. Actually we have only two letters, both written by Marcuse, but from them one can easily infer Heidegger's remarks.[85] Marcuse met and spoke with Heidegger in Todtnauberg after the war, and in the first letter, dated 28 August 1947, he mentions issues that still trouble him from his visit. Specifically he expresses his disappointment and distress because his former teacher has never publicly disavowed his earlier ties to National Socialism. Heidegger evidently replied late in January of 1948. He appealed apparently to the difficulty of discussing these matters with those who themselves did not remain in Germany and experience National Socialism firsthand, but Marcuse correctly counters that the difficulty lies less in a possible incongruity of experience than in the Nazi's perversion of language and feelings, and the ready acceptance of this perversion by large sectors of the German population. What is most offensive and revealing about Heidegger's response, however, is his equation of the mass murder of the Jews with the allied policy toward Germans in Eastern countries, the so-called Ostdeutsche. With some justification Marcuse is enraged by Heidegger's disingenuous line of argument:

> With this proposition [equating the Holocaust to the treatment of the Eastern Germans] do you not stand outside of the dimension in which a discussion can still be conducted between human beings—outside of the logos? For only completely outside this "logical" dimension is it possible to explain, to excuse, to comprehend a crime by insisting others would have also done the same thing. Moreover, how is it possible to place the torture, maiming, and annihilation of millions of human beings on the same level with the forced relocation of groups when none of these horrible deeds occurred (save in some exceptional cases)? Today's world is such that the difference between inhumanity and humanity lies precisely in the difference between Nazi concentration camps and the deportations and internment camps of the postwar period.

Heidegger's arguments quite obviously followed an apologetic conservative line, and until recently, when an equally pernicious variation was picked up by Ernst Nolte, Andreas Hillgruber, and other conservatives in the "Historikerstreit" (historians' debate), such an apology for the attempted annihilation of the Jews was considered illicit in the public sphere.[86] What Marcuse's letters tell us therefore is that the man many tout as the foremost philosopher of the twentieth century was unable to cope with the most elementary ethical distinctions, and that, at least with regard to Germany and the Second World War, he himself was an illustration as well as the advocate of anti-Enlightenment thought and values.

As in the case of de Man, the central question here is what connection, if any, does Heidegger's politics have with his philosophy. The issue is perhaps a bit more complicated and momentous for two reasons: First, unlike de Man, whose life can be divided into a period of youthful mistakes and mature theoretical pronouncements, Heidegger held and acted upon repugnant political views at a time when he was in his philosophical prime. *Sein und Zeit (Being and Time),* the most important book of his early period, had appeared just six years before the assumption of his rectorship; *Kant und das Problem der Metaphysik (Kant and the Problem of Metaphysics)* was published in 1929. The *Einführung in die Metaphysik (Introduction to Metaphysics)* and *Ursprung des Kunstwerks (The Origin of the Work of Art)* are both products of the mid-thirties, and much of his writing on Nietzsche stems from lectures delivered to students during the Third Reich. In contrast to de Man's oeuvre, there is no significant hiatus separating a politicized, journalistic phase and a more serious, reflected philosophical stance. Second, despite the wide respect de Man enjoyed in critical circles in the United States, his influence is in no way comparable to Heidegger's. Indeed, it is fair to say that French philosophy from the middle of the twentieth century—and by extension recent developments in Western theory that include de Man's work—is unthinkable without him. Thus if Heidegger's work is somehow politically implicated in conservative or even fascist ideological movements, we might feel compelled to reexamine a good deal of what has been written under his considerable influence, and to try at the very least to determine how and whether politically dangerous tendencies have been incorporated. Some of this reexamination could rely on work that has already been done in Germany. The political implications of Heidegger's philosophy, including its possible connection with National Socialism, have been dealt with in some detail by Alexander Schwan, Theodor Adorno, Robert Minder, Jürgen Habermas, and Hugo Ott.[87] Even if Farias had not provided additional evidence for his proximity to fascism, it would behoove us to renew our interest in these studies and in general to take more seriously the ramifications of the seemingly abstract turn to ontology and the search for a realm of more fundamental being.

Although adherents and friends of deconstruction have not turned primarily to the sources I suggested, many have been extremely concerned about Heidegger's politics. This is especially true for the French and for those American deconstructors who have a more philosophical inclination. In the late eighties Heidegger's involvement with National Socialism was treated directly or indirectly in books by Derrida, Lacoue-Labarthe, and Jean-François Lyotard, and each of these short monographs was dutifully rendered into English shortly thereafter. *Critical Inquiry* devoted a large part of an issue in the winter of 1989 to a "Symposium on Heidegger and Nazism,"[88] and in the same year *Diacritics* published a double issue on the question of Heidegger on art and politics.[89] The French Heidegger controversy also prompted responses in several other journals, both from critics who aligned themselves with deconstruction or with Heideggerianism and from those who were critical of these directions. Articles on this topic could even be found in popular magazines and newspapers. Most recently a German documentation and commentary of Heidegger's involvement in National Socialism appeared in English translation.[90] Thus, although in the United States the Heidegger affair did not have the shock value it did in France, nor did the response take on the proportions it did in Europe, it has hardly gone unnoticed.

To some degree, however, deconstructors in this country were reticent to understand the attack on Heidegger's politics as in any way related to the deconstructive project. This sentiment is expressed most succinctly perhaps in the course of the de Man controversy by J. Hillis Miller. Replying to Jon Wiener, who placed Heidegger as the "intellectual progenitor" of deconstruction, Miller maintains that "the facts are far otherwise. Both de Man and Derrida have been consistently, carefully, patiently critical of what Heidegger says. Heidegger has been one of the major targets of so-called 'deconstruction,' not its progenitor."[91] The ability to excise Heidegger from the deconstructive project, to make him exclusively an object of its criticism, rather than its most important philosophical source, inspiration, and dialogic partner is a peculiarity of the American reception of deconstruction and thus a consequence of the crossing of borders to which this book is dedicated. In France, deconstruction was conceived primarily as a philosophical project that has ramifications for all texts, including literary texts. All the main French figures associated with it in this country—I am thinking of Derrida, Lacoue-Labarthe, Nancy, and Lyotard—consider themselves philosophers and are concerned institutionally not with literary studies, but with the place of philosophy in the French educational system. Imported into the United States, however, deconstruction becomes a "literary theory" in the eyes of most of its American practitioners. The Yale School consisted solely of professors of French,

English, and comparative literature, and outside of a few maverick philosophers on the margins of the discipline in the States, deconstruction has been fairly invisible in that area of knowledge.

One of the results of this reception is that the philosophical roots of deconstruction, which may be found in the critique of the phenomenological tradition, have been largely ignored. In particular, the relationship to Heidegger, who himself plays an ambivalent role in phenomenology and whose relationship to this tradition altered from the appearance of *Sein und Zeit* in the late 1920s to the works of the 1950s, has been given short shrift in most American discussions. There are some notable exceptions to this rule. Gayatri Spivak's excellent introduction to the English version of *Grammatology* demonstrates in a number of areas Derrida's indebtedness to Heidegger, and Rodolphe Gasché's work, in particular in *The Tain of the Mirror*, emphasizes that an adequate understanding of the deconstructive project cannot be achieved without a grasp of Heideggerian thought.[92] Perhaps it is not insignificant that both these critics are themselves rooted in foreign traditions, especially since the most popular introductions to deconstruction published in the English-speaking world have played down this connection. Typically misleading on the connection between Heidegger and deconstruction is Jonathan Culler's *On Deconstruction*, in which Heidegger is mentioned only a half dozen times in passing. Culler's central concern, like those of the Yale School and its disciples, appears to be reading, in particular the reading of literary texts; the relationship between deconstruction and continental philosophy is a matter of secondary importance. This philosophically impoverished notion of deconstruction, which has come to predominate in the American understanding of the term, is contradicted by French and German proponents, as well as opponents, of deconstruction. Whether one refers to Vincent Descombes, who sees Derrida's early work as a "radicalization of phenomenology," or Luc Ferry and Alain Renaut, who place Heidegger's thought at the very center of the philosophical efforts of the sixty-eighters;[93] or whether one turns to Jürgen Habermas, who sees in Derrida a continuation of Heideggerianism, or Manfred Frank, who likewise believes that deconstruction is an outgrowth of a particular reading of Heidegger's thought;[94] there is general continental agreement on the link between the philosopher of *Dasein* and the inaugurator of deconstruction.[95] Indeed, the fact that Heidegger's notion of *Destruktion* appears in Derrida's *De l'esprit* as *déconstruction*,[96] or that Lacoue-Labarthe asserts the "indissociable" connection between "the question of Being" and "the project of deconstruction," discloses the Heideggerian connection at the very origin of Derrida's philosophical project.[97]

The American conception of deconstruction as a strategy for churning out new interpretations of novels and poetry, or for examining the rhetoric and meaning in literary texts, may explain why the Heidegger controversy was of less consequence than the de Man affair in the United States, while the reverse was true in the French public sphere. It may also serve to clarify the nature of the discussions around Heidegger's politics in *Critical Inquiry* and in *Diacritics.* In the former journal Arnold I. Davidson collects texts from some of the major commentators on the Heidegger affair. A short piece by Gadamer and a translation of Habermas' introduction to the Farias book are the German contributions, while a few sections from Derrida's *De l'esprit* and three newspaper articles by Maurice Blanchot, Lacoue-Labarthe, and Emmanuel Levinas, respectively, constitute the French reaction. The only piece by a non-European is Davidson's introductory remarks. That the debate around National Socialism was really a European affair is also confirmed by the essays in *Diacritics.* Although the issue appeared almost two years after Farias' book was published, most of the contributors do not refer to this book, nor to any of the German sources I cited above. Examining the Works Cited lists for these essays is instructive. Besides references to Heidegger, the most frequently cited author was Derrida. The books by Derrida, Lyotard, and Lacoue-Labarthe are all subjects of lengthy review, while the most sustained reference to Farias occurs in a review by Lacoue-Labarthe, which appeared as an article in *Le journal littéraire* and as an appendix in his *La fiction du politique.* Ott's authoritative monograph is cited only once; the books by Schwan and Adorno are ignored entirely; and the only time Habermas' name surfaces is in a ridiculous attempt to uncover latent anti-Jewish prejudice in his critique of Derrida.[98] Here the European nature of the debate on Heidegger and politics is narrowed to a particular French perspective that is itself under the influence of Heidegger's thought. Dissenting voices—as authors of reviews, as authors of books reviewed, and even as authors of books cited—are diacritically excluded from consideration.

Deconstruction obviously did have something at stake in the question of Heidegger and his National Socialist background. Although the standard deconstructive line on Heidegger is that he never escapes the metaphysical tradition that is the object of his "destruction," for the French in particular his thought is foundational for deconstructive strategies. For this reason we find some of the same defensive and offensive strategies in the discussions of the Heidegger affair that we encountered in the apologies for de Man. Derrida, for example, repeats his exaggerated claims that the thrust of criticism in the Heidegger affair was directed not against Heidegger himself, but against (1) the reading of Heidegger and (2) those directions in philosophy that are indebted to Heidegger, in particular deconstruction.[99] "It was not only, but it also was, rather evidently, a question of banning the reading of Heidegger and of exploiting what was believed to be a strategic advantage, in France, in France above all, against all thought that took Heidegger seriously, even if in a critical or deconstructive mode."[100] These contentions are preposterous. In all of the critiques of Heidegger I have read not a single author suggests that we should cease reading and discussing Heidegger's works, and, as usual, Derrida produces no evidence that anyone ever advocated such a ludicrous prohibition. Furthermore, although there are occasional, albeit not very credible, connections made between Heidegger's politics and deconstructive politics, I have seen no substantive argument invoked that would discredit those philosophical directions influenced by Heidegger's thought. Such an attempt would be unserious and foolhardy. As Derrida himself points out, it would involve discrediting most philosophy in the twentieth century, and I would add not only and not primarily deconstruction but directions in hermeneutics, critical theory, and marxism that would include such writers as Hans-Georg Gadamer, Herbert Marcuse, Jean-Paul Sartre, and Lucien Goldman. The point here, however, is that there is no endeavor to ban Heidegger and all thought influenced by him. The threats imputed to these enemies of thought in general and of Derrida's philosophy in particular are either figments of a paranoid imagination or defensive strategies to protect the inviolably sacred turf of deconstruction. As in the de Man apology, the desired effect of the straw-man technique employed by Derrida is to foreclose genuine debate on issues and to secure a rhetorical advantage.

Jean-François Lyotard resorts to similarly questionable strategies in his account of Heidegger that appeared in *Heidegger et "les Juifs."* Perhaps most disturbing is his insistence that we follow four rules that he deems appropriate in any discussion of Heidegger's National Socialism. If we do not adhere to them, he suggests, then our comments are illicit. We have to admit (1) that Heidegger is one of the great thinkers of our century, (2) that his thought has been compromised in a nontrivial manner by his involvement with National Socialism, (3) that we do not invoke rule (1) to cancel rule (2), or vice versa, and (4) that we neither separate his politics from his philosophy nor connect them precipitously.[101] Like Derrida in his discussion of the de Man affair, Lyotard would have us accept a priori what he should be trying to prove with analysis and argument. That Heidegger is one of the greatest thinkers of our century *based on the impact of his philosophy* is beyond dispute. But that we should be prohibited from reevaluating his greatness in light of his politics, his personal life, or historical changes is a ridiculous and dogmatic proposition. Similarly we should not be enjoined from making any connections between Heidegger's philosophy and his politics. What is called for is not a set of regulations by which only Lyotard can offer a proper and correct explanation of these difficult relations, but arguments based on a careful reading of texts and a thorough knowledge of the local and historical circumstances in which Heidegger acted. Lyotard may want to argue that we should not confound Heidegger's thought with his politics because "a thought exceeds its contexts,"[102] but his interdiction of bringing them together and his penchant for mitigating the complicity of Heidegger's texts with claims of influence and greatness bring his thought dangerously close to the apologetic strategies that marked too much of the debate around de Man.

Both Lyotard and Derrida are in fundamental agreement about the way to understand Heidegger's philosophy and politics, but this peculiarly deconstructive understanding is articulated most cogently in the work of a third philosopher whose book on Heidegger has been well received in deconstructive circles. Philippe Lacoue-Labarthe's *Heidegger, Art and Politics* was conceived prior to the Farias affair as an endeavor to come to terms with Heidegger's politically repugnant actions. To his credit Lacoue-Labarthe refuses to attribute Heidegger's commitment to National Socialism to "a failing or a sudden loss of vigilance, or even, more seriously, to the pressure of a thinking as yet insufficiently disengaged from metaphysics."[103] Although he does not invoke this argument, which has become a commonplace among Heidegger's supporters, he does contend that Heidegger recognized his error in 1934 and considered Nazism as a continuation of precisely what he thought it should fight against. Citing other European intellectuals of the left and right who became politically active during the thirties, Lacoue-Labarthe asserts that it is Heidegger's "merit" to "have succumbed for only ten months to this Janus-headed illusion of 'new times.'"[104] Such an argument, which lumps the struggle for socialism together with the support of fascism, shows an inordinate amount of respect for Heidegger's own apologetic explanations and would have to be revised on the basis of evidence presented in Farias' book. More disturbing than Lacoue-Labarthe's penchant for taking Heidegger at his word, however, is the manner in which he explains Heidegger's acceptance of certain distasteful features of National Socialism: "Heidegger overestimated Nazism and probably wrote off as merely incidental certain things which were already in evidence before 1933 to which he was, in fact, staunchly opposed: anti-semitism, ideology ('politicizied science') and peremptory brutality."[105] Even if we accept that Heidegger opposed all of these "incidental" features of Nazism—it is, of course, a matter of considerable dispute whether Heidegger was "staunchly opposed" to antisemitism—this explanation misses the political point. It is precisely Heidegger's willingness to buy into a system and a party that vocally and uninhibitedly supported these "incidentals" that defines his ethical and political values. That other intellectuals did likewise is not a serious argument for Heidegger's "merit." To reach an understanding of Heidegger's politics we are not best served if we are directed away from the education and intellectual climate that allowed Heidegger and so many others to ignore these "incidentals." Rather, we can reach a better understanding of political alternatives, as Heidegger lived and practiced them, only if we view much of his work during the thirties as the philosophical expression of a much larger, conservative, and elite German mandarin stratum.[106] Heidegger's ability to place the most uncomfortable and repugnant features of Nazism at the margins (if he was indeed opposed to them at all) is not unimportant, but rather the very essence of a politics that he shared with many of his conservative contemporaries.

Let me be fair to Lacoue-Labarthe. Although he does not pursue a line of investigation that seeks to foreground those elements of conservative education and ideology that could explain Heidegger's involvement with National Socialism, neither does he agree that the matters Heidegger "probably" considered marginal were, in fact, incidental to the Third Reich. His argument is rather that antisemitism was essential to Nazism and that Heidegger committed himself to this form of racism when he joined the party and became rector at Freiburg. But Lacoue-Labarthe does not propose that racism and National Socialism were fundamentally linked in order to demonstrate that Heidegger was at fault for lending his prestige to the fascist cause. He agrees instead with Hannah Arendt, who postulated that many of the people who supported fascism were caught in their own intellectual constructions of what fascism was and did not promote in any direct fashion the final outcome of war and Shoah. Heidegger is criticized, rather, for his failure to confront the situation in retrospect, for his refusal to discuss and analyze the events to which he indirectly contributed. Referring to the notorious comparison Heidegger drew between the Holocaust and the "motorized food industry," Lacoue-Labarthe voices his most severe criticism of Heidegger: "The fact that Heidegger was not even able, nor probably even wished to state this difference [between the mass extermination of the Jews and the agricultural industry] is what is strictly—and eternally—intolerable."[107] And later on in his book, he reiterates this sentiment: Heidegger's "silence after the war—his silence on the Extermination—is unpardonable."[108] Lacoue-Labarthe thus locates the failure of Heidegger not in action before the war, but in reflection during postwar years; not in an inability to think through consequences, but in an inability to account for what occurred; not in an insensitivity to the dignity and humanity of other living beings, but in a neglect of proper commemoration for the dead.

What connects Lacoue-Labarthe's text with other deconstructive treatments of Heidegger's politics is not his condemnation of postwar silence, a criticism that he uniquely stresses, but rather three features that repeatedly emerge in the course of his argument. The first is the leveling of differences among various political phenomena in the twentieth century. We have already seen that Lacoue-Labarthe freely mixes leftist and fascist commitment in his discussion of Heidegger's "merit," and from the remarks at the beginning of his seventh chapter it appears that he has adopted from Arendt her outdated totalitarianism thesis.[109] Citing Brecht and Benjamin's insistence on a "politicization of art" to counter the Nazi "aestheticization of politics," Lacoue-Labarthe brings their slogan into the proximity of the "politicized science" that Heidegger opposed in his rectorial address. Politicization, he claims, "is the starting point of 'totalitarian logic,' from which absolutely no one seems to have been immune during this period."[110] This accords fairly well with Derrida, whose stated goal in *De l'esprit* was to demonstrate the commonalities of National Socialism and anti–National Socialism.[111] Indeed, this leveling extends beyond the comparison of extreme right and left. Both Lacoue-Labarthe and Derrida suggest that liberal democracy and, indeed, all intermediate political forms are "mirror images" (Derrida). This judgment is made from the perspective of "the Age of Technology,"[112] in other words from the perspective of a Heideggerian analysis of the state of the world. The problem with this view is that it vitiates most of the distinctions that really matter for politics as they have been and are practiced by human beings on this planet. Thus while we might want to agree with Lacoue-Labarthe that we should not validate liberal democracy simply because "we do not have (too many) police breathing down our necks" or because "our labour is not (too) exploited,"[113] this does not mean that *from a political perspective* liberal democracy can be equated with socialism, communism, fascism, and racism. That some liberal democrats, some Jews, and some fascists have all made racist statements does not mean that all are equally implicated in one monolithic racist ideology.[114] Lacoue-Labarthe (and the rest of the Heideggerians, both orthodox and critical) can suggest such a leveling because he accepts the *philosophically based* notion of humanism that Heidegger propounded after the war. Indeed, perhaps the most perverse and significant moment of Lacoue-Labarthe's zeal for leveling political difference is his thesis that "Nazism is a humanism."[115] Only from the totalized philosophical perspective of an abstract Heideggerianism does this statement make any sense. As a political statement, however, it is an absurdity that, as far as I can see, only dogmatic Heideggerians subscribe to. With this thesis it is obvious why deconstruction has been unable to offer a viable political analysis of both the de Man and the Heidegger affair. For all the things that affect people in their daily lives, for all the struggles that have been carried out against oppression and fascism, for the lived reality of the twentieth century, deconstruction is simply unable to supply analyses that matter.

At the same time that deconstruction levels political differences it elevates philosophy, in particular Heidegger's philosophy, above other types of discourse. Deconstructors take their lead, as usual, from Heidegger himself, who always sought to separate himself from "vulgar" Nazis. Lyotard reproduces Heidegger's derogatory statement concerning National Socialist leaders—"Diese Leute waren viel zu unbedarft im Denken" (these people were much too impoverished in their thinking)—and uses it as evidence for Heidegger's distance from the Nazi party. Heidegger was not like Krieck, Rosenberg, or Goebbels, who were all flagrant propagandists; his error consisted in believing that a genuine thinker like himself could become part of the political vanguard.[116] Lacoue-Labarthe also emphasizes the distance between "the greatest thinker of our age,"[117] evidently a nondisputable fact for him, and the Nazi regime he came to represent. Thus the "truth of Nazism," or at least what Heidegger considers its truth (as expounded in the 1935 lectures on metaphysics), is valid and defensible for Lacoue-Labarthe. Heidegger, indeed, recognized his mistake in 1934, he contends: "Not about the truth of Nazism, but about its reality." The philosophy of the man who is "incontestably the greatest thinker of the age"[118] must be divorced from and elevated above the crude reality of Nazism. We cannot understand Heidegger by comparison with Nazi hacks; we must rise "to the level of Heidegger's questioning," to regions that are above and beyond the common multitude. The deception in this elevation strategy is that there are half-truths in it: Heidegger as a "philosopher" is in no way comparable to the Nazi demagogues, and he probably did not want the same things they wanted. Nor was his vision of the party, of Germany, of the West, of the possibilities for the future, identical to that of most party propaganda. His superiority in intellect, however, should make him more, and not less, culpable. Others with less intellect, but more political sense and courage, were able to see through National Socialism without much effort. Moreover, Heidegger was not the only person whose visions were not matched by the reality of the Nazi regime. Many adherents to the party were neither antisemites, nor warmongers. Each person had different, sometimes contradictory, reasons for supporting Hitler's regime. To portray Heidegger's *political* motives as any better than those of his compatriots, to validate the philosophical daydream of Heidegger's National Socialism, is to engage in a form of apologetic discourse that exculpates the intellectual elite, that validates the superior spirit, the preeminence of *Geist*.

The third feature found in the deconstructive discussion of Heidegger is exclusion and exclusivity. As in the defense of de Man, Heidegger is found to be the only real source for achieving an understanding of his own fascist ties. Other approaches to him are dismissed as complicit with metaphysics or humanism; they are therefore invalid since they putatively repeat the very ideological stance they are invoked to refute. Paradoxically this feature is the only one that does not have direct support in Heidegger's own statements. The leveling of ideologies of left, right, and center, the view of all thought since the Greeks as metaphysical and humanist, and the elevation of Heidegger's own utterances above those of Nazi rabble are derived from the texts of the philosopher himself. But Heidegger, unlike his deconstructive disciples, never applied his philosophy to his own (mis)deeds; nor did he ever seek to explain fascism in terms of his own thought. For orthodox deconstruction, however, there is apparently no other legitimate approach to these matters. Derrida, for example, reaches an understanding of Heidegger's momentary slip into "spiritual" and metaphysical thought through a careful consideration of what Heidegger himself had to say about "spirit" *(Geist)* before and after his fascist interlude. And Lyotard, in a shameless comparison recalling Felman's likening of de Man and Primo Levi in the de Man debate, brings Heidegger's notion of *Andenken an das Vergessene* (Remembrance of what has been forgotten) into the proximity of Elie Wiesel.[119]

It is again Lacoue-Labarthe, however, who states the deconstructive line most openly and emphatically. We have seen that all along he, like Derrida and Lyotard to varying degrees, depends on arguments drawn from Heidegger to bolster his interpretations and contentions. In two places he makes his dependence on Heidegger more explicit. (1) At the start of his eighth chapter he embarks on a discussion of the topos of the aestheticization of politics, a thesis propounded most prominently by Walter Benjamin in the thirties. His argument for the necessity of consulting Heidegger depends on a radicalization of Benjamin, on an idiosyncratic notion of fascism as "the *truth* of the political." There is, Lacoue-Labarthe contends, an "unseverable link between art and politics"; "the political ('religion') is the truth of art." Because Heidegger is seen as the thinker who dealt with the nature of art most profoundly, he is the most insightful for an analysis of fascism. "Heidegger, in so far as his project in the 1930s explicitly consists in 'overcoming' aesthetics, gives a privileged access—and perhaps the only possible access—to the essence of the political that is simultaneously veiled and unveiled by National Socialism."[120] (2) Toward the close of his book Lacoue-Labarthe entertains the thought that Heidegger's writings could be classified as "archi-fascist." Despite appearances, this is in no way a suggestion that Heidegger's thought is in some way complicit with National Socialism. Rather, Lacoue-Labarthe maintains that an understanding of Heidegger as "archi-fascist" is possible only if fascism is emptied of its biologism and racism, and only if the *archi* is understood in a nonmetaphysical sense. One wonders what all this really means. Lacoue-Labarthe appears to be proposing that if fascism is nonracist and nonmetaphysical (and thus *antifascist* in the binary Heideggerian/deconstructive scheme), then Heidegger was indeed an archi-fascist. *Archi* comes to mean *anti*, except that this "archi/anti" cannot be recuperated into the logic that informs all the other fascisms and antifascisms. What remains certain for Lacoue-Labarthe then is that Heidegger broke definitively with National Socialism after his Rectorship (a fact disproven by Farias), and that this break coincides with the abandonment of ontology and the "determination of Nazism's truth." After the notorious *Kehre* or "turn" in Heidegger's thought, the philosopher reached insights that are essential for an understanding of fascism: Heidegger "taught us to think philosophically, what fascism, plain and simple, is about.... Who in our age has said so much of such 'profundity' on fascism—and consequently on our 'world'?"[121] "Who in our age has said so much nonsense about fascism?" we are tempted to retort. Lacoue-Labarthe would have us believe that the person who proudly wore his party pin in 1936 (after his major essay on art), who never publicly or privately renounced National Socialism and his involvement with it, and who never in the postwar period reflected directly on the most horrific consequences of Germany's fascist regime is the only reliable source for a comprehension of his own involvement with Nazism and of Nazism as a European phenomenon. Such a conclusion can be maintained only by someone who has already and without critical questioning accepted the major propositions of the very philosophy which Heidegger's fascist proclivities should compel us to rethink.

In contrast to the de Man affair, the deconstructive discussion of Heidegger in the United States has been represented most forcefully by translations from the French, rather than by native contributions. Most American deconstructors failed to involve themselves with Heidegger's relationship to National Socialism, either because it seemed irrelevant to the deconstructive project, or because it had been adequately treated by their more philosophically inclined French colleagues. Perhaps the most interesting contribution that originated on this side of the Atlantic comes from William V. Spanos, a Heideggerian whose relationship to deconstruction has been somewhat ambiguous. Spanos is more of a "pure" Heideggerian than adherents of deconstruction. He continues to advocate Heidegger's original project outlined in *Being and Time,* which, as Spanos conceives it, involves the retrieval of "the temporality of being (the differences that temporality disseminates), which the representational (metaphysical/aesthetic) discourse and practice of the Occident, especially in the wake of the Enlightenment, had virtually spatialized/reified."[122] Spanos' difference from deconstruction is thus a difference conceived within Heideggerianism, and for the most part he adheres to tenets that are usually associated with critical or dissident Heideggerians. His brand of Heideggerianism might be best characterized by an insistence that the seminal insights deconstruction has attained were already part of Heidegger's project, even though Heidegger himself at times fell short of his own standards. Thus, although he originally conceived of his renewal of "destructive criticism" as a rival for deconstruction, the differences between these two Heideggerian offsprings are fewer than their shared premises and strategies.[123]

Perhaps because he relies more directly on Heidegger than do his deconstructive colleagues, Spanos' discussion is more openly apologetic. He employs, of course, the rhetorical strategy of conceding "at once and in no uncertain terms" that Heidegger was guilty of a "lapse in human sensitivity."[124] His "no uncertain terms" return later in his essay when he admits Heidegger's "indefensible callousness to the enormity of both the calculated barbarism of the Nazis' program to exterminate the Jews and of the unspeakable human suffering that was its consequence."[125] Spanos does not intend to produce, he insists, the "flagrantly reductive project of exonerating Heidegger's discourse and practice in the period of the Rectorship and after,"[126] as orthodox Heideggerians such as Jean Beaufret, François Fedier, and Gérard Granel have done. But these concessions are surrounded by such a consistently defensive argument that they lose all persuasive force. Like Derrida in the de Man affair, Spanos devotes most of his efforts and argumentation to excusing Heidegger's words and deeds. Framed as an attack against Arnold I. Davidson's presentation of different positions in the *Critical Inquiry* symposium, Spanos' response to the Heidegger affair, despite his occasional disclaimers, places him squarely in the apologetic camp.

In his lengthy, eighty-page essay this apology takes many paths and many forms, and my treatment of Spanos' arguments here must therefore remain partial. Particularly troubling is the reasoning and evidence he employs to defend Heidegger's initial involvement with the National Socialists. In retrospect, Spanos admits, the decision to join the Nazi cause "seems unpardonably reactionary." At the time, he continues, Heidegger's allegiances are "quite understandable, if not very wise."[127] Citing the notorious passage from the *Introduction to Metaphysics* concerning Germany's position "in a pincer" between American capitalism and socialist bureaucratism, Spanos utilizes the familiar elevating strategy to make Heidegger's motives seem at least philosophically legitimate. Heidegger was interested in the fate of the world in the face of the onslaught of technology, we are told; he was advocating not a German nationalism, but a return to the pre-Socratic Greeks. This is a pleasant story, but it is one that lacks attention to historical context. The facts are that Heidegger's depiction of Germany as the "nation in the middle" had been a conservative and reactionary topos for decades. The only thing "genial" about his version is the philosophical dressing he provides for what was customarily considered direct right-wing propaganda. Similarly his discussions of technology, as both Jeffrey Herf and Michael E. Zimmerman have shown,[128] were drawn largely from well-worn conservative thought of the Weimar era. Nor can we agree with Spanos' contention that "many other leading European intellectuals besides Heidegger, both of the right and the left, either succumbed to the lure of a national socialism or found little in National Socialism to resist."[129] The only list of these leading European intellectuals that Spanos produces is taken from Lacoue-Labarthe's leveling discourse mentioned above. It includes Hamsun, Benn, Pound, Blanchot, Drieu, and Brasillach.[130] This is a rather meager offering. Again the facts are very different. Although many university professors in Germany supported the fascists, they were usually among the mediocre.[131] The foremost intellectuals of Germany and of Europe, including most of the left, either opposed National Socialism or remained neutral. As evidence for this we need only remember that the Hitler regime was responsible for the decimation of German scholarship and the arts; it was enthusiastically supported by only a few stellar personalities, and unfortunately Heidegger was one of them. One can better explain Heidegger's attraction to Nazism on the basis of his mandarin background and his conservative, antidemocratic, antisocialist proclivities. But such an explanation for reprehensible allegiances is very different from the sympathetic understanding Spanos advocates.[132]

The bulk of Spanos' essay deals not with Heidegger's "understandable" commitment to National Socialism, however, but rather with the single public remark he made about the destruction of European Jewry. I have already referred to it above in connection with Lacoue-Labarthe, but since Spanos devotes so much energy and space to it, it should be quoted in its entirety. The occasion for this remark was a lecture from 1949:

> Agriculture is now a mechanized food industry. As for its essence, it is the same thing as the manufacture of corpses in the gas chambers or the death camps, the same thing as blockades and reduction of countries to famine, the same thing as the manufacture of hydrogen bombs.[133]

The statement is obviously shocking. It appears that incommensurate items are being equated, and for a German, only four years after the war, to compare the Holocaust with agricultural methods is surely callous at the very least. Lacoue-Labarthe discusses this passage extensively in his book, criticizing Heidegger's comparison by pointing to the singularity of the Holocaust. Davidson adds a tone of moral reproach. Spanos will have none of this. He concedes a "remarkable insensitivity," but sets out to defend the validity of the statement. This can be accomplished, of course, rather easily. If we emphasize the phrase "as for its essence," and add a dose of Heidegger's philosophical reflections on humanism and technology, then all of these seemingly unequal items could be considered similar. Spanos does this as follows:

> The essence, if not the worldly manifestation, of this relay of violent practices is the same. However unevenly materialized and distributed its worldly manifestations at any historically specific time and place in Modernity, they are the consequences of the *technologization* or alternatively the *reification* of the temporality of being, the process, that is, which Heidegger discovers to be intrinsic to the discursive practices of humanism.[134]

The problem with this reading, which would no doubt accord well with Heidegger's intentions, is that it makes the notion of essence and manifestation rather trivial. If everything, from methods of agriculture to gas chambers, from moral reproaches to Nazi propaganda, from liberal democracy to fascism, from antifascist humanism to racism, is a manifestation of some megalo-essence, then meaningful debate and meaningful political practices have ceased.

Even Spanos, however, is ultimately not satisfied with this simplistic (and totalized) view of a technologized essence and its protean manifestations. A large part of his essay is therefore devoted to the task of proving that the worldly manifestations of this essence have more in common than precipitous critics have conceded. This is not easily accomplished. Blockades are indeed tactics used to pressure a country to capitulate on some demand, and if the country being blockaded does not do so, it may be reduced to famine, and human life may be lost. But the result of many blockades, such as the Berlin blockade, to which Spanos believes Heidegger was referring, is not the loss of human life, but rather a negotiated settlement between the country initiating the blockade and the country blockaded. This is obviously not the outcome of the "manufacture of corpses in the gas chambers," where the result was death, and the strategic or tactical value was nil. The manufacture of the hydrogen bomb could also have led to the loss of life—if the bomb had been used. But although Spanos produces numerous instances of bombings—from the fire bombing of Dresden to the atomic bombing of Hiroshima and Nagasaki—this is not what Heidegger's comparison mentions by name. Heidegger spoke specifically about a specific type of bomb, the hydrogen bomb, which served as a deterrent in numerous cases during the postwar era, but which was never employed as a weapon. And he speaks of not its employment, but only its *manufacture*. It is difficult to see the mere manufacturing of a weapon, no matter how horrible, as commensurate with the intentional annihilation of human beings. Finally, Spanos takes us to Vietnam in a farfetched attempt to convince us that the exportation of American agricultural methods into this country was tantamount to mass murder. After pages of description of how the United States shamelessly laid waste to the countryside of Vietnam, a genocidal action that is in fact comparable to the "manufacturing of corpses in the gas chambers," he puts forth the incredible proposition that "the introduction of IR 8, the higher-yielding and faster-growing...rice strain," shows the "essential continuity" between misguided agricultural assistance and military intervention.[135] But this is patently absurd. The United States has given similar agricultural aid to many countries without bombing their civilian populations. Certainly we might be able to hypothesize that certain forms of aid have evidenced an insensitivity to foreign cultures, and no one wants to minimize the violation that often accompanies this insensitivity. But who could place this on the same level, or mention this in the same breath, with direct and calculated murder. If these are the kinds of distinctions Heideggerians, replying on the wisdom of their mentor, are incapable of drawing, then they ought to be questioning the value of their philosophical outlook for practical and political action—not the humanism of critics.

Perhaps the most interesting aspect of Spanos' essay is not his defense of Heideggerian antihumanism, but his attempt to rewrite the history of the Vietnam war and the opposition to this war in terms of poststructuralism. In a sweeping gesture typical of the totalizing discourse that speaks incessantly in the name of nontotalization Spanos equates metaphysics, ethnocentricity, and racism. United States involvement in Southeast Asia is ultimately a sign of our metaphysical proclivities; our destruction of Vietnamese villages a consequence of humanism; our murder, torture, and rape of the Vietnamese an essentially humanist activity. The Vietnamese, on the other hand, are proto-poststructuralists. According to Spanos we were annoyed by their tactics of guerrilla warfare because we, trapped in our metaphysical narratives, expected direct confrontation, not "the differential nomadic counter-strategy of the NLF [National Liberation Front] and NVA [North Vietnamese Army]."[136] We were confused and frustrated "by the enemy's decentered 'invisibility.'"[137] Indeed, the Vietnamese were the real-life counterpart of absolute difference, never allowing us to accomplish our metaphysically constituted battle strategies: "It was...the subversion of their inscribed assumption of presence and desire for and expectation of *closure*—the resolution of the narrative that promised decisive victory—that, after 1965, provoked the full fury of American technology against all the Vietnamese."[138] The philosophical and the military battlefield are made to correspond here, recalling the "slippage" so characteristic of deconstructive marxism, and so it is only fitting that the home front is conceived as a struggle between ethnocentric/liberal/metaphysical humanists and a heroic battalion of Heideggerian disciples. Confronting the "liberal humanist establishment" of Robert McNamara, McGeorge Bundy, William Bundy, Walt Rostow, and John McNaughton[139] was the antihumanist, anti-anthropological contingent "enabled in some degree or other by Heidegger's interrogation." By name Spanos mentions Derrida, Lacan, Althusser, Foucault, Lyotard, and Kristeva. All of them "got their historically specific impetus in the period of the Vietnam War."[140] And this incessant need to dichotomize the world in terms of Heideggerian categories is also extended into the present. Davidson, whose evenhanded introduction to the Heidegger dossier is criticized for not mentioning the Vietnamese, has to bear the full brunt of Spanos' fulminations. His "project" joins not only the conservative critique of William Bennett and Allan Bloom, and the "revisionary representations of the Vietnam war in film, video, fiction, and journalistic writing," but also "the State's neo-colonial initiative in the Third World, especially in Latin American and the Middle East, that threatens to repeat the pattern of American involvement in Vietnam."[141]

Like Derrida in his defense of de Man, Spanos has come slightly unwound here. His Heideggerianism is so firm and so dogmatic that he is unable to register crucial political distinctions and make coherent arguments. The Vietnamese struggle against the United States was surely not a manifestation of antihumanism, but, on the level of doctrines, a product of two ideologies firmly tied to what Spanos labels the humanist tradition: nationalism and socialism. One need only read the statements of the Vietnamese to confirm this. Just as surely one can state that the political morals of Heidegger's texts would not necessarily lead one to oppose oppression in the "third world." As evidence for this we need only turn to Heidegger himself, who to my knowledge never went on record for any non-European liberation movement (nor any liberation movement at all). Nor for that matter did any of his most prominent German followers. Furthermore, that Davidson is taken to task for current American policy and for his "silence" on Vietnam is ludicrous. Indeed, no other critic except Spanos found it necessary to devote two-thirds of an essay on Heidegger's National Socialism to Vietnam. Of course, I am not saying that Vietnam cannot be brought into play in connection with these issues, but only that it can hardly be made a requirement for speaking about Heidegger's politics. Finally, Spanos is simply historically inaccurate when he presents the native opposition of the sixties as derivative from Heideggerianism. The most prominent spokespersons—Spanos himself names Noam Chomsky, Susan Sontag, Tom Hayden, I. F. Stone, Bernard Fall, Jean-Paul Sartre, and Bertrand Russell[142]—were themselves unquestionably "humanistic" in their thinking and in their reasons for opposing the war. Only a failure to develop adequate political categories, based on simplistic Heideggerian assumptions, could place these anti-establishment intellectuals in the same camp as the perpetrators of American foreign policy. In France it may very well be true that deconstruction and other forms of neo-Heideggerianism surfaced in the struggles of May 1968. But their reception in the United States, as I have been at pains to demonstrate in this book, was much different. Through most of the years of intense struggle against Vietnam, deconstruction was almost exclusively known in a few departments of French and comparative literature at the most elite universities. Only after translations in the mid and late seventies did it gain a broader academic reading public, and its peak of popularity probably coincides with the era of Reagan and Thatcher, not with popular unrest and the antiwar movement. Spanos' attempt to politicize Heideggerianism is thus dependent on a dismissal of the most obvious features of the historical record and a narrow scheme in which antihumanism constitutes the only authentic opposition.[143] In these tendencies he joins ranks with the chief deconstructors in their defense of de Man and Heidegger.

Politics after Poststructuralism

In my discussions of the controversies around de Man and Heidegger I have tried to show how deconstruction has contributed to its own demise as a form of political criticism. By adopting a rigid scheme according to which only neo-Heideggerianism is accorded philosophical and political acumen, adherents of deconstruction have acted in a sectarian and dogmatic fashion. In the course of their contributions to these debates they have wittingly or unwittingly exhibited various types of apologetic discourses, unwarranted abuse of differing opinions, fear of engaged dialogue, fuzzy and inaccurate reading, strained argumentation, and paranoid reaction. In my view the discredit that deconstruction has reaped for this collective performance is unfortunate. Most of the defensive and offensive strategies used in the contributions to these debates have nothing to do with the best features of deconstruction, as they are manifested in earlier texts of Derrida, de Man, and various other practitioners. What became obvious, however, is that deconstruction, a textual practice that itself had waged an unremitting struggle against sclerotic thinking and writing, was itself constituted of certain dogmatic premises and beliefs that had to be defended at all costs. On the basis of new and old information it would have been refreshing to find someone identifying him or herself as a deconstructor who questioned or even doubted that the key to understanding fascism was an exhaustive reading of de Man and Heidegger. No one associated with deconstruction even entertained the possibility that de Man may have been attracted to "apolitical" literary criticism as a reaction to his early journalistic activity, i.e., that he exhibited throughout his academic career what the Germans call "Ideologieverdacht" (suspicion of ideology), and that this led him from various forms of phenomenology to a nonpolitical variant of deconstruction. And no neo-Heideggerian even thought of doubting that Heidegger is the greatest philosopher of our time, although such a doubt could be easily justified in light of his extensive complicity with National Socialism and conservative political thought, documented by Farias and Ott. What was lacking in the collective deconstructive response was integrity and openness, a willingness to learn from and enter into productive dialogue with other opinions.

Unfortunately the manner in which deconstruction responded to the crises around its spiritual leaders de Man and Heidegger has been too often the way in which many American practitioners have treated deconstruction since its inception in the United States. There has been an unfortunate tendency to adopt, in an uncritical fashion, the results of subtle deconstructive readings, or to accept neo-Heideggerian "truths" as a substitute for real political analysis. During the eighties deconstruction as dogma became an unfortunate by-product of its popularization in the United States, and this unquestioning adherence to doctrine extended beyond the knee-jerk acceptance of the party line in the de Man and the Heidegger discussions. Two examples may serve to clarify the type of uncritical theoretical assumptions that have proliferated in work of the eighties. Both of my illustrations come from the same volume, a book entitled *Postmodernism and Politics,* edited by Jonathan Arac in 1986.[144] This collection of essays consisted of selected contributions that originally appeared in a double issue of *boundary 2* in 1982–83, and this origin may explain the inclusion of the word "postmodernism" in the title. The description attached to *boundary 2,* which was started in 1972 by Spanos, is "an international journal of postmodern literature and culture." Thus, although most essays do not thematize postmodernism at all—it occurs as a word in only three of the nine pieces—it seems to have been retained as a general signifier of art and theory of the contemporary period.

One of the essays that does have a postmodern and a deconstructive bent is Andrew Parker's "Ezra Pound and the 'Economy' of Anti-Semitism."[145] Parker is probably best categorized as a political deconstructor similar to those I discussed in Chapter 8. He contributed to a special issue of *Diacritics* entitled "Marx after Derrida," where he seeks to reconcile the German political economist with the French deconstructor through an extended consideration of Louis Althusser.[146] The project on which he was working when *Postmodernism and Politics* appeared had the working title "Re-Marx: Studies in Marxist Theory and Criticism 'After Derrida.'"[147] Because he values political critique, his essay on Pound's antisemitism is even more troubling. Parker undertakes an analysis which seeks to uncover a more profound explanation for Pound's racist attitudes. His thesis is that "Pound's animus against Judaism ultimately will be legible as an animus against (his own) writing as such, a 'turn' of events that will produce an aberrant economy discernible in the workings of his poetry and prose alike."[148] For his analysis he depends considerably on Aristotle's *Politics* and its notion of usury, but the theoretical inspiration for his remarks is obviously of a more modern, deconstructive vintage. Parker wants to make Pound's antisemitism boomerang, to show that he is actually involved in self-cancellation. To do this he postulates that excess is "the most significant of the 'Jewish elements' that Pound would purge."[149] As anyone familiar with the French scene knows, however, excess is also a quality associated with writing *(écriture)*, particularly among deconstructors. Equating both excesses, Parker can then posit "Pound's irreducible Jewishness,"[150] thus interpreting his antisemitism as an aspect of the aporia of writing against writing. In typical poststructuralist fashion, and parallel to Hartman's apology for de Man, this analysis therefore trivializes the political by making it a function of linguistic games. Pound's statements about Jews are ripped out of their historical context and placed instead in an abstract philosophical realm that encompasses everything from Aristotle to Derrida.

Rather than using logical connections, Parker employs the more questionable but unfortunately popular device of analogy. Without explaining why, Parker assumes that the mere appearance of "excess" in both discourses can replace an argument that would link them causally or logically. Indeed, the very uncertainty of Parker's entire undertaking can be seen in his repeated use of conditional sentences at key points in his essay:

> If this excess by which writing is characterized can be understood (provisionally) as "an experience of the infinitely other"...we might then infer that Judaism conveys a rhetorically similar experience, for it forms an analogous, unassimilable "excess" on the margins of the dominant Western culture.

> If...both Jews and money can function as alternate figures for "writing," each term will maintain with the other a "relationship of reciprocal metaphoricity in which the Jews represent money and money represents them." [?]

> If, then, it were admitted that usury and rhetoric share an identical structure of "excess," it would not be unreasonable to expect that Pound will fulminate against rhetoric and writing in the same ways that he attacks usury and Judaism.

> Since, in Derrida's words, "writing will appear to us more and more as another name for this structure of supplementarity"—and since we previously discovered [!] that "usury," "rhetoric," and "Judaism" may figure as alternate names for this structure as well—we then may infer that this supplementary logic would equally subvert all the dichotomies on which Pound's writings are founded....[151]

The problem here is that the dependent clauses are all so hypothetical that we should avoid drawing any conclusions from them at all. It is worth noting as well that in the first two sentences the conclusions do not follow even if we admit the condition. But deconstructors employing such arguments, heavily dependent as they are on both the vocabulary and the style of Derrida, are apparently undaunted by such minor matters as logic and consistency. It is more persuasive—since rhetoric is more essential than logic anyway—to invoke the master deconstructor himself, to work with vague and imprecise associations as if they were proven connections, and to build arguments progressively on any piece of speculation that strikes one's fancy. Since much of this type of analysis appears to be written increasingly for the initiated anyway, no one has to fear being called to account for his or her reasoning. In an essay about a novel or some obscure metaphysical point such a tactic might be merely the occasion for a good laugh. But when the politics of antisemitism is treated with the same type of "logical" rigor that legitimated the mass murder of European Jewry, the matter is rather more pernicious in its ramifications. Parker's fall into the apologetic trap is thus related closely to those we have examined above. Through an uncritical acceptance of deconstruction as dogma, he finds himself, despite his obvious political progressiveness, trivializing a moment in

Pound's life when he allied himself with the most despicable features of European fascism.

My second illustration is taken from Rainer Nägele's essay "The Scene of the Other."[152] Nägele has been one of the most interesting, provocative, and innovative writers in American German studies and, like Parker, his political allegiances are decidedly on the left.[153] More than any scholar dealing with German literature and theory in the United States, he has been forging a connection between poststructuralist thought and the progressive parts of the German tradition. For him this has meant, in particular, the Frankfurt School, and, accordingly, his essay seeks to establish connections between the Negative Dialectic of Theodor W. Adorno and various aspects of poststructuralism. In contrast to Parker, therefore, who applies a poststructuralist approach and style to a political issue, Nägele relates poststructuralism and politics by means of a third party. His analysis, similar to sections in Michael Ryan's *Marxism and Deconstruction,* relies on the political credentials of the Frankfurt School to demonstrate the oppositional valence of modern French theory. Because he takes up a limited (although hardly simple) task, this essay is extremely persuasive. Nägele is able to demonstrate parallels that exist in the work of Adorno and in the thought of the most seminal poststructuralists, especially in their opposition to a unified subject and to thinking in systemic totalities. Adorno is thus brought into the proximity of two notions commonly associated with deconstruction. What would have to be examined more closely, of course, is whether these points of similarity are themselves political in the way Nägele wants them to be, and how they relate to the political context of both their own times and ours. Nägele seems to assume that the critique of subjectivity, as undertaken by Adorno and Derrida/Lacan, is an imminently political act, but he does not endeavor to connect this primarily epistemological concern with ethics or action. Ultimately he too, therefore, falls back on deconstructive dogma to persuade the reader of the progressive nature of his enterprise. Like the contributors to the de Man and Heidegger debates he identifies the establishment, without differentiation, as humanists. Near the beginning of his essay he ridicules the anxiety in the American academy speaking "in the name of humanistic scholarship and scientific objectivity."[154] The real radicals, Nägele would have us believe, are those who adhere, as he does, to post-Freudian—that is, Lacanian and Derridean—modes of reading. This sort of dichotomization is familiar from previous discussions, and my doubts about its accuracy and usefulness do not disappear because of the frequency with which it is repeated. With regard to Nägele's particular version we should perhaps admit that an anxiety about various forms of poststructuralism exists among some more conservative scholars, but note that it has been vastly overstated by those who wish to appear marginalized and persecuted. Far more disturbing for me is the tendency in many contemporary humanities departments to instill another type of anxiety. It is most manifest among young critics and students who find that in the current academic climate, particularly among theorists, it is not chic to embrace any principles except those that maintain the inevitability of aporia, contradiction, and nihilism. This is a much more troubling anxiety because it is so widespread and because it has most often served to inhibit, rather than enhance, discussion of real political issues. It has been disseminated in particular in many poststructuralist discourses since poststructuralism's reception in the United States, and only in recent years, with the self-induced demise of deconstruction, has it begun to lose some of its force.

We might think of this anxiety as the anxiety of appearing naive. As all of us who deal with theory know, naiveté is probably the worst possible error into which one can fall. Being wrong is nowhere near as damaging to our professional reputations since this can still entail a great amount of knowledge and theoretical sophistication. Indeed, a variety of theorists in the past two decades have spent considerable time arguing that strong theoretical positions are beyond such petty judgments as right and wrong, or that a certain amount of error is a necessity for any interesting theoretical proposition.[155] To be naive, on the other hand, is to be outside of the discourse that matters. It entails a lack of knowledge, rather than a strong application of knowledge, a recourse to things obsolete and hackneyed, a state of having been surpassed. This anxiety of appearing naive is pervasive in the academy and accounts, I would contend, for the uncritical imitation that deconstruction has suffered at the hands of limited and unskilled epigones. I have not referred to any of the most crude mimics of deconstruction in this section, but they frequently populate scholarly conferences and are found in relatively large numbers among junior faculty and in graduate programs at various universities. Living in fear of appearing naive to their colleagues and students, these epigones are condemned to invoke the most trendy words and phrases from writings found in the deconstructive canon. When pressed about their arguments, they can offer only clichés as defense, but this rarely deters them from continuing to search out and employ the latest jargon.

But the anxiety of appearing naive, which has been largely a by-product of deconstruction's reception in the United States, also extends into many other types of discourse, where it inhibits precisely the type of political dialogue that should be fostered. Let me give another instance of the hasty affirmation of premises that usually accompanies this anxiety. In connection with his postulate of a humanistic anxiety, Nägele mentions in a dismissive fashion Georg Lukács's *The Destruction of Reason* (1954), a one-sided but hardly useless analysis of the ideological and philosophical history of German fascism. For most poststructuralists and critical theorists the later Lukács is the epitome of an outmoded political orthodoxy; to cite any of his works written after 1930 in a positive fashion is to label oneself naively doctrinaire. It is probably not coincidental that Andreas Huyssen, one of the very best critics in German studies today, alludes to Lukács in a similar circumstance, revealing I think the precise complex to which I have made reference. Defending his own critical but largely affirmative views on contemporary culture, Huyssen speaks of the fear of becoming the Lukács of the postmodern.[156] He is referring, of course, to Lukács's attacks on expressionism and other modernist forms in the 1930s and is observing as a truism that we would not want to place ourselves in an analogous position vis-à-vis postmodernism. What is interesting in this implied admonition is Huyssen's phrasing. It suggests that we as critics or theorists, in order not to appear naive or obsolete, must validate what is new, current, and "in," and implies that there is some necessary or natural connection between the theoretical or artistic avant-garde and the political avant-garde. Some of these presuppositions are precisely those that have served deconstruction so well over the past two decades. The problem with this stance, however, is that it departs from the very political perspective Huyssen otherwise embraces. For one thing it treats Lukács's views on modernism too simplistically. The real problem with Lukács's perspective was its dogmatic adherence to an epistemological and aesthetic prejudice, not his opposition to certain tendencies in modernism. In positing cognition and clarity as the chief features of our literary interaction with texts, he is compelled to adopt a formalist valorization of realism. For all his railing against formalism, Lukács is the most rigid formalist of all. From our perspective it should therefore be evident that it is the foundation of Lukács's critique of modernism which is faulty, not or not exclusively its political objectives. What would have been needed—and what is needed today for an evaluation of deconstruction, postmodernism, poststructuralism, and any of the other various "posts" flourishing in contemporary culture—is a differentiation based on political categories. Modernism as such is neither reactionary nor progressive, although certain types of modernism may fit either label very well. Brecht and T. S. Eliot, both well-known modernists, cannot be lumped together politically; they are similar only by dint of formal and aesthetic, not political, distinctions.

The real question, of course, is how to develop or locate these political categories so that they encompass various political projects and do not remain sectarian. My suggestion is the following. In contrast to the poststructuralist prejudice for valorizing language and text over action and effect, I would insist that these categories, if they are to be truly political, must be derived from praxis. Politics, whether it is conceived as the interpretation of a literary text or the struggle for a specific cause, is a fundamentally ethical proposition. In this appeal to the ethical as a primary category for political theory I am not at all differing from the best advocates of deconstruction. Indeed, in recent years Derrida has consistently affirmed that his is primarily an ethical project. The difficulty is in bringing the strategies employed by Derrida and the best of political deconstruction into play with the political field of reality that exists in the contemporary United States. To do so we have to avoid the types of exclusive projects that dominated political theory in the early part of the twentieth century and that proved to be ideological pillars for repression in Eastern Europe throughout the cold war. We have to avoid, therefore, recourse to uncriticizable premises such as the cynical, orthodox marxist proposition that we derive our morality from the class struggle—since this has more often than not been the pretext for the abuse of ethics. In short, in consonance with the antifoundational movements in theoretical discourse, we have to work with propositions that are tentative, revisable, and, most important, products of democratic processes.

Since Nietzsche's famous dictum of the death of God, which was really anticipated by Heine a half century earlier, ethics can be conceived in two ways. The conservative lineage from Nietzsche himself to the present conceives the loss of transcendental entities or instances as a liberation from the moralizing inherent in everything from organized religion to Kant's categorical imperative. As Nietzsche himself attested, if God is dead, then everything is allowed. For him this means that the love-thy-neighbor ethic of the Christian world is no better than the hierarchization of societies expounded in the caste system of India. Indeed, in various works he suggests that the latter may be more honest and "natural" than the former. The lesson he and other conservative thinkers draw from the demise of the deity is that society can be structured according to a hierarchy of power, enforced if necessary by violence. Democracy and socialism are nothing more than various disguises for an obsolete Christian ethics. Since there are no transcendent rules, no prohibitions from a divine source, no guidelines to behavior other than what instinct allows, we are responsible to no one other than ourselves. Built into this position is also a convenient defense mechanism against opposing arguments. Anyone who continues to propound a system of "good and evil" versus the preferred nondichotomy of "good and bad" is simply trying to gain the upper hand in the power struggle. The very notion of morality and the various systems derived from it are thus seen as a ploy to maintain the supremacy of mediocre and weak, albeit cunning, individuals.

There is another way to look at the liberation from conventional morality that Nietzsche proclaims. Instead of viewing it as an invitation for the exercise of hegemony, we can read it as a call to human responsibility. Rather than envisioning a hierarchization of society based on power and violence, we can interpret it as a reminder of our fundamental obligation to democracy and the respect for otherness. The disappearance of a transcendent source for our ethical systems throws the burden back on us. With no God, no commandments, and no imperatives from above, we are left to develop our own ethical precepts in a constant interaction with each other. Viewed in this fashion, the various systems of ethics that have dominated human thought do not have to be scrapped entirely either, even if they were based on the existence of transcendental norms. For in them there may well be hints and anticipations of the interactive and democratic ethics that can evolve from intersubjective exchange. The love-thy-neighbor ethic of Christianity is perhaps not only an instance of a furtive will to power, but also a premonition of social values that could only be realized once its transcendent foundation has been destroyed. Similarly Kant's categorical imperative is not just an abstract product of an outmoded and illusory Enlightenment belief in Reason, but one result of abstract utopianism based on a democratically achieved *sensus communis.* To characterize the two Nietzschean tendencies even more schematically than I have thus far, one could say that the first has recourse to an individual and an individual consciousness in order to establish legitimacy for one group over another. The second accepts the death of God as a collective, intersubjective charge in order to secure equality and rights within a democratic community.

It seems to me that most variants of poststructuralism, including deconstruction, are stuck in the first of the post-Nietzschean paradigms while gesturing toward the second. In their radicalization of

Nietzsche's epistemological and ethical positions, the French and their American followers have been unable to rethink the premises of the great tradition as it might affect collective action. Their ethical stance therefore vacillates between an anarchic libertarianism and a conservative affirmation of the status quo, both of which remain eternally virtual as consequences of an abstract philosophical critique. The central strategies for overcoming this ethical and political conundrum, which have been the topic of much of the previous chapter, have been largely unsuccessful. Either they force a political valence onto a mode of analysis that remains impervious or indifferent to it, or they take a preformed and undifferentiated schema, developed by the conservative German cultural criticism of the late nineteenth and twentieth centuries, and try to twist this into a progressive politics. Nietzsche's political views had the virtue of being consistent; they were a logical extension of his philosophical insights. From the perspective of the individual, whether Zarathustra or overman, morality was a big lie. Democracy, socialism, and all other leveling political movements were little more than secularized versions of *ressentiment,* of Christian ethics turned loose in the public arena. Nietzsche's conclusion was that there were not "good" (in the sense of nonmoral) arguments against elitism, hierarchy, social class, or even racism. Some of this rejection of traditional morality accounts no doubt for his appeal to the right wing, as well as his attraction for Heidegger. Deconstruction has been inconsistent with the heritage on which it most relies. Accepting the framework within which a conservative and antidemocratic heritage developed, it was able to sustain a critique of the status quo, but was unable to show itself as progressive or leftist except by oppositional gestures. It could support the black cause in South Africa, feminism, and gay rights, but not within the confines of its philosophical presuppositions. Every time it advocated something progressive and democratic, it began to push against the limits of its own theoretical assumptions.

As I have suggested in my presentation of a second variant of post-Nietzschean ethics, what is needed is not necessarily a rejection of the criticism of morals, but rather a perspective that eliminates the dependence on the individual consciousness as the bearer and arbiter of moral and amoral precepts. In contemporary philosophical and social thought such a perspective has been best articulated in the work of the school of communicative ethics, in particular in the writings of Jürgen Habermas.[157] In humanities circles in the United States, the reception of Habermas has been effectively blocked by some of the very mechanisms that I outlined in my discussion of reception theory in the first two chapters. His thought has been unfairly seen as a throwback to values of the European Enlightenment. Nothing, of course, has been more disdained than the Enlightenment by avant-garde theorists since the Second World War. From Adorno and Horkheimer's savage attack in *Dialectic of Enlightenment,* which is occasionally less one-sided than it would appear, to the more recent work of Derrida and Foucault, the ideals of the Enlightenment, particularly reason, have been eagerly besieged by theories that claim to know better. The works of Heidegger and de Man are heavily indebted to this tradition as well, and part of a politicized reexamination of their work might also involve the implications of their rejection of Enlightenment thought. But Habermas is not a theoretical dinosaur who wants to turn back the clock to the Age of Reason. He shares with most contemporary theorists a skepticism regarding the way in which reason has been instituted in the contemporary world, but he insists that regarding reason monolithically leads to irrationalism or contradiction. With respect to poststructuralist theorists he presents his arguments in more detail in *The Philosophical Discourse of Modernity.*[158] His claim in this volume is that theory remains trapped in a modern problematic that is first enunciated by Hegel and that Habermas calls "the philosophy of the subject." The endeavor of philosophers from Heidegger to Derrida to escape its reach never actually succeeds. Indeed, the strength of Habermas' own project, which is expounded most extensively in *The Theory of Communicative Action,* is that it is an attempt not to overcome the Enlightenment, but rather to rethink its premises from an intersubjective, communicative perspective.[159] Habermas' reliance on a reduced and interactive notion of reason allows him to avoid both irrationalism and performative contradiction. By placing dialogue and exchange at the center of his concerns, he is able to postulate and to exemplify a nondogmatic, democratic, and infinitely criticizable political practice.

The notion that a genuine political practice must distance itself from deconstructive dogma and interact democratically with actual concerns is articulated in the work of many progressive critics. Indeed, in the very volume which includes the essays of Parker and Nägele we find Cornel West advocating a more skeptical attitude toward the political potentials in the United States for the Francophilic heritage.[160] He frames his comments in a consideration of Fredric Jameson's marxism, and although he does not rely specifically on Habermas, communicative ethics, or values associated with the Enlightenment, I do not believe that his discussion is incompatible with my criticisms and suggestions. West's main point is that Jameson assumes a homology between epistemology and ethics and thus too readily accepts poststructuralist and deconstructive methods as politically relevant. This has been the substance of my claim above with regard to the two paths leading from Nietzsche's philosophy. I believe that West is also correct in reproaching Jameson—and by extension others who too readily apply deconstruction to politics—for not examining deconstructionist strategies themselves as modes of ideological activity. The various forms of poststructuralism, West argues, live in a symbiotic relationship with the very philosophical tradition they purport to subvert. The question he poses is therefore not how to integrate deconstruction or neo-Heideggerianism into political theory; rather, he favors historicizing these enterprises themselves:

> The Marxist lesson here is that only if one has taken metaphysics, epistemology, and ethics seriously will one be attracted by Heideggerian rhetoric about going beyond metaphysics or Nietzschean rhetoric about going beyond good and evil. If one instead takes history seriously—as do Marx and after 1844 American pragmatism at its best—then metaphysics, epistemology, and ethics are not formidable foes against which to fight nor are the Ali-like shuffles of the deconstructions that "destroy" them impressive performances. On this view, deconstructionists become critically ingenious yet politically deluded ideologues, who rightly attack bourgeois humanism, yet who also become the ideological adornments of late-monopoly-capitalist academies.[161]

Although West polemicizes heavily here against ethics, he does not mean to exclude this realm from a politicized theory. From the context of his essay he obviously understands ethics here as part of the metaphysical, Western tradition that has to be overcome if we are to achieve a viable political perspective. He therefore criticizes Jameson's work precisely for leaving "little or no space for either highlighting issues of political praxis within its theoretical framework or addressing modes of political praxis in its own academic setting."[162] The task West envisions is thus not to go beyond existing discourses or to integrate them into a marxist framework, but rather to transform "present practices...against the backdrop of previous discursive and political practices, against the 'dead past.'"[163]

A similar complaint can be heard in bell hooks's recent essay "Postmodern Blackness."[164] Like West, hooks is skeptical of the contribution that avant-garde (white, elitist) theory can make toward real political change, and critical of its distance from societal praxis in the United States. She points out that much of the terminology most frequently encountered in the texts of postmodern theorists is insensitive and often at cross-purposes to black experience. Similar to West, she claims that it partakes in and bolsters the very discourse that it seeks to overturn.

> It is sadly ironic that the contemporary discourse which talks the most about heterogeneity, the decentered subject, declaring breakthroughs that allow recognition of otherness, still directs its critical voice primarily to a specialized audience, one that shares a common language rooted in the very master narratives it claims to challenge.

With regard to the critique of identity, a favorite topos of most varieties of neo-Heideggerian thought, she notes that it is posited too absolutely, thus excluding a place for the very "otherness" it purportedly promotes. "Given a pervasive politics of white supremacy which seeks to prevent the formation of radical black subjectivity, we cannot cavalierly dismiss a concern with identity politics." Although she obviously sees advantages in a critique of essentialism and in the affirmation of multiple identities, her point is that the postmodern critique, as it is presently articulated, is too undifferentiated to account for the complexity of lived experience in the black community. She ends up endorsing some tenets related to a weak notion of the postmodern, but her central concerns are to find modes of resistance that are primarily ethical, political, and practical.

The reason that I feel this resistance can be aided by communicative ethics, democratically informed dialogue, and the interactive reason bequeathed to us by the Enlightenment is that only when we engage such principles do we actually make connections with the most important political movements of our time. I would insist that the Enlightenment heritage is not antithetical to progressive politics, but the very core of any meaningful political movement. Enlightenment, conceived in its widest sense, entails emancipation from imposed hegemony, whether this hegemony appears in the form of a church, a state, linguistic structuration, or discourse. Although a good deal has been made of the fiction of the autonomous subject and of the necessity for antihumanism as political prerequisites in the postmodern age, there is no evidence that these notions appear either desirable or progressive to anyone except those inside a small circle of academicians, chiefly in humanities departments in the most advanced Western nations. This is verified by examining any progressive force in our society or in the world. The women's and civil rights movements, as well as gay and lesbian rights movements, appear to be extremely "old-fashioned," perhaps even "reactionary," to most avant-garde theorists, since they demand the very kind of individual autonomy and validation of subjectivity that is currently declared a metaphysical delusion. The blacks in South Africa and the Palestinians in the Middle East would similarly be "retrograde"—or at least theoretically naive—by the postmodernist yardstick when they struggle for peace, freedom, and democracy, without outside interference or intervention. Indeed, if we observe the key goals and demands from the most concrete political movements in this country and throughout the world—demands for which many have sacrificed their lives—it will be difficult to find deconstructive leaders or a substantial deconstructive contribution. More frequently we would find the "obsolete" notions that postmodernism consigns to the historical dustbin. I am not suggesting that we have nothing to learn from poststructuralism or from deconstruction. Nor am I questioning the political integrity of those who have become politically active through their appropriation of French theory. Indeed, Foucault's notion of power, Derrida's deconstructive readings of Western philosophy, Lacan's reconception of the unconscious, are undoubtedly important contributions to our understanding of our history, our present, and ourselves. It would be foolish to think that these theories cannot be useful inside the framework of a political strategy for change. But these theories, once they crossed the border into the United States, forfeited their inherent native political value, and if they are to be important again, they must drop their claim to exclusive political correctness and begin to develop in consonance with the demands posed by contemporary American society. If theory in the humanities is going to contribute politically, it must concern itself less with grand radical gesturing, which is frequently allied with a nihilistic refutation of our ability to control our own destiny through reason, cooperation, and mutual respect, and more with an alliance with those forces seeking the realization of the uncompleted task of modernity.

Notes

Index

Notes

Chapter 1. Resistance and Rivalry

1. Joel Conarroe, Editorial, *PMLA* 95 (1980): 3–4.

2. When referring to reception theory I mean the general shift in criticism from concerns with the author or the text to a focus on the reader, the audience, or the relationship between text and recipient. The most prominent names associated with this movement have been Wolfgang Iser and Hans Robert Jauß, both of whom teach at the University of Constance.

3. Hans Robert Jauß, "Literaturgeschichte als Provokation der Literaturwissenschaft," in *Literaturgeschichte als Provokation* (Frankfurt: Suhrkamp, 1970), pp. 144–207. The essay in this volume is an expanded version of his inaugural address. An abbreviated and poorly translated English version of this essay was published under the title "Literary History as a Challenge to Literary Theory" in *New Literary History* 2 (1970) and then in Ralph Cohen, ed., *New Directions in Literary History* (Baltimore: Johns Hopkins University Press, 1974), pp. 11–41. A complete and decent translation, however, was available only in 1982 with the publication of a collection of Jauß's essays, *Toward an Aesthetic of Reception* (Minneapolis: University of Minnesota Press, 1982), pp. 3–45.

4. Gunter Grimm, *Rezeptionsgeschichte: Grundlegung einer Theorie* (Munich: Fink, 1977), pp. 354–80.

5. The papers from this conference were published in Walter Müller-Seidel, ed., *Historizität in Sprach- und Literaturwissenschaft* (Munich: Fink, 1974).

6. The response to reception theory has been evident in the Netherlands as well. In 1974, for example, the *Amsterdamer Beiträge zur neueren Germanistik* devoted an entire issue to matters pertaining to reception, and scholars like Ferdinand van Ingen, Horst Steinmetz, Douwe Fokkema, and Elrud Kunne-Ibsch contributed to reception studies in that country. In addition, two French journals, *Oeuvres et Critiques* in 1977–78 and *Poétique* in 1979, published issues on this method. Nothing comparable can be found in the United States.

7. My own study, *Reception Theory: A Critical Introduction* (London: Methuen, 1984), finally filled this gap.

8. Richard E. Amacher and Victor Lange, eds., *New Perspectives in German Literary Criticism: A Collection of Essays* (Princeton: Princeton University Press, 1979). Amacher and Lange took selected essays from the "Poetik and Hermeneutik" series, the proceedings of a colloquium held at Constance every second year, but in weighting their selection toward the early colloquia from the sixties, they ignored much of reception theory.

9. See Susan R. Suleiman and Inge Crosman, eds., *The Reader in the Text: Essays on Audience and Interpretation* (Princeton: Princeton University Press, 1980); and Jane Tompkins, ed., *Reader-Response Criticism: From Formalism to Post-Structuralism* (Baltimore: Johns Hopkins University Press, 1980). Significant for the latter collection is that only Wolfgang Iser is anthologized; references to other German reception theorists are limited to the bibliography.

10. Murray Krieger and L. S. Dembo, eds., *Directions for Criticism: Structuralism and Its Alternatives* (Madison: University of Wisconsin Press, 1977).

11. Ong's essay appeared in *PMLA* 90 (1975): 9–21. The essay won the William Riley Parker Prize for the outstanding essay in the *PMLA* for that year.

12. Harald Weinrich, "Für eine Literaturgeschichte des Lesers," *Merkur* 21 (1967): 1026–38.

13. The original German version of this essay, "Die Appellstruktur der Texte," was Iser's inaugural lecture at Constance. It first appeared in English in *Aspects of Narrative: Selected Papers from the English Institute*, ed. J. Hillis Miller (New York: Columbia University Press, 1971), pp. 1–45, and is now more readily available in a collection of Iser's essays entitled *Prospecting: From Reader Response to Literary Anthropology* (Baltimore: Johns Hopkins University Press, 1989), pp. 3–30.

14. Steven Mailloux, "Reader-Response Criticism?" *Genre* 10 (1977): 413–31.

15. Iser still teaches at Constance; Jauß retired in the late eighties, although he is still an influential member of the Constance community. His student Karlheinz Stierle was named as his replacement.

16. See Hans Robert Jauß and Herbert Nesselhauf, *Gebremste Reform: Ein Kapitel deutscher Hochschulgeschichte* (Constance: Universitätsverlag Konstanz, 1977).

17. See Klaus L. Berghahn, "Wortkunst ohne Geschichte: Zur werkimmanenten Methode der Germanistik nach 1945," *Monatshefte* 71 (1979): 387–98.

18. See *Kursbuch* 15 (1968), especially Hans Magnus Enzensberger, "Gemeinplätze, die neuste Literatur betreffend," pp. 187–97.

19. Hans Robert Jauß, "Paradigmawechsel in der Literaturwissenschaft," *Linguistische Berichte* 3 (1969): 44–56.

20. Walter J. Slatoff, *With Respect to Readers: Dimensions of Literary Response* (Ithaca: Cornell University Press), p. 169.

21. My views here discount perhaps too much the influence of critics like Louis Kampf, who was president of the Modern Language Association in 1971, or Richard Ohmann, the author of *English in America: A Radical View of the Profession* (New York: Oxford University Press, 1976), as well as other leftist professors from the seventies. Their influence, however, never extended to a substantial revision of dominant literary paradigms, particularly not in literary theory, and not at the key graduate institutions in the United States. It would be absurd to maintain that there was no leftist movement in English and the modern languages during the late sixties and early seventies, and that this movement had no effect on literary studies. But I would still insist that the central focus of any leftist movement that did exist was not literary theory and its reform, and that the more significant protests at universities were carried out around concrete political issues, not around the way we approach literary texts.

22. Geoffrey H. Hartman, *Beyond Formalism: Literary Essays, 1958–1970* (New Haven: Yale University Press, 1970), p. 42.

23. Paul de Man, Introduction, *Studies in Romanticism* 18 (1979): 498–99.

24. Jonathan Culler, "Structuralism and Grammatology," *boundary 2* 8 (1979): 75–85; here pp. 76–78.

25. See Jonathan Culler, "Beyond Interpretation: The Prospects of Contemporary Criticism," *Comparative Literature* 28 (1976): 244–56.

26. Maria Ruegg, "The End(s) of French Style: Structuralism and Post-Structuralism in the American Context," *Criticism* 21 (1979): 186–216; here pp. 197–98.

27. For example Hannelore Link, "'Die Appellstruktur der Texte' und ein 'Paradigmawechsel in der Literaturwissenschaft,'" *Jahrbuch der deutschen Schillergesellschaft* 17 (1973): 532–83.

28. For example in Robert Crosman, "Discontinuities," review of *The Implied Reader*, by Wolfgang Iser, *Novel* 8 (1975): 182–83; William Ray, "Recognizing Recognition: The Intra-Textual and Extra-Textual Critical Persona," *Diacritics* 7 (1977): 20–33; Ed Bloch, review of the *The Act of Reading*, by Wolfgang Iser, *Western Humanities Review* 34 (1980): 189.

29. That Iser has actually had quite different concerns is made most obvious from his recent work in literary anthropology. If it was ever in doubt, it should now be clear that the problems of most interest to him are not textual and therefore not in the tradition of New Criticism.

30. Wolfgang Iser, *The Implied Reader: Patterns of Communication in Prose Fiction from Bunyan to Beckett* (Baltimore: Johns Hopkins University Press, 1974), p. xii.

31. Link, "'Die Appellstruktur,'" p. 555.

32. The ahistorical nature of Iser's project became even more apparent in the eighties. In the collection of essays from 1989, to which I referred above *(Prospecting: From Reader Response to Literary Anthropology)*, the bias toward anthropology that was already contained in his early work becomes stronger. Iser's main arguments are riddled with ahistorical assumptions and claims. Too often we read what literature or fiction is, or what it does; about "our own experience" (p. 7) or "the required activity of the recipient" (p. 244). Both the phenomenological model from which Iser proceeds and the anthropological goal to which he aspires are ultimately conceived as norms or ideals outside of the real history of literature and reader response.

33. For example, Iser's concern with distinguishing between literary texts and other writing—a concern of the Russian Formalists at the beginning of the century—and his repeated reference to the "meaning" of a piece of literature.

34. Wallace Martin, review of *The Act of Reading*, *Criticism* 21 (1979): 262.

35. For a discussion of the concept of the "horizon of expectation," see Heinrich Anz, "Erwartungshorizont: Ein Diskussionsbeitrag zu H. R. Jauß' Begründung einer Rezeptionsästhetik der Literatur," *Euphorion* 70 (1970): 398–408.

36. Jauß, *Aesthetic of Reception*, p. 24.

37. Jauß, *Aesthetic of Reception*, p. 25.

38. See my "Reception Theory and Russian Formalism," *Germano-Slavica* 3 (1980): 271–86.

39. Jauß, *Aesthetic of Reception*, p. 45.

40. His works had already been reviewed in previous issues of *Diacritics* by William Ray, as noted above, and Robert Scholes, "Cognition and the Implied Reader," *Diacritics* 5 (1975): 13–15.

41. The third interviewer, Stanley Fish, withdrew from the interview at the last moment, preferring evidently to contribute to the debate with his diatribe against Iser "Why No One's Afraid of Wolfgang Iser," *Diacritics* 11 (1981): 2–13. A more

detailed consideration of this review and Iser's response to it will be included in the second chapter.

42. Rudolf E. Kuenzli, "The Intersubjective Structure of the Reading Process: A Communication-Oriented Theory of Literature," *Diacritics* 10 (1980): 47–56; here esp. p. 50.

43. Wolfgang Iser, *The Act of Reading: A Theory of Aesthetic Response* (Baltimore: Johns Hopkins University Press, 1978), p. 151.

44. See, e.g., *The Act of Reading*, p. 218.

45. John Paul Riquelme, "The Ambivalence of Reading," *Diacritics* 10 (1980): 75–86; here p. 81.

46. Among them Crosman, who feels that phenomenological criticism "comes to history bringing not peace, but a sword" ("Discontinuities," p. 283).

47. Riquelme, "The Ambivalence of Reading," p. 85.

48. For the best orientation to the criticism of Fish see his *Is There a Text in This Class: The Authority of Interpretive Communities* (Cambridge: Harvard University Press, 1980). This volume collects all his important theoretical pieces from the seventies.

49. See, for example, Fish's treatment of Milton in "Interpreting the *Variorum*," *Critical Inquiry* 2 (1976): 465–85, esp. pp. 471–73.

50. How well Fish can play his game is shown by the ingenuity in his response to critics, for example to Douglas Bush and John Reichert. See "Interpreting 'Interpreting the *Variorum*,'" *Critical Inquiry* 3 (1976): 191–96; and "A Reply to John Reichert; or, How to Stop Worrying and Learn to Love Interpretation," *Critical Inquiry* 6 (1979): 173–78. Both essays are anthologized in *Is There a Text in This Class.*

Chapter 2. Confrontations with Radicalness

1. *Toward an Aesthetic of Reception*, trans. Timothy Bahti (Minneapolis: University of Minnesota Press, 1982); *Aesthetic Experience and Literary Hermeneutics*, trans. Michael Shaw (Minneapolis: University of Minnesota Press, 1982); and *Question and Answer: Forms of Dialogic Understanding*, ed. and trans. Michael Hays (Minneapolis: University of Minnesota Press, 1989). Iser also published three books in English in the eighties: *Walter Pater: The Aesthetic Moment*, trans. David Henry Wilson (Cambridge: Cambridge University Press, 1987); *Laurence Stern: Tristram Shandy*, trans. David Henry Wilson (Cambridge: Cambridge University Press, 1988); and Prospecting: From Reader Response to Literary Anthropology (Balitmore: Johns Hopkins University Press, 1989).

2. Vassilis Lambropoulos and David Neal Miller, eds., *Twentieth-Century Literary Theory: An Introductory Anthology* (Albany: SUNY Press, 1987).

3. Peter J. Rabinowitz, "Whirl without End: Audience-Oriented Criticism," in *Contemporary Literary Theory*, ed. G. Douglas Atkins and Laura Morrow (Amherst: University of Massachusetts Press, 1989), pp. 81–100.

4. Robert Magliola, "Like the Glaze on a Katydid-Wing: Phenomenological Criticism," in Atkins and Morrow, *Contemporary Literary Theory*, pp. 101–16; Joel Weinsheimer, "Hermeneutics," in ibid., pp. 117–36.

5. Vincent B. Leitch, *American Literary Criticism from the 30s to the 80s* (New York: Columbia University Press, 1988), pp. 231–34.

6. Hans Robert Jauß, "The Theory of Reception: A Retrospective of Its Unrecognized Prehistory," in *Literary Theory Today*, ed. Peter Collier and Helga Geyer-Ryan (Ithaca: Cornell University Press, 1990), pp. 53–73.

7. For example in his *The Institution of Criticism* (Ithaca: Cornell University Press, 1982) and in *Building a National Literature: The Case of Germany, 1830–1870*, trans. Renate Baron Franciscono (Ithaca: Cornell University Press, 1989).

8. Samuel Weber, "Caught in the Act of Reading," *Demarcating the Disciplines: Philosophy Literature Art*, Glyph Textual Studies 1 (Minneapolis: University of Minnesota Press, 1986), pp. 181–214; here p. 181.

9. For a more detailed consideration than the one I provided above, see Robert C. Holub, *Reception Theory: A Critical Introduction* (London: Methuen, 1984), pp. 5–12.

10. Holub, *Reception Theory*, pp. 147–63.

11. Stanley Fish, "Why No One's Afraid of Wolfgang Iser," *Diacritics* 11, no. 1 (1981): 2–13.

12. Wolfgang Iser, "Talk Like Whales: A Reply to Stanley Fish," *Diacritics* 11, no. 3 (1981): 82–87.

13. Iser, "Talk Like Whales," p. 83.

14. Iser, "Talk Like Whales," p. 83.

15. Paul de Man, Introduction, *Toward an Aesthetic of Reception*, by Hans Robert Jauß (Minneapolis: University of Minnesota Press, 1982), pp. vii–xxv.

16. Fish, "Why No One's Afraid," p. 2.

17. De Man, Introduction, p. xviii.

18. De Man, Introduction, p. xvii.

19. De Man, Introduction, p. xvii.

20. De Man, Introduction, p. xix.

21. See Rainer Warning, "Rezeptionsästhetik als Literaturwissenschaftliche Pragmatik," in *Rezeptionsästhetik: Theorie und Praxis*, ed. Warning (Munich: Fink, 1975), pp. 9–41; and Walter Benjamin, "Die Aufgabe des Übersetzers," *Illuminationen: Ausgewählte Schriften* (Frankfurt: Suhrkamp, 1980), pp. 50–62. While it is true that certain citations can be produced that indicate Benjamin may have been opposed to approaches resembling reception theory, other citations from his texts indicate precisely the opposite.

22. De Man, Introduction, p. xvi.

23. De Man, Introduction, p. xxii.

24. De Man, Introduction, p. xxiii.

25. See Weber, "Caught in the Act of Reading."

26. Weber, "Caught in the Act of Reading," p. 195.

27. Wolfgang Iser, *The Act of Reading: A Theory of Aesthetic Response* (Baltimore: Johns Hopkins University Press, 1978), pp. 3–10.

28. Weber, "Caught in the Act of Reading," p. 210.

29. Weber, "Caught in the Act of Reading," p. 199.

30. De Man, Introduction, p. xxii.

31. De Man, Introduction, pp. xix–xx.

32. Weber, "Caught in the Act of Reading," p. 199.

33. Weber, "Caught in the Act of Reading," p. 212.

34. Fish, "Why No One's Afraid," p. 3.

35. Weber, "Caught in the Act of Reading," p. 200.

36. See W. J. T. Mitchell, *Against Theory: Literary Studies and the New Pragmatism* (Chicago: University of Chicago Press, 1985).

Chapter 3. French Theory and German Scholarship

1. Vincent Descombes, *Modern French Philosophy*, trans. L. Scott-Fox and J. M. Harding (Cambridge: Cambridge University Press, 1980).

2. See Martin Schwab, Foreword to Manfred Frank's *What Is Neostructuralism?* trans. Sabine Wilke and Richard Gray (Minneapolis: University of Minnesota Press, 1989), p. xiii.

3 For example in the writings of Hans Peter Duerr, Dietmar Kamper, and Christoph Wulf. Despite their works and continued publication by a number of young philosophers and literary critics, I believe that poststructuralism still exerts a rather minor influence on most major intellectuals. Many German theorists have obviously relied on Jürgen Habermas' discussion in *The Philosophical Discourse of Modernity*, trans. Frederick Lawrence (Cambridge: MIT Press, 1987), which appeared in Germany in 1985 and was the first work by a major figure to deal with poststructuralist thought. However, volumes occasionally appear that indicate that poststructuralism has penetrated to a level of general familiarity. See, for example, Jürgen Fohrmann and Harro Müller, eds., *Diskurstheorien und Literaturwissenschaft* (Frankfurt: Suhrkamp, 1988), or, on a more philosophical plane, Manfred Frank, Gérard Raulet, and Willem van Reijen, eds., *Die Frage nach dem Subjekt* (Frankfurt: Suhrkamp, 1988). More significant for Germany are discussions of postmodernism, which occasionally also touch on poststructuralist concerns. See, for example, Andreas Huyssen and Klaus R. Scherpe, eds., *Postmoderne: Zeichen eines kulturellen Wandels* (Reinbeck: Rowohlt, 1986); Dietmar Kamper and Willem van Reijen, eds., *Die unvollendete Vernunft: Moderne versus Postmoderne* (Frankfurt: Suhrkamp, 1987); Christa Bürger and Peter Bürger, eds., *Postmoderne: Alltag, Allegorie und Avantgarde* (Frankfurt: Suhrkamp, 1987); or Peter Kemper, ed., *'Postmoderne' oder Der Kampf um die Zukunft* (Frankfurt: Fischer, 1988). See also Ingeborg Hoesterey, *Verschlungene Schriftzeichen: Intertextualität von Literatur und Kunst in der Moderne/Postmoderne* (Frankfurt: Athenäum, 1988). Hoesterey's book is to be commended for its sensitivity to the differences in the reception of both the postmodern and poststructuralism in Germany and in the United States.

4. Other names one encounters in anthologies and footnotes include: Richard Faber, Heinrich Fink-Eitel, Jürgen Fohrmann, Wolfgang Hübener, Harro Müller, and Georg Christoph Tholen.

5. Kittler and Frank will be discussed below. Hörisch has done extremely interesting work with texts from German literature and, more recently, with hermeneutics. See Jochen Hörisch, *Gott, Geld und Glück: Zur Logik der Liebe in den Bildungsromanen Goethes, Kellers und Thomas Manns* (Frankfurt: Suhrkamp, 1983); and *Die Wut des Verstehens: Zur Kritik der Hermeneutik* (Frankfurt: Suhrkamp, 1988). Bolz, whose primary concern has been philosophy, has also contributed to the critique of the hermeneutic tradition, as well as to other topics. His most recent publications include *Stop Making Sense* (Würzburg: Königshausen und Neumann, 1989), *Theorien der neuen Medien* (Munich: Raben-Verlag, 1989), and *Auszug aus der entzauberten Welt: Philosophischer Extremismus zwischen den Weltkriegen* (Munich: Fink, 1989). Hamacher was prominently involved in the de Man debate in the late

eighties. With Neil Hertz and Thomas Keenan he edited both Paul de Man's *Wartime Journalism 1939–1943* (Lincoln: University of Nebraska Press, 1988) and *Responses: On Paul de Man's Wartime Journalism* (Lincoln: University of Nebraska Press, 1989).

6. Friedrich Kittler, "Fleur de Lys," *Fugen: Deutsch-Französisches Jahrbuch für Text-Analytik* 1 (1980): 99–113. As far as I can tell, only one issue of this "yearbook" appeared.

7. Norbert Bolz, "Das innere Ausland der Philosophie," in *Wer hat Angst vor der Philosophie* (Paderborn: Schöningh, 1982), pp. 95–136.

8. Bolz, "Das innere Ausland," p. 105.

9. Bolz, "Das innere Ausland," p. 107.

10. Friedrich Kittler, "Kratylos: Ein Simulacrum," in *Fugen*, pp. 247–51.

11. Georg Wilhelm Friedrich Hegel, *Der Geist des Christentums: Schriften, 1796–1800*, ed. Werner Hamacher (Frankfurt: Ullstein, 1978).

12. Werner Hamacher, "pleroma—zur Genese und Struktur einer dialektischen Hermeneutik bei Hegel," Introduction to Hegel, *Der Geist des Christentums*, pp. 310–11.

13. Werner Hamacher, "—in letzter Sekunde," in *Wer hat Angst vor der Philosophie*, pp. 283–314.

14. Friedrich Kittler, ed., *Austreibung des Geistes aus den Geisteswissenschaften* (Paderborn: Schöningh, 1980).

15. Manfred Frank, *Das Sagbare und das Unsagbare: Studien zur neuesten französischen Hermeneutik und Texttheorie* (Frankfurt: Suhrkamp, 1980), p. 7.

16. Norbert W. Bolz, Einleitung, in *Wer hat Angst vor der Philosophie*, p. 9.

17. Bolz, Einleitung, p. 10.

18. Bolz, Einleitung, p. 13.

19. Bolz, Einleitung, p. 12.

20. Friedrich Kittler, Einleitung, in *Austreibung des Geistes*, p. 10.

Chapter 4. Michel Foucault among the Germans

1. Even in the year of his death there were a significant number of book-length studies on Foucault. See *University Publishing*, no. 13 (Summer 1984): 16 for a bibliography of books on Foucault in English from the early eighties. The issue contains ten pieces commemorating Foucault's death.

2. Paul Rabinow, ed,. *The Foucault Reader* (New York: Pantheon, 1984); and David Couzens Hoy, *Foucault: A Critical Reader* (Oxford: Blackwell, 1986).

3. See Michael Clark, *Michel Foucault: An Annotated Bibliography: Tool Kit for a New Age* (New York: Garland Publications, 1983).

4. In literary and cultural criticism I am thinking in particular of Frank Lentricchia and Edward Said.

5. If we consider that a good deal of the work under the rubric "New Historicism" may be influenced by him, then this statement would have to be modified. Much of the work done for and around the journal *Representations* could be considered, with some justification, Foucauldian. See, for example, Catherine Gallagher and Thomas Laqueur, eds., *The Making of the Modern Body: Sexuality and Society in the Nineteenth Century* (Berkeley: University of California Press, 1987); Paul Rabinow, *French Modern: News and Forms of the Social Environment* (Cambridge: MIT Press,

1987); and Laqueur's recent study of sexuality, *Making Sex: Body and Gender from the Greeks to Freud* (Cambridge: Harvard University Press, 1990).

6. Foucault's reception in the German Democratic Republic, which I will not treat here, was even more restricted than in the Federal Republic. Indeed, only in the last few years of its existence does one find any reference to French poststructuralist theory that is not accompanied by outright dismissal.

7. Michel Foucault, "Die Spuren des Wahnsinns," *Kursbuch*, no. 3 (1965): 1–11.

8. Clemens Kammler, *Michel Foucault: Eine kritische Analyse seines Werks* (Bonn: Bouvier, 1986).

9. Dietmar Kamper and Christoph Wulf, eds. *Das Schwinden der Sinne* (Frankfurt: Suhrkamp, 1984). This volume contains the proceedings of an interdisciplinary seminar held in Paris in 1982. The proceedings of a previous seminar held in Berlin in the spring of 1981 are collected in *Die Widerkehr des Körpers* (Frankfurt: Suhrkamp, 1982). In recent years Kamper and Wulf have continued to edit volumes on themes that suggest a Foucauldian tradition: *Andere Körper* (Berlin: Verlag Mensch und Leben, 1984); *Die erloschene Seele: Disziplin, Geschichte, Kunst, Mythos* (Berlin: Reimer, 1988); *Schicksal der Liebe* (Weinheim: Quadriga, 1988); *Transfigurationen des Körpers: Spuren der Gewalt in der Geschichte* (Berlin: Reimer, 1989). Kamper has edited *Über die Wünsche: Ein Versuch zur Archäologie der Subjektivität* (Munich: Hanser, 1977) and written books such as *Zur Geschichte der Einbildungskraft* (Munich: Hanser, 1981) and *Soziologie der Imagination* (Munich: Hanser, 1986).

10. See the bibliography in Kammler, *Michel Foucault*, pp. 264–73, and his introduction, pp. 13–17.

11. See, for example, Heidrun Hesse, "Denken in der Leere des verschwundenen Menschen: Überlegungen zu Foucaults Konzept von Geschichte und Kritik," *Konkursbuch*, no. 3 (1979): 81–98; and Hinrich Fink-Eitel, "Michel Foucaults Analytik der Macht," in *Austreibung des Geistes aus den Geisteswissenschaften*, ed. Friedrich A. Kittler (Paderborn: Schöningh, 1980), pp. 38–78. We should also note that Peter Sloterdijk, whose *Critique of Cynical Reason* was one of the cult books of the eighties, was one of the first in Germany to discuss Foucault. See his essay "Michel Foucaults strukturale Theorie der Geschichte," *Philosophische Jahrbuch* 79 (1972): 161–84. An introductory monograph written by Hinrich Fink-Eitel appeared in 1989 under the title *Foucault zur Einführung* (Hamburg: Junius Verlag).

12. Reinhart Koselleck and Wolf-Dieter Stempel, *Geschichte—Ereignis und Erzählung*, Poetik und Hermeneutik, Vol. 5 (Munich: Fink, 1973). The reference to Foucault appears in the contribution by Herbert Dieckmann, "Naturgeschichte von Bacon bis Diderot," pp. 95–114, on p. 96.

13. "Register," *Der Spiegel* 38, no. 27 (2 July 1984): 172.

14. Lothar Baier, "Die Vernunft ist der Wahnsinn: Zum Tode des Philosophen Michel Foucault," *Die Zeit* 39, no. 28 (6 July 1984): 30.

15. Jürg Altwegg, "Empörung gegen die vorschreibende Vernunft: Michel Foucaults Auseinandersetzung mit den Erben der Aufklärung," *Frankfurter Allgemeine Zeitung* (3 Nov. 1984), n.p. (in section "Bilder und Zeiten").

16. Konrad Adam, "Der Preis für das Werk: Zum Tode von Michel Foucauld [*sic*]," *Frankfurter Allgemeine Zeitung* (28 June 1984), n.p.

17. Wolfgang Eßbach, one of the few sociologists in Germany to show an interest in Foucault, points out that even his most natural allies, the German left, have ignored and misunderstood him. See his "Michel Foucault und die deutsche Linke," *Links*, no. 174 (September 1984): 28–29.

18. Jean Améry, "Wider den Strukturalismus: Das Beispiel Michel Foucault," *Merkur* 27 (1973): 468–82; here p. 469.

19. Jean Améry, "Michel Foucaults Vision des Kerker-Universums," *Merkur* 31 (1977): 389–94; here p. 389.

20. Améry, "Wider den Strukturalismus," pp. 473–77.

21. Jean Améry, "Archäologie des Wissens: Michel Foucault und sein Diskurs der Gegenaufklärung," *Die Zeit* 33, no. 14 (31 March 1978); 44–45; here p. 44.

22. Améry, "Archäologie," p. 44.

23. In his later work the political motivation for the rejection of humanism is more explicit. "By humanism I mean the totality of discourse through which Western man is told: 'Even though you don't exercise power, you can still be a ruler. Better yet, the more you deny yourself the exercise of power, the more you submit to those in power, then the more this increases your sovereignty.' . . . In short, humanism is everything in Western civilization that restricts the *desire for power*." From "Revolutionary Action: 'Until Now,'" *Language, Counter-Memory, Practice: Selected Essays and Interviews*, ed. Donald F. Bouchard (Oxford: Basil Blackwood, 1977), pp. 218–33; here p. 221. Foucault's rejection of "humanism" is thus obviously much different from the totalized neo-Heideggerian version that I will discuss in the last part of the book.

24. In fact, Foucault denies that he is saying that humanity does not progress. See "Prison Talk," in Michel Foucault, *Power/Knowledge: Selected Interviews and Other Writings, 1972–1977*, ed. Colin Gordon (Brighton: Harvester Press, 1980), pp. 37–54; here p. 50.

25. See, for example, the essay by Altwegg; or Wilfried Gottschalch, "Foucaults Denken—eine Politisierung des Urschreis?" in *Literaturmagazin 9: Der neue Irrationalismus* (Hamburg: Rowohlt, 1978), pp. 66–73.

26. Jean Améry, "Bericht über den 'Gauchismus,'" *Merkur* 29 (1975): 271–79; here p. 274.

27. Améry, "Michel Foucaults Vision," p. 393.

28. Améry, "Archäologie," p. 44.

29. Jean Améry, "Französische Tendenzwende? Politische und philosophische Aporien im Lande des Cartesius," *Merkur* 31 (1977); 1040–53; here p. 1048. See also Gottschalch; "Foucault's thought—this much I understand—has political consequences, and these are obviously counterrevolutionary" ("Foucaults Denken," p. 66.).

30. Jürgen Habermas, "Modernity versus Postmodernity," *New German Critique*, no. 22 (Winter 1981); 3–14; here p. 13.

31. See his somewhat more sympathetic piece in *University Publishing*, pp. 5–6. This article is a translation of a piece that appeared in the *Berliner Tageszeitung (taz)* on 7 July 1984, p. 13, and is thus something of an obituary for Foucault. Habermas's more in-depth opinions concerning Foucault in the *Philosophical Discourse of Modernity* (1985) will be discussed below.

32. See, for example, Luc Ferry and Alain Renaut, *French Philosophy of the Sixties: An Essay on Antihumanism*, trans. Mary Schnackenberg Cattani (Amherst: University of Massachusetts Press, 1990).

33. Hayden White, "Michel Foucault," in *Structuralism and Since: From Lévi-Strauss to Derrida*, ed. John Sturrock (Oxford: Oxford University Press, 1979), pp. 81–115; here p. 82.

34. See, for example, Michael Sprinker, "The Use and Abuse of Foucault," *Humanities in Society* 3, no. 1 (1980): 1–20; Edward Said, "Traveling Theory," *Raritan* 1, no. 3 (1982): 41–67; and Frank Lentricchia, "Reading Foucault I and II (Punishment, Labor, Resistance)," *Raritan* 1, no. 4 (1983): 41–70. For a general discussion of the marxist reception in France, see Alan Sheridan, *Michel Foucault: The Will to Truth* (London: Tavistock, 1980), pp. 209–18. Of particular importance is Dominique Lecourt, *Pour une critique de l'épistémologie (Bachelard, Canguilhem, Foucault)* (Paris: François Maspero, 1972), pp. 98–133.

35. Améry has erroneously identified the "episteme" with Otto Spengler's *Kulturseele* (soul of culture), thus associating Foucault in the process with the worldview of the reactionary side of *Geistesgeschichte.*

36. Michel Foucault, *The Archaeology of Knowledge,* trans A. M. Sheridan Smith (London: Tavistock, 1972), p. 191. The French version appeared in 1969.

37. Foucault, *Archaeology,* p. 159.

38. For an excellent critique of Foucault on this point see David Carroll, "The Subject of Archaeology or the Sovereignty of the Episteme," *Modern Language Notes* 93, no. 4 (1978): 695–722. A similar criticism is voiced by Manfred Frank in *What Is Neostructuralism?* (Minneapolis: University of Minnesota Press, 1988).

39. Michel Foucault, "The Subject of Power," Afterword to Hubert L. Dreyfus and Paul Rabinow, *Michel Foucault: Beyond Structuralism and Hermeneutics* (Chicago: University of Chicago Press, 1982), pp. 208–26; here p. 209.

40. Schütz was at the New School for Social Research in New York from 1952 until his death in 1959. His works had a strong appeal in the Federal Republic during the seventies. During this decade the Suhrkamp publishing house brought out three of his books—*Das Problem der Relevanz* (1971), *Der sinnhafter Aufbau der sozialen Welt* (1974), and *Strukturen der Lebenswelt* (1979)—as well as his correspondence with Talcott Parsons, *Zur Theorie sozialen Handelns* (1972). He is quoted frequently in phenomenologically oriented literary studies and was influential for Habermas as well, who was particularly interested in his sociologically informed notion of the "lifeworld."

41. This is one of the central contentions that Dreyfus and Rabinow make.

42. Alfred Schütz and Thomas Luckmann, *Strukturen der Lebenswelt* (Frankfurt: Suhrkamp, 1979), p. 47.

43. See Ulrich Rauf, "Das normale Leben: Michel Foucaults Theorie der Normalisierungsmacht," Diss. Marburg 1977.

44. Jürgen Habermas, "A Review of Gadamer's *Truth and Method,* " in *Understanding and Social Inquiry,* ed. Fred R. Dallmayr and Thomas A. McCarthy (Notre Dame: University of Notre Dame Press, 1977), pp. 335–63; here, p. 360.

45. Jürgen Habermas, *The Theory of Communicative Action,* Vol. 1, trans. Thomas McCarthy (Boston: Beacon, 1984), p. 392.

46. Habermas, *Communicative Action,* p. 398.

47. Habermas, *Communicative Action,* p. 287.

48. Habermas, *Communicative Action,* p. 42.

49. It is interesting to note, of course, the similarities between the Habermasian notion of discourse and the humanistic view of something like a university seminar.

50. Robert C. Holub, *Jürgen Habermas: Critic in the Public Sphere* (London: Routledge, 1991).

51. Foucault, *Archaeology,* p. 55.

52. Even in what Foucault called his "transitional stage" he poses a much different notion of discourse: "We must conceive discourse as a violence that we do to things, or, at all events, as a practice we impose upon them; it is in this practice that the events of discourse find the principle of their regularity." Michel Foucault, "Orders of Discourse," trans. Rupert Swyer, *Social Science Information* 10, no. 2 (1971): 7–30; here p. 22. This was Foucault's inaugural lecture delivered at the Collège de France on 2 December 1970.

53. For a discussion of how Foucault tries to accomplish this see David Carroll, "Disruptive Discourse and Critical Power: The Conditions of Archaeology and Genealogy," *Humanities in Society* 5, no. 3 (1982): 175–200. Foucault's own discussion of this issue, found in *The Archaeology of Knowledge* (pp. 205–11), is somewhat evasive and inadequate.

54. Dreyfus and Rabinow, *Michel Foucault*, p. 130.

55. Jonathan Arac in "The Function of Foucault at the Present Time," *Humanities in Society* 3, no. 1 (1980): 73–86, supplies an insightful comparison of Foucault and Habermas (pp. 79–83); for a comparison of Foucault and the Frankfurt School, see Barry Smith, *Foucault, Marxism and Critique* (London: Routledge, 1983), pp. 132–37. See also Dietmar Kamper, "Die Auflösung der Ich-Identität: Über einige Konsequenzen des Strukturalismus für die Anthropologie," in *Austreibung des Geistes aus den Geisteswissenschaften*, pp. 79–86.

56. Habermas's chapters on Foucault are taken from lectures he delivered before Foucault's death. An earlier version of his views on Foucault was published under the title "Genealogische Geschichtsschreibung: Über einige Aporien im machttheoretischen Denken Foucaults," *Merkur* 38 (1984): 745–53. I think it is fair to say that of all French theorists Habermas considered Foucault's thought most productive for his own work.

57. Jürgen Habermas, *The Philosophical Discourse of Modernity*, trans. Frederick Lawrence (Cambridge: MIT Press, 1987), p. 278.

58. Habermas, *Philosophical Discourse*, p. 279.

59. Habermas, *Philosophical Discourse*, p. 290.

60. Axel Honneth, *Kritik der Macht: Reflexionsstufen einer kritischen Gesellschaftstheorie* (Frankfurt: Suhrkamp, 1985), pp. 168–69.

61. Honneth, *Kritik der Macht*, pp. 176, 191, 192, 195.

62. Honneth, *Kritik der Macht*, p. 216. For a brief discussion of Luhmann's theory and Habermas' debate with him, see the fifth chapter of my *Jürgen Habermas: Critic in the Public Sphere*.

63. See, for example, Christa Karpenstein-Eßbach, *Einschluß und Imagination: Über den literarischen Umgang mit Gefangenen* (Tübingen: Konkursbuchverlag, 1985).

64. This lack of familiarity became most evident, as we shall see, in considerations of fascism in connection with de Man and Heidegger.

65. Friedrich Kittler and Horst Turk, Einleitung, in *Urszenen: Literaturwissenschaft als Diskursanalyse und Diskurskritik* (Frankfurt: Suhrkamp, 1977), pp. 9–43.

66. Foucault, *Archaeology*, p. 37.

67. Kittler and Turk, Einleitung, p. 33.

68. Kittler and Turk, Einleitung, p. 38.

69. Kittler and Turk, Einleitung, p. 39.

70. Michel Foucault, *Discipline and Punish: The Birth of the Prison,* trans. Alan Sheridan (Middlesex: Penguin, 1979), p. 29. The French edition appeared in 1975.

71. Kittler and Turk, Einleitung, pp. 39–40.

72. Found in Foucault, *Language,* pp. 113–38. The French original of this essay appeared in 1969.

73. Kittler and Turk, Einleitung, p. 41.

74. Dreyfus and Rabinow, *Michel Foucault,* p. 89.

75. Michel Foucault, "Two lectures," in *Power/Knowledge,* pp. 78–102; here p. 85.

76. For a contrasting view of classical theories of power, see Niklas Luhmann, "Klassische Theorie der Macht," *Zeitschrift für Politik* 16, no. 2 (1969): 149–70.

77. For a critique of Foucault's repression hypothesis, see Mark Poster, "Foucault's Three Discourses," *Humanities in Society* 2, no. 2 (1979): 153–66.

78. Foucault, "Prison Talk," in *Power/Knowledge,* pp. 37–54; here p. 39. As far as I can tell, most German theorists adhere to what Foucault calls a juridical model of power based on prohibitions and restraints. A notable exception is Elias Canetti in *Masse und Mensch* (Frankfurt: Fischer, 1980). He suggests different ways of conceiving power. His discussion of the question-and-answer situation (pp. 317–23) and the secret (pp. 323–31) demonstrates his sensitivity to the same type of mechanisms that Foucault feels are important.

79. Foucault, "Intellectuals and Power," in *Language,* pp. 205–17; here p. 213.

80. Foucault, "Intellectuals and Power," p. 216.

81. As far as I can tell, the first German critique of Foucault from a feminist perspective came in Claudia Honneger's" Überlegungen zu Michel Foucault's Entwurf einer Geschichte der Sexualität," Diss. Bremen 1980. Because of Foucault's popularity in the United States, there is much more discussion about him in the context of feminism. See, for example, Irene Diamond and Lee Quinby, *Feminism and Foucault: Reflections on Resistance* (Boston: Northeastern University Press, 1988); and Nancy Hartsock, "Foucault on Power: A Theory for Women?" in *Feminism/Postmodernism,* ed. Linda J. Nicholson (New York: Routledge, 1990), pp. 157–75.

82. The first four terms were used by Said, "Traveling Theory," pp. 64–66; the fifth and sixth by Sprinker, "Use and Abuse of Foucault," p. 11, and Lentricchia, "Reading Foucault," p. 51, respectively.

83. Foucault, "Prison Talk," p. 52.

84. Leo Bersani, "The Subject of Power," *Diacritics* 7, no. 3 (1977): 2–21; here, p. 6.

85. The insensitivity to a Foucauldian problematic is probably the chief deficiency in the otherwise excellent study by Klaus Weimar, *Geschichte der deutschen Literaturwissenschaft bis zum Ende des 19. Jahrhunderts* (Munich: Fink, 1989).

86. Paul A. Bové, "The End of Humanism: Michel Foucault and the Power of Disciplines," *Humanities in Society* 3, no. 1 (1980): 23–40; here p. 36.

87. An English version was printed in *Humanities in Society* 3, no. 1 (1980): 87–111. A German version with the title of the French original, *Oublier Foucault,* was published in Munich by Raben Verlag in 1978.

88. Foucault, "Prison Talk," pp. 53–54.

89. Michel Foucault, "The History of Sexuality," in *Power/Knowledge,* pp. 183–93; here p. 190.

Chapter 5. Peter Szondi and the Missed Opportunity

1. See Gert Mattenklott, "Peter Szondi als Komparatist," in *Vermittler,* ed. Jürgen Sieß (Frankfurt: Syndikat, 1981), pp. 127–41.

2. Peter Szondi, *Theorie des modernen Dramas* (Frankfurt: Suhrkamp, 1956). The English translation by Michael Hays appeared as *Theory of the Modern Drama* (Minneapolis: University of Minnesota Press, 1987).

3. Peter Szondi, *On Textual Understanding and Other Essays,* trans. Harvey Mendelsohn (Minneapolis: University of Minnesota Press, 1986).

4. Since his death, under the series titles *Schriften* and *Poetik und Geschichtsphilosophie* most of Szondi's lectures, including major studies of Celan and Hölderlin, have appeared in German.

5. Szondi's most extensive discussion of Schleiermacher may be found in his *Einführung in die literarische Hermeneutik* (Frankfurt: Suhrkamp, 1975), pp. 155–91. This volume consists of lectures Szondi held in Berlin during the winter semester 1967/68. Lectures 9 and 10, in which he deals with Schleiermacher, were reworked for the essay "L'herméneutique de Schleiermacher," *Poetique* 2 (1970), 141–55, which appears in *On Textual Understanding* in English translation.

6. Fr. D. E. Schleiermacher, *Hermeneutik,* ed. Heinz Kimmerle (Heidelberg: Carl Winter, 1959).

7. See Frank's introduction to Schleiermacher's *Hermeneutik und Kritik* (Frankfurt: Suhrkamp, 1977), pp. 7–67 and his book *Das individuelle Allgemeine: Textstrukturierung und -interpretation nach Schleiermacher* (Frankfurt: Suhrkamp, 1977).

8. Szondi, *Textual Understanding,* p. 17.

9. Thomas S. Kuhn, *The Structure of Scientific Revolutions,* 2nd enlarged ed., International Encyclopedia of Unified Science, Vol. 2, no. 2 (Chicago: University of Chicago Press, 1970).

10. Szondi, *Textual Understanding,* p. 97.

11. Szondi, *Textual Understanding,* p. 100.

12. Schleiermacher's "decisive shift" is in fact not as decisive as Szondi makes it out to be. When he has recourse to speech, he suggests that even in this face-to-face situation we must engage in a hermeneutical process. Thus speech is not seen as logically primary or prior to writing, but rather as communication which cannot be distinguished from writing for the purposes of interpretation. It is in this regard that his theory is related to Derrida's *Of Grammatology,* a work Szondi specifically cites in the text.

13. For a more complete discussion of Szondi's uneasy relationship to Schleiermacher see Norbert Altenhofer, "Geselliges Betragen—Kunst—Auslegung: Anmerkungen zu Peter Szondis Schleiermacher-Interpretation und zur Frage einer materialen Hermeneutik," in *Studien zur Entwicklung einer materialen Hermeneutik,* ed. Ulrich Nassen (Munich: Fink, 1979), pp. 165–211.

14. Szondi, *Textual Understanding,* p. 13.

15. Szondi, *Textual Understanding,* p. 14.

16. Szondi, *Textual Understanding,* p. 103.

17. Szondi, *Textual Understanding,* p. 5.

18. Hans Robert Jauß, "Literary History as a Challenge to Literary Theory," in *Toward an Aesthetic of Reception,* trans. Timothy Bahti (Minneapolis: University of Minnesota Press, 1982), p. 22.

19. Hayden White, *Metahistory: The Historical Imagination in Nineteenth Century Europe* (Baltimore: Johns Hopkins University Press, 1973), and Dominick LaCapra, *Rethinking Intellectual History: Texts, Context, Language* (Ithaca: Cornell University Press, 1983).

20. Altenhofer, "Geselliges Betragen," p. 204.

21. Szondi, *Textual Understanding*, p. 171.

22. Szondi, *Textual Understanding*, p. 169.

Chapter 6. Manfred Frank as Mediator

1. Manfred Frank, *Das Problem "Zeit" in der deutschen Romantik* (Munich, 1972; revised version Paderborn: Schöningh, 1990).

2. Manfred Frank, *Der unendliche Mangel an Sein: Schellings Hegelkritik und die Anfänge der Marxschen Dialektik* (Frankfurt: Suhrkamp,1975).

3. Manfred Frank, *Das individuelle Allgemeine: Textstrukturierung und -interpretation nach Schleiermacher* (Frankfurt: Suhrkamp, 1977).

4. F. W. J. Schelling, *Philosophie der Offenbarung: 1841/1842*. ed. Manfred Frank (Frankfurt: Suhrkamp, 1977); Friedrich Schleiermacher, *Hermeneutik und Kritik*, ed. Manfred Frank (Frankfurt: Suhrkamp, 1977); F. W. J. Schelling, *Ausgewählte Schriften*, ed. Manfred Frank (Frankfurt: Suhrkamp, 1985); Manfred Frank, *Einführung in Schellings Philosophie* (Frankfurt: Suhrkamp, 1985); *Die unendliche Fahrt: Ein Motiv und sein Text* (Frankfurt: Suhrkamp, 1979); *Der kommende Gott* (Frankfurt: Suhrkamp, 1982); *Gott im Exil: Vorlesungen über die neue Mythologie* (Frankfurt: Suhrkamp, 1982).

5. Manfred Frank, "Eine fundamental-semiologische Herausforderung der abendländischen Wissenschaft: Jacques Derrida," *Philosophische Rundschau* 23 (1976): 1–16.

6. Manfred Frank, *Das Sagbare und das Unsagbare: Studien zur neuesten französischen Hermeneutik und Texttheorie* (Frankfurt: Suhrkamp, 1980).

7. Manfred Frank, *Was ist Neostrukturalismus?* (Frankfurt: Suhrkamp, 1983); *What is Neostructuralism?* trans. Richard Gray and Sabine Wilke (Minneapolis: University of Minnesota Press, 1989).

8. Frank, *Neostructuralism*, pp. 21–22.

9. An appendix to the German volume, which was omitted from the English translation, includes two lectures on the relationship between hermeneutics and poetics in Derrida.

10. Frank, *Neostructuralism*, p. 6.

11. Frank, *Neostructuralism*, p. 14. I have translated "die oberste Spitze" as "the current high point" rather than "the present tip" since I believe it reflects more accurately Frank's positive evaluation of neostructuralism.

12. Frank, *Neostructuralism*, p. 191.

13. Manfred Frank, *Einführung in Schellings Philosophie* (Frankfurt: Suhrkamp, 1985).

14. Dieter Henrich, "Fichte's 'Ich,'" in *Selbstverhältnisse: Gedanken und Auslegungen zu den Grundlagen der klassischen deutschen Philosophie* (Stuttgart: Reclam, 1982), pp. 57–82.

15. John H. Smith, "The *Transcendance* of the Individual,," *Diacritics* 19, no. 2 (1989): 80–98. Smith's essay, which concentrates primarily on Frank's work, is probably the best discussion of his works to appear thus far in English.

16. Manfred Frank, *Die Unhintergehbarkeit der Individualität* (Frankfurt: Suhrkamp, 1986), p. 17.

17. Frank, *Neostructuralism,* pp. 10–11.

18. Frank, *Neostructuralism,* p. 287. Further reflections by Frank on this topic are contained in the essay "Subjekt, Person, Individuum," in *Die Frage nach dem Subjekt,* ed. Manfred Frank, Gérard Raulet, and Willem van Reijan (Frankfurt: Suhrkamp, 1988), pp. 7–28. These matters continue to occupy Frank's attention today, even though the contribution of poststructuralism to his thinking has receded in recent years.

19. Gerd Gemünden, "Der Unterschied liegt in der Differenz: On Hermeneutics, Deconstruction, and Their Compatibility," *New German Critique,* no. 48 (1989): 176–92.

20. The word *nach* in German means both "after" and "according to."

21. Frank, *Neostructuralism,* p. 284.

22. In "The will to Consensus: Manfred Frank on Derrida," *Modern Language Notes* 105, no. 3 (1990): 596–609, Hans Hauge presents a one-sided distortion of Frank's theory when he claims: "Frank argues that there are no codes or rules, there is only the individual" (p. 601). This is a gross misrepresentation of what Frank actually contends. Frank speaks so often of the existence of codes and codified signs that one would have to ignore his texts completely to arrive at Hauge's conclusion that he conducts a "crusade against rules, codes, and conventions" (p. 602). The implication that Frank's theory is ultimately "religious" and based on the individual life of Jesus, just because he relies on Schleiermacher, who wrote *Das Leben Jesu,* is equally ludicrous. In Hauge's essay we witness the kind of depths some critics will stoop to when they encounter a theorist who dares to question poststructuralism or deconstructive dogma.

23. Frank, *Die Unhintergehbarkeit,* p. 17.

24. Smith, "The *Transcendance,* p. 94.

25. Frank, *Das individuelle Allgemeine,* pp. 196–97.

26. Frank, *Neostructuralism,* p. 408.

27. Frank, *Neostructuralism,* p. 432.

28. Manfred Frank, "Die Grenzen der Beherrschbarkeit der Sprache: Das Gespräch als Ort der Differenz von Neostrukturalismus und Hermeneutik," in *Text und Interpretation,* ed. Phillippe Forget (Munich: Fink, 1984), pp. 181–213. This book presents the German version of the "encounter" between Gadamer and Derrida that appeared in English in the volume *Dialogue and Deconstruction,* ed. Diane P. Michelfelder and Richard E. Palmer (Albany: SUNY Press, 1989). Portions of Frank's essay were translated for that volume by Palmer and given the title "Limits of the Human Control of Language: Dialogue as the Place of Difference between Neostructuralism and Hermeneutics" (pp. 150–61).

29. Jonathan Culler, *On Deconstruction: Theory and Criticism after Structuralism* (Ithaca: Cornell University Press, 1982).

30. Rodolphe Gasché, *The Tain of the Mirror: Derrida and the Philosophy of Reflection* (Cambridge: Harvard University Press, 1986); Christopher Norris, *The Deconstructive Turn: Essays in the Rhetoric of Philosophy* (London: Methuen, 1983); *The Contest of Faculties: Philosophy and Theory after Deconstruction* (London: Methuen, 1985); and *Derrida* (Cambridge: Harvard University Press, 1987).

31. Frank, *Neostructuralism,* pp. 208, 319.

32. Frank, *Neostructuralism,* p. 184.
33. Frank, *Neostructuralism,* p. 342.
34. Frank, *Die Unhintergehbarkeit,* p. 11.
35. Manfred Frank, "Kleiner (Tübinger) Programmentwurf: Philosophie heute und jetzt: Ein paar Überlegungen," *Frankfurter Rundschau* (5 March 1988), p. ZB 3.

Chapter 7. Friedrich Kittler as Discursive Analyst

1. See my discussion of Kittler and Turk's introduction to *Urszenen* above.
2. Friedrich Kittler, *Der Traum und die Rede: Eine Analyse der Kommunikationssituation Conrad Ferdinand Meyers* (Bern: Francke, 1977).
3. Gerhard Kaiser and Friedrich Kittler, *Dichtung als Sozialisationsspiel: Studien zu Goethe und Gottfried Keller* (Göttingen: Vandenhoeck & Ruprecht, 1978).
4. Friedrich Kittler, *Aufschreibesysteme 1800–1900* (Munich: Fink, 1985); *Discourse Networks 1800/1900,* trans. Michael Metteer, with Chris Cullens (Stanford: Stanford University Press, 1990).
5. Kittler, *Discourse Networks,* p. 451.
6. Kittler, *Discourse Networks,* p. 369.
7. Kittler, *Discourse Networks,* p. 278.
8. David E. Wellbery, Foreword to *Discourse Networks,* p. ix.
9. Kittler, *Discourse Networks,* p. 189.
10. For a more detailed investigation of this new technology see Kittler's *Grammophon Film Typewriter* (Berlin: Brinkmann & Rose, 1985). "With the historical co-temporaneity of movies, phonographs, and typewriting the optic, acoustic, and written data flow are separated and made autonomous" (p. 27).
11. Kittler, *Discourse Networks,* p. 209.
12. Kittler, *Discourse Networks,* p. 215.
13. Kittler, *Discourse Networks,* p. 258.
14. Kittler, *Discourse Networks,* p. 206.
15. Kittler, *Discourse Networks,* p. 214.
16. Kittler, *Discourse Networks,* p. 227.
17. Kittler, *Discourse Networks,* p. 222.
18. Kittler, *Discourse Networks,* p. 212.
19. Kittler, *Discourse Networks,* p. 312.
20. Kittler, *Discourse Networks,* p. 336.
21. Kittler, *Discourse Networks,* pp. 336–37.
22. Kittler, *Discourse Networks,* p. 11.
23. For a more detailed criticism of Kittler's methods in this work see the extended review by Thomas Sebastian, "Technology Romanticized: Friedrich Kittler's *Discourse Networks 1800/1900,*" *Modern Language Notes* 105, no. 3 (1990): 583–95. Sebastian's central objection is that Kittler reduces historical differences illicitly to the substrate of media technology, thereby ignoring or obscuring the historical specificity of his material.
24. Kittler, *Discourse Networks,* pp. 211–12.
25. Kittler, *Grammophon,* p. 33.
26. Wellbery claims that the first component of Kittler's program is the "presupposition of exteriority" (*Discourse Networks,* p. xii).

Chapter 8. Marxist Deconstruction

1. For a brief review of the leftist criticism of the Vietnam era see Vincent B. Leitch, *American Literary Criticism from the 30s to the 80s* (New York: Columbia University Press, 1988), pp. 366–79.

2. Jacques Derrida, *Of Grammatology,* trans. Gayatri Spivak (Baltimore: Johns Hopkins University Press, 1976). The French original appeared in 1967.

3. Jacques Derrida, "Où commence et comment finit un corps enseignant," in *Politique de la philosophie,* ed. Dominique Grisoni (Paris: Grasset, 1976), pp. 60–61.

4. See Jacques Derrida, *The Ear of the Other: Otobiography, Transference, Translation,* ed. Christie V. McDonald (New York: Schocken, 1982). The remarks to which I am referring here are drawn from the essay "Otobiographies: The Teaching of Nietzsche and the Politics of the Proper Name," translated by Avital Ronell, pp. 1–38 of this volume, particularly pp. 28–29. The text of this essay was evidently presented at the University of Montreal in October of 1979.

5. Maria Ruegg, "The End(s) of French Style: Structuralism and Post-Structuralism in the American Context," *Criticism* 21, no. 3 (1979): 203–16.

6. Vincent B. Leitch, "The Lateral Dance: The Deconstructive Criticism of J. Hillis Miller," *Critical Inquiry* 6, no. 4 (1980): 593–607.

7. Leitch, "Lateral Dance," p. 607.

8. J. Hillis Miller, "Theory and Practice: Response to Vincent Leitch," *Critical Inquiry* 6, no. 4 (1980): 609–14.

9. Miller, "Theory and Practice," p. 612.

10. Karl Marx, "Zur Kritik der Politischen Ökonomie," in *Marx Engels Werke,* Vol. 12 (Berlin: Dietz, 1961), pp. 8–9.

11. See, for example, Jacques Derrida, "Racism's Last Word," trans. Peggy Kamuf, *Critical Inquiry* 12 (1985): 290–99; and Jacques Derrida and Mustapha Tlili, eds., *For Nelson Mandela* (New York: Henry Holt, 1987).

12. Derrida, "Où commence," pp. 60–64.

13. Fynsk's argument appeared in a review of *Qui a peur de la philosophie* with the title "A Decelabration of Philosophy," in *Diacritics* 8, no. 2 (1978): 80–90. Such an endeavor to separate the project of Derrida from his American followers has become a commonplace in criticism. Derrida himself, however, has consistently refused to divorce himself from his American followers. On the contrary, he has even suggested at times that he is better understood in the United States. In *Memoires for Paul de Man* (New York: Columbia University Press, 1986), for example, he remarks: "America *is* deconstruction [l'Amérique, mais c'est la deconstruction]. *In this hypothesis,* America would be the proper name of deconstruction in progress, its family name, its toponymy, its language and its place, its principal residence" (p. 18). In an interview in *Le Nouvel Observateur* from 6 November 1988 he indicated that the debates that really interest him are better developed in the United States, and that they are conducted more openly and with more important results.

14. Derrida, "Où commence," pp. 60–89.

15. Fynsk, "A Declaration," pp. 86–87. We might note that in the eighties Derrida increasingly emphasized the ethical nature of this project, but that he too has been unable or unwilling to give a good sense of what this entails.

16. Art Berman, *From the New Criticism to Deconstruction: The Reception of Structuralism and Post-Structuralism* (Urbana: University of Illinois Press, 1988), p. 301.

17. Michael Ryan, "Self-Evidence," *Diacritics* 10, no. 2 (1980): 2–16.

18. Ryan, "Self-Evidence," p. 2.
19. Ryan, "Self-Evidence," pp. 2, 10, 4, 15, 12, 14.
20. Ryan, "Self-Evidence," p. 4.
21. Ryan, "Self-Evidence," pp. 13–14.
22. Ryan, "Self-Evidence," pp. 2–3.
23. Ryan, "Self-Evidence," pp. 9, 11, 15.
24. Interview with Jacques Derrida, "Positions," *Diacritics* 3, no. 1 (1973): 33–34.
25. Ryan, "Self-Evidence," p. 11.
26. Ryan, "Self-Evidence," p. 11.
27. Michael Ryan, *Marxism and Deconstruction: A Critical Articulation* (Baltimore: Johns Hopkins University Press, 1982), p. 181.
28. Ryan, *Marxism and Deconstruction*, p. 41.
29. With regard to the Jews this argument was advanced during the Third Reich, and by right-wing conservatives in the postwar period. In the "historians' debate" of the mid-eighties, after existing for forty years in the mindless apologetics of neo-Nazis, it even found its way into the mainstream public sphere when Ernst Nolte claimed that Hitler may have been justified in treating Jews as prisoners of war. At issue is a statement made by Chaim Weizmann in a letter to Neville Chamberlain on behalf of the Jewish Agency on 29 August 1939 to the effect that the Jewish people would fight with England against Germany in the Second World War. Jürgen Kocka cleared up the inaccuracies in Nolte's hasty account in "Hitler sollte nicht durch Stalin und Pol Pot verdrängt werden," an article that originally appeared in the liberal *Frankfurter Rundschau.* Weizmann was president of the World Zionist Organization in 1929–31 and 1935–46. The Jewish Agency represented the World Zionist Organization for Palestine, which was under British authority at the time. As Kocka points out, the offer to fight with the British and in fact the entire letter has to be seen in the context of the relationship of the Jewish Agency and the British governing authorities in Palestine. Kocka's statement may be found in *"Historikerstreit": Die Dokumentation der Kontroverse um die Einzigartigkeit der nationalsozialistischen Judenvernichtung* (Munich: Piper, 1987), pp. 132–42. Ryan, of course, is hardly a neoconservative like Nolte. But my point here is only that this type of pseudodeconstructive reading can, without much effort, be used for the support of some very dubious ideological enterprises.
30. Although Derrida argues in connection with de Man, as we shall see later, that deconstruction is the only discourse effective in combating textual totalitarianism, he came to recognize in the eighties that there was no simple political dichotomy to be drawn on the basis of deconstructive practices. In the letter to Gerald Graff included at the end of *Limited Inc* (Evanston, Ill.: Northwestern University Press, 1988), Derrida writes: "I have come to understand that, *sometimes, certain* bitter and compulsive enemies of deconstruction stand in a more certain and more vital relationship, even if not theorized, to what is in effect at stake in it than do *certain* avowed 'deconstructionists'" (140). Even in this admission, however, we cannot fail to note the smug conviction that ultimately and inherently deconstruction is the political vanguard position of theory. Those who are politically progressive, but enemies of deconstruction—and we should note that the term "enemy" is an odd, polemical, and unproductive notion for describing a critic of deconstruction—are unwittingly and untheoretically on the side of deconstruction.
31. Michael Sprinker, "Criticism as Reaction," *Diacritics* 10, no. 3 (1980): 2–14.

32. Sprinker, "Criticism as Reaction," p. 4.

33. Sprinker, "Criticism as Reaction," p. 4.

34. Graff's views on deconstruction have moderated significantly in the past few years. In an essay included in the *Responses* volume, he admits his more positive evaluation and separates himself from the real conservative criticism of deconstruction. Essentially Graff now appreciates the sophisticated philosophical arguments that the best deconstructors have to offer. Graff's role in the publication of Derrida's debate with John Searle in *Limited Inc* is evidence of his altered views on deconstruction. See Gerald Graff, "Looking Past the de Man Case," *Responses: On Paul de Man's Wartime Journalism*, ed. Werner Hamacher, Neil Hertz, and Thomas Keenan (Lincoln: University of Nebraska Press, 1989), pp. 246–54.

35. Sprinker, "Criticism as Reaction," p. 3.

36. Edward Said, "Roads Taken and Not Taken in Contemporary Criticism," *Contemporary Literature* 17, no. 3 (1970): 348.

37. Gerald Graff, *Literature against Itself: Literary Ideas in Modern Society* (Chicago: University of Chicago Press, 1979).

38. Sprinker, "Criticism as Reception," p. 12.

39. Gayatri Spivak, "Revolutions That As Yet have no Model," *Diacritics* 10, no. 4 (1980): 29–49.

40. Spivak, "Revolutions," p. 47.

41. Spivak, "Revolutions," p. 46.

42. Spivak, "Revolutions," p. 47.

43. Spivak, "Revolutions," p. 47.

44. Spivak, "Revolutions," p. 47.

45. Spivak, "Revolutions," p. 47.

46. Spivak, "Revolutions," p. 48.

47. Spivak, "Revolutions," p. 48.

48. Spivak, "Revolutions," p. 49.

49. See Michael Ryan and Douglas Kellner, *Camera Politica: The Politics and Ideology of Contemporary Hollywood* (Bloomington: Indiana University Press, 1988); Mike Davis and Michael Sprinker, eds., *Reshaping the US Left: Popular Struggles in the 1980s* (London: Verso, 1988); and Gayatri Chakravorty Spivak, *In Other Worlds: Essays in Cultural Politics* (London: Methuen, 1987).

50. See, for example, Ryan's more modest remarks on deconstruction in *Politics and Culture: Working Hypotheses for a Post-Revolutionary Society* (Baltimore: Johns Hopkins University Press, 1989). In the introduction Ryan gives some ground to "German rationalists" in their critique of French theory. Although he does include a wholly negative review of Habermas' *Theory of Communicative Action* in his initial chapter (pp. 27–45), he also shows that he has some appreciation for "German" objections: "I have also come to feel that we who work on the French side would be wrong to ignore the insistent point the German thinkers make: that the measures of reason are necessary instruments for attaining a good society" (p. 2). In a later discussion, he seems to argue that deconstruction in and of itself has no political valence: "It would be a mistake to become too uncritically starry eyed in its [deconstruction's] regard without taking the obvious problem that if it has its radical use, it also has its conservative ones, into account" (p. 70).

51. Christopher Norris, "On Marxist Deconstruction: Problems and Prospects," *Southern Review* 17 (1984): 203–11. See also my reply to this essay, "Counter-Episte-

mology and Marxist-Deconstruction: A Reply to Christopher Norris," *Southern Review* 18 (1985): 206–14.

52. Norris, "On Marxist Deconstruction," p. 210.

53. Norris, "On Marxist Deconstruction," p. 208.

54. Norris, "On Marxist Deconstruction," p. 296.

55. Jacques Derrida, "Entre crochets: Entretien avec Jacques Derrida," *Digraphe,* no. 8 (1976); here p. 113.

Chapter 9. The Uncomfortable Heritage

1. Typical in this regard is Derrida's response to Anne McClintock and Rob Nixon, who criticized Derrida's essay "Racism's Last Word," *Critical Inquiry* 12 (1985): 290–99. McClintock and Nixon supply valuable material on the history of racism in South Africa and in general criticize Derrida for his concentration on the word "apartheid." Derrida responds with sarcasm and condescension. See Anne McClintock and Rob Nixon, "No Names Apart: The Separation of Word and History in Derrida's 'Le Dernier Mot du Racisme,'" *Critical Inquiry* 13 (1986): 140–54; and Jacques Derrida, "But, beyond . . . (Open Letter to Anne McClintock and Rob Nixon)," *Critical Inquiry* 13 (1986): 155–70.

2. Avital Ronell gives us some insight into how crudely and flippantly the "in-group" reacts to criticism from even eminent European intellectuals. She reports a remark made by Philippe Lacoue-Labarthe concerning Jean-François Lyotard's willingness to engage in a debate with Habermas: "Why take seriously a kind of dinosaur from the *Aufklärung?* And why go after him?" Evidently openness and dialogue are not traits cultivated by deconstruction in recent times. Cited in Avital Ronell, "The Differends of Man," *Diacritics* 19, no. 3–4 (1989): 63–75; here p. 70.

3. The complete wartime writings are available in Paul de Man, *Wartime Journalism, 1939–1943,* ed. Werner Hamacher, Neil Hertz, and Thomas Keenan (Lincoln: University of Nebraska Press, 1988).

4. See, for example, the accounts gathered by James Atlas in his article, "The Case of Paul de Man," *New York Times Magazine* (28 August 1988), pp. 36–37, 60, 66–69.

5. In *Signs of the Times: Deconstruction and the Fall of Paul de Man* (New York: Poseidon, 1991), David Lehman uses this sort of argument. Lehman has done some useful and sometimes revealing journalistic work on the de Man affair, but he exhibits a poor and simplistic understanding of deconstruction in particular and of literary theory/philosophy in general. An abbreviated version of his position may be found in the staged debate (with Walter Kendrick) under the title "Oh no, [de] Man again!" *Lingua Franca* 1, no. 4 (April 1991): 26–33. There are, of course, many less extreme forms in which this argument has been expressed. Several more sophisticated critics view de Man's theoretical proclivities as in some fashion complicit with a "cover-up," although few believe seriously that de Man was consciously and intentionally using deconstruction to avoid confronting his past. In the volume *Responses: On Paul de Man's Wartime Journalism,* ed. Werner Hamacher, Neil Hertz, and Thomas Keenan (Lincoln: University of Nebraska Press, 1989), the contributions by Stanley Corngold, "On Paul de Man's Collaborationist Writings" (pp. 80–84), and Jeffrey Mehlman's "Perspectives: On Paul de Man and *Le Soir*" (pp. 324–33), fall into this group. In general the "Responses" are what one might expect

from contributors consisting primarily of de Man's friends, colleagues, and former students. Although there are a few critical pieces, most enter into some discourse of apology.

6. Christopher Norris, *Paul de Man: Deconstruction and the Critique of Aesthetic Ideology* (London: Routledge, 1988). Norris appears to have been in a difficult position. He apparently had already finished his manuscript on de Man, in which he had argued for de Man's political relevance, when the early journalism was discovered. His essay in the *London Review of Books,* and the postscript, "On de Man's Early Writings in *Le Soir,*" are thus ex post facto justifications of the book he had completed.

7. Christopher Norris, "Paul de Man's Past" *London Review of Books* 10 no. 3 (4 February 1988): 7–11.

8. Geoffrey Hartman, "Paul de Man, Fascism, and Deconstruction: Blindness and Insight," *New Republic* (7 March 1988); pp. 27–31.

9. Hartman, "Paul de Man, Fascism, and Deconstruction."

10. Werner Hamacher, "Fortgesetzte Trauerarbeit: Paul de Mans komplizierte Strategie: Eine Erwiderung," *Frankfurter Allgemeine Zeitung* (24 February 1988). Indeed, the controversy about de Man in Germany has been more strident than one would expect considering the meager reception of deconstruction in literature and philosophy departments in the Federal Republic. The German interest in this matter seems to stem as much from their own recent controversies about the past, the so-called "historians' debate" *(Historikerstreit),* as from an inherent interest in de Man and deconstruction.

11. Lindsay Waters asserts that "many of de Man's students were former activists from the 1960s; and they were not wrong—we can now appreciate—to see his thought as a meditation on, around, and about literature and politics." "Paul de Man: A Sketch of Two Generations," in *Responses,* pp. 397–403; here p. 402. But most of the people to whom I have spoken and who were at Yale when de Man arrived confirm that he was not perceived as a political figure for the French or Comparative Literature Department, that he was considered somewhat apolitical. Although former activists may have gone into his seminars, I have seen no testimony that indicates political activists emerged from these seminars.

12. "In Memorium," *Yale French Studies* 69, *The Lesson of Paul de Man* (1985): 3–15.

13. Printed in Paul de Man, *The Resistance to Theory* (Minneapolis: University of Minnesota Press, 1986), pp. 73–105.

14. De Man, *Resistance to Theory,* p. 102.

15. Paul de Man, Introduction to Hans Robert Jauß, *Toward an Aesthetic of Reception* (Minneapolis: University of Minnesota Press, 1982), pp. vii–xxv. See my discussion of this in the second chapter of this book.

16. For a recent example of how de Man might be recruited for political arguments, see Frederick M. Dolan, "Crisis in the Gulf, by George Bush, Saddam Hussein, et alia: As Told to the *New York Times,*" *Postmodern Culture* 1, no. 2 (1991). (Since *Postmodern Culture* is a journal received by electronic mail, there are no consecutive page numbers. It is accessible by corresponding on electronic mail to the editors at pmc@ncsuvm.ncsu.edu. I was told that hard copies would be sold to libraries in the future).

17. Norris, "Paul de Man's Past," p. 10. A quick perusal of three recently published volumes of de Man's work turns up only a handful of passing references

to Marx, Adorno, and Althusser, and although I am obviously not as acquainted with de Man's work as Norris is, I fail to remember any of his later published essays that took up issues of ideology or politics in any but an oblique fashion.

18. Hartman, "Paul de Man, Fascism, and Deconstruction," p. 31. The absolute determinism Hartman offers as apology here shows exactly how questionable deconstructionist politics can be that rely on an absolute notion of system or code.

19. See notes 3 and 5.

20. Shoshana Felman, "Paul de Man's Silence," *Critical Inquiry* 15 (1989): 704–44.

21. Felman, "Silence," p. 710.

22. Felman, "Silence," p. 711.

23. Found on p. 45 of de Man's *Wartime Journalism*.

24. For a good contextualization of intellectuals in the German setting see Jeffrey Herf, *Reactionary Modernism: Technology, Culture and Politics in Weimer and in the Third Reich* (New York: Cambridge University Press, 1984).

25. For example, in the *Responses* volume, the contributions by Jacques Derrida, Richard Klein, and Peggy Kamuf.

26. De Man, *Wartime Journalism*, pp. 323–26. The article originally appeared on 20 August 1942.

27. Those contributors to the *Responses* volume who recognize the existence of this article are perhaps worse than those who insist on the singularity of de Man's article in *Le Soir*. Rodolphe Gasché in "Edges of Understanding" (pp. 208–20) considers both articles a sign of "naiveté and confusion" and states unbelievably that "making due allowances" (whatever this means) "they are rather harmless" (p. 209). And Hans-Jost Frey in "Literature, Ideology" (pp. 185–92) has the temerity to ask parenthetically: "But then, how anti-Semitic is it?" (p. 190). The insensitivity of these writers to racial prejudice is apt to make one wonder about their critical acumen in general.

28. Felman, "Silence," p. 717.

29. Felman, "Silence," p. 719.

30. Felman, "Silence," p. 722.

31. Paul de Man, *Allegories of Reading* (New Haven: Yale University Press, 1979), p. 299.

32. Felman, "Silence," p. 737.

33. Felman, "Silence," p. 705.

34. Felman, "Silence," pp. 707–8.

35. Karl Jaspers, *The Question of German Guilt*, trans. E. B. Ashton (New York: Capricorn Books, 1947).

36. Felman, "Silence," p. 708.

37. Felman, "In Memorium," *Yale French Studies*, p. 9.

38. Jacques Derrida, "Like the Sound of the Sea Deep within a Shell: Paul de Man's War," *Critical Inquiry* 14 (1988): 590–652.

39. Derrida, "Paul de Man's War," p. 592.

40. Jon Wiener, "Deconstructing de Man," *Nation* (9 January 1988), pp. 22–24. Wiener's version of things contains some unfortunate inaccuracies and distortions. Also his view of deconstruction, which he appears to have gotten secondhand, is woefully inadequate. These failures on Wiener's part should not cloud the issues that are at the center of his essay: that de Man wrote for a collaborationist newspaper and that he authored antisemitic statements in his articles.

41. Derrida, "Paul de Man's War," p. 607.
42. Derrida, "Paul de Man's War," p. 607.
43. Derrida, "Paul de Man's War," p. 623.
44. De Man, *Wartime Journalism,* p. 45.
45. Derrida, "Paul de Man's War," p. 625.
46. Derrida, "Paul de Man's War," p. 629.
47. De Man, *Wartime Journalism,* p. 45.
48. Derrida, "Paul de Man's War," p. 636.
49. This letter was reprinted in the *Responses* volume on pp. 475–77.
50. A Belgian colleague provided a somewhat different explanation for this misidentification. He stated that de Man simply liked to make up stories about his past. In either interpretation, the letter does not speak very strongly for de Man's candor.
51. *Responses,* p. 476.
52. Derrida, "Paul de Man's War," p. 642.
53. Derrida, "Paul de Man's War," p. 640.
54. Derrida, "Paul de Man's War," p. 641.
55. Derrida, "Paul de Man's War," p. 644.
56. Derrida, "Paul de Man's War," p. 640.
57. Derrida, "Paul de Man's War," p. 645.
58. Derrida, "Paul de Man's War," p. 646.
59. Derrida, "Paul de Man's War," p. 647.
60. Derrida, "Paul de Man's War," p. 651.
61. Perhaps more significant than the objections that have appeared is the unanimous approval of Derrida's essay on the part of his faithful coterie of deconstructors. As far as I can tell, not one disciple has sounded a critical word against the master. Essays by the various deconstructors in the *Responses* volume read like a litany of praise for the high priest. Timothy Bahti writes that the situation in Belgium was "carefully and sensitively analyzed" by Derrida (p. 1), whose views are "immensely clarifying" (p. 4). J. Hillis Miller calls "Paul de Man's War" "a balanced essay" (p. 338); Andrzej Warminski states that Derrida "resists better than anyone" the suspension of reading that would lead to totalitarianism (pp. 387–88); and Samuel Weber agrees that we should submit ourselves passively to Derrida's restrictive rules for reading the de Man case (p. 410). With regard to the article "Les Juifs" Derrida is praised without the slightest contradiction. Peggy Kamuf agrees with Derrida's suggestion that de Man was very likely smuggling contraband into a collaborationist journal, thus turning him into a selfless and courageous hero of the resistance (p. 264). Rodolphe Gasché concurs with the interpretation of "vulgar antisemitism" as an attempt to call antisemitism "vulgar" (p. 209). And Ian Balfour calls Derrida's analysis "a painstaking reading of the article" and "an excellent point of departure for future thinking about these matters" (p. 17). The failure of any of these critics (or any others who are prominent in deconstruction) to exercise an independent judgment is troubling and further evidence of the cultlike character of deconstruction in recent years. When you enter the deconstructive church, you evidently have to check any independence of intellect at the door.
62. Most centrally in the volume *On Deconstruction* (Ithaca: Cornell University Press, 1982).

63. Jonathan Culler, "'Paul de Man's War' and the Aesthetic Ideology," *Critical Inquiry* 15 (1989): 777–83; here p. 783.

64. Culler, "Aesthetic Ideology," p. 780.

65. Jacques Derrida, "Biodegradables: seven Diary Fragments," *Critical Inquiry* 15 (1989): 812–73.

66. Derrida, "Biodegradables," pp. 817, 819, 821, 838, 820, 823, 872.

67. Derrida, "Biodegradables," p. 822.

68. Derrida, "Biodegradables," p. 823.

69. Derrida, "Biodegradables," p. 852.

70. Derrida, "Biodegradables," p. 825.

71. Derrida, "Biodegradables," pp. 829–31.

72. Jon Wiener, "The Responsibilities of Friendship: Jacques Derrida on Paul de Man's Collaboration," *Critical Inquiry* 15 (1989): 797–803; here p. 801; W. Wolfgang Holdheim, "Jacques Derrida's Apologia," *Critical Inquiry* 15 (1989): 784–96; here p. 789; John Brenkman and Jules David Law, "Resetting the Agenda," *Critical Inquiry* 15 (1989): 804–11; here p. 809.

73. Derrida, "Biodegradables," p. 825.

74. Holdheim, "Apologia," p. 794.

75. Brenkman and Law, "Agenda," p. 805.

76. Derrida, "Biodegradables," p. 826.

77. Marjorie Perloff, "Response to Jacques Derrida," *Critical Inquiry* 15 (1989): 767–76; here p. 775.

78. Derrida, "Biodegradables," p. 827.

79. Derrida, "Biodegradables," pp. 825, 850.

80. The most notable of these was perhaps Frank Lentricchia in *After the New Criticism* (Chicago: University of Chicago Press, 1980), pp. 282–317.

81. This section on the "Defense of Paul de Man" was written before the appearance of the fall 1990 issue of *Diacritics*, published in the late spring of 1991, which was devoted exclusively to Paul de Man and extensively to the "de Man affair." Since *Diacritics* has been a journal that has consistently promoted Derrida, de Man, and deconstruction, it is not surprising to find a strict adherence to the deconstructive party line. The first article, written by Neil Hertz, provides an interesting and speculative analysis of de Man's reception of William Empson's *Seven Types of Ambiguity*. More significant for our purposes, however, is Hertz's treatment of the death of de Man's mother and de Man's reaction to it. Hertz cites the story that Edouard Colinet told in the *Responses* volume: after Paul's brother died in an accident, his mother committed suicide; the fifteen-year-old Paul discovered the body of his mother; and Paul's father was so disturbed by the two violent deaths that for a time Paul had to be cared for by his uncle Henri (in *Responses*, p. 427). This version, which de Man apparently told to Colinet and repeated throughout his life to various members of his family, is directly contradicted by his cousin Jan, who evidently wrote to Hertz in 1988. Jan reports that Paul's father discovered the body, and that since Paul was seventeen at the time, his uncle did not need to take care of him. Hertz confirms that the dates match Jan's versions of the story and thus contradict the version told by his more illustrious cousin Paul.

What should one conclude from these two versions, or from the very fact that two versions exist? Hertz psychoanalyzes the whole event and its recounting as follows: "What he chose to tell provides the germ for what I find obliquely inscribed at various points in his writing—a tableau of uncertain agency, of someone confronting a suspended body, himself suspended between feelings of matricidal guilt and the intensified innocence of the bereft, immobilized in the act of having 'kill[ed] the original by discovering that the original was already dead'" (p. 7). But a much more commonsense reading of the different versions (which could then also be subjected to psychoanalytic analysis) is that here we have simply another instance of de Man's lack of candor concerning his own past. As we have seen in his letter to Poggioli, de Man often distorted or falsified what he had done. Former students have also reported that he was less than truthful about his wartime activities. But Hertz, although an otherwise perceptive literary critic, does not see this motif, or does not want to see it. In ignoring the obvious problems de Man had in confronting and reporting honestly about his own life, he displays here precisely the type of blindness that has led de Man's friends and supporters to exhibit so little insight into their former mentor and/or colleague.

Other articles follow familiar patterns as well. Deborah Esch repeats the facile argument that the de Man affair was a pretext for attacking "theory," as if no one has a legitimate claim to theoretical reflection outside of the French and their followers. Her discussion relies almost exclusively on those who defend de Man. Cynthia Chase (the special editor of this issue of *Diacritics*), Werner Hamacher, Geoffrey Hartman, Rodolphe Gasché, Samuel Weber, Barbara Johnson, and Andrzej Warminski are cited repeatedly with approval; totally absent is any criticism of obvious flaws in the arguments offered by Derrida or other adherents to deconstruction. (pp. 28–49). Marc Redfield, occasionally pillorying Frank Lentricchia for daring to criticize the master (even before his wartime journalism came to light), (re)produces the familiar claim that de Man's politics become evident in his late essays on "aesthetic ideology." Redfield, like others who pursue this line, can make de Man a political being only by parroting de Man's own idiosyncratic understanding of "ideology": the confusion of natural with linguistic reality (pp. 50–70). The essay by Arne Melberg, which treats Kierkesgaardian and de Manian repetition, mercifully avoids the wartime writings and thus produces no direct apologetics (pp. 71–87).

But with the final essays we return to more agonistic turf again. The last piece in the issue, penned by Jean-Luc Nancy, is the more abstract and less combative of the two. Nancy admits that he lacks the competence, the motivation, and the linguistic ability in English to furnish a significant contribution to the debate. Most of his essay concentrates therefore on matters with which he has a greater acquaintance: Heideggerian themes in philosophy. He supplies a useful and persuasive account of how Heideggerian *Destruktion* is the intellectual progenitor of deconstruction and then reflects speculatively on notions of ideology and history. His initial remarks on the de Man affair differ from the usual deconstructive fare in that they are neither uninteresting nor dogmatic, although he, like others in the deconstructive camp, subscribes to a rather narrow view of what racism entails (in order to place de Man outside its boundaries) and fails to note anything offensive in the essay in *Het Vlaamsche Land*. He situates the wartime journalism correctly in a milieu of intellectual revolution and uncertainty, and identifies de Man with an "artistic nationalism" (p. 99). But his insistence on seeing everything through the rather large and distorting lens of Western thought, his unwillingness to deal with intellectual preferences and philosophical proclivities as part of a less grandiose, more historically integrated scheme, and his unfamiliarity with basic research on the roots of fascism and

National Socialism make his brief observations too general to be of much utility for the debate.

Ernesto Laclau's poorly reasoned and, at times, factually inaccurate essay is a totally different piece in tenor and aims. It amounts to a rabid defense of de Man and the deconstructive line, and a vituperative attack on those who dared to see things otherwise. At the outset Laclau relies heavily on Colinet's sympathetic interpretation of de Man's activities. Colinet asserts: (1) that de Man *reluctantly* wrote the antisemitic piece for *Le Soir,* although he provides no independent evidence of coercion (Laclau reduces the number of antisemitic articles to one, thus ignoring at the very least the antisemitic piece in *Het Vlaamsche Land*); (2) that de Man wrote only on art and literature (neither Colinet nor Laclau bothers to add that he often used his reviews as a springboard for political statements); and (3) that the article in *Le Soir* has only a "slight antisemitic flavor," a rather generous reading considering de Man's obvious indifference to the removal of Jews and the Jewish contributions from European culture and to the notion of a forced exile for European Jews. These opinions, written by de Man's university friend Colinet, are according to Laclau, what "any decent person should arrive" (p. 88). Having condemned to "indecency" anyone who still believes that de Man flirted with fascism or antisemitism, Laclau repeats the tiresome canard that the whole affair "was conceived from the start as an attempt to put 'deconstruction' on trial" (p. 89). Then, to "prove" that it is the critics of de Man, and not de Man or his defenders, who are totalitarian, Laclau has only to define "totalitarian" in line with deconstructive dogma. Proceeding from a definition that almost no social scientist would recognize, much less accept—totalitarian is "essentially to assert that there is a point of the social fabric which is the locus of both knowledge and power" (p.90)—it is a simple matter for Laclau to blast critics like John Brenkman or W. W. Holdheim (referred to condescendingly as "a certain W. W. Holdheim") for their putatively totalitarian attitudes. Much of the rest of his essay exhibits bad faith and double standards in argumentation. Laclau reproaches Brenkman for stating that de Man's wartime journalism supplies evidence that proves "beyond a reasonable doubt" that he was a fascist and an antisemite, objecting not only to the content of the assertion, but to its phrasing as well. But why is the inclusion of the phrase "beyond a reasonable doubt" rhetorically more illicit than Laclau's own claims to decency, or his own statement that his contentions are "supported by all the available evidence" (p. 93)? And how can he declare repetition itself to be a propagandistic technique employed by Brenkman et al. in their "anti-deconstructionist crusade" (p. 91), when deconstructors, as I have demonstrated, hack away continuously at the same worn points and arguments? Furthermore, why does Laclau have the only say on what fascism means? (He uses his own understanding of the word to discredit any association of de Man with fascism). How does he know about "the real reasons of his [de Man's] collaboration" (p. 91)? And why does he focus on 1940 as a pivotal year for the determination of collaboration when de Man wrote for the collaborationist press until at least 1942 and perhaps 1943? We might be tempted to characterize Laclau's tactics in this essay with the adjective "totalitarian" if the word had not been abused so much by deconstructors. Bullying the reader into accepting *his* facts, *his* definitions, and *his* standards for propriety, Laclau, like most deconstructors, demonstrates the unfortunate and authoritarian propensity for closing down discussion of the very matters that have real political substance.

82. Victor Farias, *Heidegger et la nazisme* (Paris: Lagrasse, 1987). A German edition, with a foreword by Jürgen Habermas (Frankfurt: Fischer, 1989), and an English translation (Philadelphia: Temple University Press, 1989), correct some errors that appeared in the French volume.

83. For the French reactions see Luc Ferry and Alain Renaut, *Heidegger and Modernity*, trans. Franklin Philip (Chicago: University of Chicago Press, 1990); and Richard Wolin, "The French Heidegger Debate," *New German Critique*, no. 45 (1988): 135–61. This issue of *New German Critique* contains for the first time in English translation many of Heidegger's shorter political statements from his time as Rector of the University of Freiburg (pp. 96–114) as well as the English translation of Karl Löwith's account of a meeting with Heidegger in Rome in 1936 (pp. 115–16).

84. Martin Heidegger, "Nur noch ein Gott kann uns retten": Spiegel-Gespräch mit Martin Heidegger am 23. September 1966," *Der Spiegel* 30 (31 May 1976): 193–219. An English version was published in Thomas Sheehan, ed., *Heidegger: The Man and the Thinker* (Chicago: Precent Publishing, 1981), pp. 45–67.

85. Herbert Marcuse, "Gegen die Aufrechnung des Leidens" (letters to Martin Heidegger from 28 August 1947 and 13 May 1948), *Pflasterstrand* 209 (4–17 May 1985): 43–44. An English translation of these letters appeared in *New German Critique*, no. 53 (1991): 28–32.

86. See *"Historikerstreit": Die Dokumentation der Kontroverse um die Einzigartigkeit der nationalsozialistischen Judenvernichtung* (Munich: Piper, 1987). See also my discussion of the historian's debate in the final chapter of *Jürgen Habermas: Critic in the Public Sphere* (London: Routledge, 1991).

87. Alexander Schwan, *Politische Philosophie im Denken Heideggers*, 2d rev. ed. (Opladen: Westdeutscher Verlag, 1989); Theodor W. Adorno, *The Jargon of Authenticity*, trans. Knut Tarnowski and Frederic Will (Evanston, Ill.: Northwestern University Press, 1973); Robert Minder, "Heidegger und Hebel oder die Sprache von Meßkirch," *Hölderlin unter den Deutschen und andere Aufsätze zur deutschen Literatur* (Frankfurt: Suhrkamp, 1968), pp. 86–153; Jürgen Habermas, *The Philosophical Discourse of Modernity*, trans. Frederick G. Lawrence (Cambridge: MIT Press, 1987); Hugo Ott, *Martin Heidegger: Unterwegs zu seiner Biographie* (Frankfurt, 1988). In German literature of the postwar period Günter Grass in his novel *Hundejahre* (1963) was one of the first to attack and satirize Heidegger and Heideggerian language.

88. "Symposium on Heidegger and Nazism," ed. Arnold I. Davidson, *Critical Inquiry* 15 (1989): 407–88. Except for Davidson's introduction, all contributions come from Europe: Gadamer, Habermas, Derrida, Blanchot, Lacoue-Labarthe, and Levinas are the authors.

89. *Diacritics* 19, no. 3–4 (1989).

90. Günther Neske and Emil Kettering, *Martin Heidegger and National Socialism: Questions and Answers* (New York: Paragon House, 1990), The German book was called simply *Antwort: Martin Heidegger in Gespräch.* (Pfüllingen: G. Neske, 1988).

91. J. Hillis Miller, "An Open Letter to Professor Jon Wiener," *Responses*, pp. 334–42; here p. 338.

92. Rodolphe Gasché, *The Tain of the Mirror: Derrida and the Philosophy of Reflection* (Cambridge: Harvard University Press, 1986).

93. Vincent Descombes, *Modern French Philosophy*, trans. L. Scott-Fox and J. M. Harding (Cambridge: Cambridge University Press, 1980); Luc Ferry and Alain Renaut, *French Philosophy of the Sixties: An Essay on Antihumanism*, trans. Mary

Schnackenberg Cattani (Amherst: University of Massachusetts Press, 1990); and *Heidegger and Modernity,* trans. Franklin Philip (Chicago: University of Chicago Press, 1990).

94. Habermas, *Philosophical Discourse of Modernity;* and Manfred Frank, *What Is Neostructuralism?,* trans. Sabine Wilke and Richard Gray (Minneapolis: University of Minnesota Press, 1989).

95. This link is, of course, not entirely absent in the best of Derrida's American and English commentators. Christopher Norris, for example, has continued to emphasize Derrida's debt to Heidegger, while showing how he differs from him. And Vincent Leitch postulates a "destructive" and a "deconstructive" Heidegger, the latter of which is the creation of Derrida. See, for example, Norris' *Deconstruction: Theory and Practice* (London: Methuen, 1982); *The Deconstructive Turn: Essays in the Rhetoric of Philosophy* (London: Methuen, 1983); and *The Contest of Faculties: Philosophy and Theory after Deconstruction* (London: Methuen, 1985); Vincent Leitch, *Deconstructive Criticism: An Advanced Introduction* (New York: Columbia University Press, 1983); and *American Literary Criticism from the 30s to the 80s* (New York: Columbia University Press, 1988).

96. Jacques Derrida, *De l'esprit: Heidegger et la question* (Paris: Galilée, 1987), p. 35. In the English edition, entitled *Of Spirit: Heidegger and the Question,* trans. Geoffrey Bennington and Rachel Bowlby (Chicago: University of Chicago Press, 1989) the passage is found on p. 16.

97. Philippe Lacoue-Labarthe, *Heidegger, Art and Politics: The Fiction of the Political,* trans. Chris Turner (London: Blackwell, 1990; orig. Paris: Christian Bourgois, 1987), p. 10.

98. This occurs in the essay by Avital Ronell, "The Differends of Man," a review-essay of Lyotard's *Heidegger et "les Juifs"*. Liberally misquoting and misciting, Ronell adopts arguments evidently found in the seminar paper written by a misguided graduate student at Berkeley. Ronell supports her student's conclusion that "Habermas characterizes Derrida as a Jewish mystic to disqualify deconstruction as a legitimate philosophical enterprise with its own set of premises and styles of argumentation" (p. 68). This insinuation of an anti-Jewish tendency in Habermas is then reinforced when Ronell produces another statement from her graduate student, claiming that Habermas "determines the Jew as mystic to exclude him/her from the order of philosophy" (p. 69). The irony of this contention (and the disgrace of this slur) is that the key citation from Habermas that Ronell uses ("a return to the Greeks, whenever it was attempted by Jews, always had about it something of a lack of power") is taken from an essay Habermas published in 1961 whose express purpose was to demonstrate, against the contention of racists in Germany, that the Jews *had* made significant contributions to German thought. In fact the essay opens with a statement from Ernst Jünger that Habermas seeks to *disprove.* Jünger maintained that "the Jew can play a creative role in nothing at all that concerns German life, neither in what is good nor in what is evil" (cited in Jürgen Habermas, *Philosophical-Political profiles,* trans. Frederick G. Lawrence [Cambridge: MIT Press, 1983], p. 21). It is perhaps not irrelevant to note here that Jünger was far and away de Man's favorite author during the early forties and a close friend of Heidegger for over three decades. Furthermore, the quote that Ronell reproduces follows Habermas' description of a confrontation between the Jewish-German philosopher Ernst Cassirer and Heidegger, after which Heidegger refused to shake Cassirer's extended hand. It is

followed by a quite positive account of Walter Benjamin's interest in the Kabbalah. Understood in its context, the quotation simply points to a fact of assimilation that Jews, like Cassirer, failed to confront. The citation has nothing to do with Derrida; it was published before Derrida had written anything for public consumption and has nothing whatsoever to do with Habermas's discussion of Derrida in the *Philosophical Discourse of Modernity,* contrary to what Ronell, by means of sloppy scholarship, would have us believe. Habermas does not criticize Derrida because he has ties to Jewish mysticism, and Ronell is simply being dishonest when she cites Habermas as follows: "as a Jewish mystic, Derrida 'degrades politics and contemporary history ... so as to romp all the more freely, and with a greater wealth of associations, in the sphere of the ontological'" (p. 68). She adds the phrase "as a Jewish mystic" to make Habermas appear anti-Jewish, whereas the actual citation has no reference to Jewish mysticism in the vicinity. Rightly or wrongly Habermas criticizes Derrida for the same reasons he criticizes Heidegger (who can hardly be accused of *Jewish* mysticism), and this is obvious enough for anyone who bothers to read what Habermas wrote. The citation from Habermas is prefaced in the source by the following sentence: "Derrida develops the history of Being . . . in another variation from Heidegger. He, too, degrades politics and contemporary history . . ." (Habermas, *Philosophical Discourse,* p. 181). His criticism of mysticism is borne equally by the Jewish and Christian tradition, which he makes clear two pages later. The contrast between Jewish philosophy and genuine philosophy Ronell wants to pin on Habermas as well as the insinuation that Habermas harbors anti-Jewish or anti-semitic sentiments is simply a fabrication of misreading, error, and poor scholarship. For all the emphasis that deconstructors place on careful and considered reading, their own scholarship all too often reflects a shoddy and unprincipled method of dealing with the texts of others.

99. These sentiments are found in Derrida's interview in *Le Nouvel Observateur* from 6 November 1988, pp. 6–12, and in his essay "Comment donner raison: How to Concede with Reasons," *Diacritics* 19, no. 3 (1989): 4–9, a text which inexplicably appears with facing French and English pages.

100. Derrida, "Comment donner raison?" p. 4.

101. Jean-François Lyotard, *Heidegger et "les Juifs"* (Paris: Galilée, 1988), pp. 88–90.

102. Lyotard, *Heidegger,* p. 97.

103. Lacoue-Labarthe, *Heidegger,* p. 19.

104. Lacoue-Labarthe, *Heidegger,* p. 22.

105. Lacoue-Labarthe, *Heidegger,* p. 21.

106. For readers of English I would recommend looking at three books for starters: Fritz K. Ringer's valuable study *The Decline of the German Mandarins: The German Academic Community, 1890–1933* (Cambridge: Harvard University Press, 1969); Herf's *Reactionary Modernism,* and, more specifically on Heidegger, Michael Zimmerman, *Heidegger's Confrontation with Modernity: Technology, Politics, Art* (Bloomington: Indiana University Press, 1990), in particular Division One.

107. Lacoue-Labarthe, *Heidegger,* p. 35.

108. Lacoue-Labarthe, *Heidegger,* p. 116.

109. The dependence of Lacoue-Labarthe on Arendt's thesis is even more obvious in an essay he published with Jean-Luc Nancy entitled "The Nazi Myth," trans. Brian Holmes, *Critical Inquiry* 16 (1990): 291–312. Their admitted ignorance of Nazi

ideology and of the history of the era (p. 291) is a mark of honesty, but it should give us pause when it comes to Lacoue-Labarthe's statements concerning Heidegger's relationship to National Socialism. More disturbing than the appropriation of Arendt's obsolete political thesis from the cold-war era, however, is the reliance on the work of Hans Jürgen Syberberg both in this essay and in Lacoue-Labarthe's book. Although Syberberg is well acquainted with National Socialism and its more mystical, irrational elements, his latest book shows why he has increasingly become a darling of the far right. In *Vom Unglück und Glück der Kunst in Deutschland nach dem letzten Krieg* (Munich: Matthes & Seitz, 1990), Syberberg makes statements that were only implicit in his film *Hitler: Ein Film aus Deutschland* from 1977, which was hailed primarily by the postmodern avant-garde. We read, for example, that the The Reich was the natural consequence of democratic liberalism; that the Jews and the left are responsible for the horrible condition of postwar culture in Germany; that Hitler was a genial figure whom we should rethink. One must wonder how much thought one can uncritically appropriate from the far right (Syberberg, Heidegger) before one's own thought becomes an unwitting dupe of an undemocratic, ultraconservative right wing.

110. Lacoue-Labarthe, *Heidegger*, p. 61.

111. As he stated in the interview in *Nouvel Observateur*.

112. Lacoue-Labarthe, *Heidegger*, p. 103.

113. Lacoue-Labarthe, *Heidegger*, p. 103.

114. It is apparently Derrida's intention to offer such an argument when he introduces various Eurocentric, racist remarks written by Husserl and Valéry (*Of Spirit*, pp. 60–61). But it is preposterous (and a sign of totalization) to contend that such remarks are essential for all discourses that refer to spirit or *Geist*, or that seek to examine the European spirit. At an earlier point in his exposition Derrida maintains that "one cannot demarcate oneself from biologism, from naturalism, from racism in its genetic form, one cannot be *opposed* to them except by reinscribing spirit in an oppositional determination, by once again making it a unilaterality of subjectivity, even if in its voluntarist form. The constraint of this program remains very strong, it reigns over the majority of discourses which, today and for a long time to come, state their opposition to racism, to totalitarianism, to nazism, to fascism, etc., and do this in the name of spirit and even of the freedom of (the) spirit, in the name of an axiomatic—for example that of democracy or 'human rights'—which directly or not, comes back to this metaphysics of *subjectivity*" (*Of Spirit*, pp. 39–40). Derrida's proof for these sweeping assertions is lacking, and the political implications are disturbing. As in the de Man affair, Derrida would seem to leave no space for any genuine political opposition except those that he condones with the label deconstruction.

115. Lacoue-Labarthe, *Heidegger*, p. 95.

116. Lyotard, *Heidegger*, pp. 105–6.

117. Lacoue-Labarthe, *Heidegger*, p. 135.

118. Lacoue-Labarthe, *Heidegger*, p. 2.

119. Lyotard, *Heidegger*, pp. 127–32.

120. Lacoue-Labarthe, *Heidegger*, p. 77.

121. Lacoue-Labarthe, *Heidegger*, p. 110.

122. William V. Spanos, "Heidegger, Nazism, and the Repressive Hypothesis: The American Appropriation of the Question," *boundary 2* 17, no. 2 (1990): 199–280; here p. 276.

123. For an overview of Spanos's arguments and developments, see Leitch, *American Literary Criticism from the 30s to the 80s*, pp. 197–204.

124. Spanos, "Heidegger," p. 207.

125. Spanos, "Heidegger," p. 256.

126. Spanos, "Heidegger," p. 265.

127. Spanos, "Heidegger," p. 270. Perhaps this is the point to note that "philosopher" is derived from the Greek meaning "friend or lover of wisdom."

128. Herf, *Reactionary Modernism;* and Zimmerman, *Heidegger's Confrontation with Modernity.*

129. Spanos, "Heidegger," p. 274.

130. Lacoue-Labarthe, *Heidegger,* p. 22. It is not insignificant that the only German intellectual Lacoue-Labarthe names is Gottfried Benn. Benn's association with National Socialism was extremely minimal and nothing at all like Heidegger's open advocacy. The fact is that Heidegger, unlike other eminent Germans of his era—from writers like Tucholsky and Ossietsky, playwrights like Brecht and Toller, novelists like Arnold Zweig and Heinrich Mann, to philosophers like Jaspers, Husserl, Cassirer—willingly lent his support to fascism. The list of "intellectuals" in Germany who supported fascism to the degree that Heidegger did would show a shocking *lack* of intellectual substance.

131. In *The Question of German Guilt,* Karl Jaspers describes the "intellectual Nazis" in the following fashion: "Many intellectuals went along in 1933, sought leading positions and publicly upheld the ideology of the new power, only to become resentful later when they personally were shunted aside. These—although mostly continuing positive until about 1942, when the course of the war made an unfavorable outcome certain and sent them into the oppositionist ranks—now feel that they have suffered under the Nazis and are therefore called for what follows. The regard themselves as anti-Nazis. In all these years, according to their self-proclaimed ideology, these intellectual Nazis were frankly speaking truth in spiritual matters, guarding the tradition of the German spirit, preventing destructions, doing good in individual cases.

"Many of these may be guilty of persisting in a mentality which, while not identical with Party tenets and even disguised as metamorphosis and opposition, still clings in fact to the mental attitude of National-Socialism and fails to clear itself. Through this mentality they may be actually skin to National-Socialism's inhuman, dictatorial, unexistentially nihilistic essence" (pp. 68–69).

Considering Jaspers' close association with Heidegger before 1933 and the fact that he was asked after the war to evaluate Heidegger's fitness for resuming a university career—Jaspers recommended against this because of Heidegger's authoritarian pedagogy, but supported Heidegger when asked again in the early fifties—we can assume that he has Heidegger in mind here.

132. Spanos' apologetic line extends even to questions of translation. He criticizes William S. Lewis' translation of Heidegger's *Volksgemeinschaft* as "national community," although this is a perfectly acceptable rendition, and insists that it should be translated as "community of the peoples," an inaccurate rendition that substitutes a vague internationalism for the obvious nationalist connotation that the word actually contains.

133. Cited from Spanos, "Heidegger," p. 210.

134. Spanos, "Heidegger," p. 213.

135. Spanos, "Heidegger," pp. 235–36.

136. Spanos, "Heidegger," p. 229.
137. Spanos, "Heidegger," p. 227.
138. Spanos, "Heidegger," p. 227.
139. Spanos, "Heidegger," pp. 232–33.
140. Spanos, "Heidegger," p. 246.
141. Spanos, "Heidegger," p. 263.
142. Spanos, "Heidegger," p. 224.
143. For an excellent analysis of an earlier episode of the humanism/antihumanism debate in *boundary 2* as well as its Heideggerian roots, see Renate Holub, "Critical Il/Literacy: Humanism, Heidegger, Anti-Humanism," *Differentia,* no. 3–4 (1989): 73–90.
144. Jonathan Arac, ed., *Postmodernism and Politics* (Minneapolis: University of Minnesota Press, 1986).
145. Andrew Parker, "Ezra Pound and the 'Economy' of Anti-Semitism," *Postmodernism and Politics,* pp. 70–90.
146. Andrew Parker, "Futures for Marxism: An Appreciation of Althusser," *Diacritics* 15, no. 4 (1985): 57–72. At the beginning of his essay Parker makes observations concerning the reception of Derrida's work in England. His claim is that Derrida's political value was immediately recognized in Britain because he was seen as a figure related to Althusser. If what Parker says is true—and I have no reason to doubt him—this might explain some of the differences between Derrida's oppositional status in England and in the United States. As I have tried to show earlier in this book, Derrida was not originally received here as part of a French May 68 movement, or as a political thinker like Althusser, but as a writer whose demanding philosophical writings appealed to literary scholars at the most elite institutions.
147. To my knowledge the book has not yet appeared.
148. Parker, "Pound," p. 71.
149. Parker, "Pound," p. 79.
150. Parker, "Pound," p. 85.
151. Parker, "Pound," pp. 80, 81, and 85.
152. Rainer Nägele, "The Scene of the Other: Theodor W. Adorno's Negative Dialectic in the Context of Poststructuralism," *Postmodernism and Politics,* pp. 91–111.
153. Nägele has written on a number of important topics and has done extensive work on the German poet Friedrich Hölderlin. His most recent book is *Theater, Theory, Speculation: Walter Benjamin and the Scenes of Modernity* (Baltimore: Johns Hopkins University Press, 1991).
154. Nägele, "Scene," p. 93.
155. For example, most prominently, Paul de Man in *Blindness and Insight: Essays in the Rhetoric of Contemporary Criticism,* 2d ed. (London: Methuen, 1983).
156. Andreas Huyssen, *After the Great Divide: Modernism, Mass Culture, Postmodernism* (Bloomington: Indiana University Press): "Who, after all, would want to be the Lukács of the postmodern . . ." (p. 43).
157. For an introduction to key issues in English, see Seyla Benhabib and Fred Dallmayr, *The Communicative Ethics Controversy* (Cambridge: MIT Press, 1990).
158. Habermas, *Philosophical Discourse of Modernity.*
159. Jürgen Habermas, *The Theory of Communicative Action,* 2 vols., trans. Thomas McCarthy (Boston: Beacon, 1984 and 1987).

160. Cornel West, "Ethics and Action in Fredric Jameson's Marxist Hermeneutics," *Postmodernism and Politics*, pp. 123–44.
161. West, "Ethics and Action," p. 138.
162. West, "Ethics and Action," p. 140.
163. West, "Ethics and Action," p. 138.
164. bell hooks, "Postmodern Blackness," *Postmodern Culture* 1, no. 1 (1990).

Index